**Criminological
Theory**

# Criminological Theory

**Foundations and Perceptions**

Edited by

**Stephen Schafer**
Northeastern University

**Richard D. Knudten**
Marquette University

**Lexington Books**
D.C. Heath and Company
Lexington, Massachusetts
Toronto

**Library of Congress Cataloging in Publication Data**
Main entry under title:

Criminological theory.

1. Crime and criminals—Addresses, essays, lectures. I. Schafer, Stephen.
II. Knudten, Richard D.

| | | |
|---|---|---|
| HV6028.C74 | 364.2 | 76-18488 |
| ISBN 0–669–00795–1 | | |

Published simultaneously in Canada

Printed in the United States of America

International Standard Book Number: 0–669–00795–1

Library of Congress Catalog Card Number: 76-18488

Dedicated To
Lili, Pauline, and Andrew Schafer
and
Ethel B. Swedlund

On July 29, 1976, criminology lost a respected and valuable leader. Stephen Schafer was a scholar of international renown who will be best remembered for his contributions to victimology and the concept of the political criminal. Dr. Schafer led an active professional life; at the time of his death he was organizing the Second International Symposium on Victimology, held in Boston in September of 1976.

Stephen Schafer's living monument is in the many victim/witness assistance programs in operation in the United States and throughout the world; his walking monument is the victim who is now remembered rather than forgotten.

# Contents

# Preface

The development of criminological theory—that is, of systematic attempts to explain crime—has occurred only within the last two hundred years. Before the middle of the eighteenth century, the notion that crime is caused by evil supernatural forces dominated the conceptualization of the crimino-legal problem. Only since that time have analysts struggled to develop a scientific understanding of the causes of crime. Although some successes have been achieved, it is obvious from the works presented in this volume that the goal is yet to be attained.

Many modern criminological theorists have offered creative insights into the nature, scope, and causes of crime. However, much of what seems to be new today is essentially a restatement in more sophisticated language of the central ideas of older theories. Only by becoming aware of our criminological heritage, therefore, can we understand the theoretical-philosophical assumptions that pervade our current ideas of crime, justice, punishment, and treatment. The articles that comprise this volume, excerpted from the works of the major theorists of the past two centuries so as to focus on the central idea of each man, the general introduction by Stephen Schafer, and the introductions to the five parts provide a glimpse into the exchange of ideas over time that has brought criminological theorizing to its present state. Richard D. Knudten concludes the volume with a discussion of the direction that criminological theorizing will take in the future and a presentation of his middle-range theory of relativity, which brings the historical panorama of criminological theorizing into contemporary focus.

Like most literary efforts, this one is also a product of many minds and hands. The editors wish to acknowledge the special assistance of Lee Nagle, John Goerdt, Lynelle Gramm, Karen McLaughlin, and Gilla McCarriston, who handled many of the tasks involved in manuscript development; the typing assistance of Carolyn Sanders, Alison Ressler, and Terry Parker; and, finally the help of our wives, Lili Schafer and Mary S. Knudten, who have served as both critics and sounding boards for ideas in the development of this volume.

*Stephen Schafer*
*Richard D. Knudten*

# Introduction: The Quest to Understand Crime

*Stephen Schafer*

## Historical Approaches to the Problem of Crime

Historically, the interpretation of and response to crime, perhaps the oldest of all recognized social problems, have passed through several consecutive but frequently overlapping phases.

In primitive societies, crime was regarded as an act of malevolence, and the idea of revenge dominated the response to the crime problem. Crimes committed against the whole community, such as treachery or treason, were constrained through collective action, but redress of an attack against an individual was held to be the responsibility of the victim, who alone or in company with family members or friends, did his best to get even with his attacker. But when the victim thus responded, the original violator defended himself against the response. The result was an ongoing conflict between the original "criminal" and his "victim" that eventually made the victim the criminal, and the criminal the victim. In this "conceptualization" of the crime problem, both attack and revenge were little more than attempts by both the victim and the offender to secure power in the given territory.[1] The continuance of such acts of revenge and counter-revenge eventually endangered community peace, and a turmoil of back-and-forth revenge-taking characterized these primitive societies.

The spread of religious ideas and the consolidation of such religious practices as asylum (sanctuary for the hunted criminal offered by the Church to stop the cycle of revenge-taking) and *treuga dei* ("peace in the name of god," to interrupt the sequel of war between criminal and his victim) caused a modification and extension of the notion of revenge. In medieval times, most "criminal" aggression was interpreted as an attack against the deity, which unless placated, would release grave misfortunes (for example, flood, earthquake, pestilence, plague) upon the community. The practice of revenge, influenced by superstition and reinforced by a capricious approach to the application of criminal responsibility, became widespread, resembling a mass madness. Demonology, mysticism, magic, and witchcraft were the dominant features of this "religious" conception of criminal justice. Cruel punishments characterized this era. Because it was believed that the criminal was a sinner who "must not only pay a debt to society; he must get right with God,"[2] this period was one of the bloodiest in human history.

By the late Middle Ages, when the state possessed unlimited power, crime was viewed as an attack against the ruler and was controlled by imposing severe punishments on the transgressor. Although the era began with a system of "com-

position"—an attempt to avoid private and blood revenge by establishing monetary or economic compensation in accordance with an intricate scale—a
philosophy of deterrence dominated the period. As urban life and commerce
developed during the first decades after the Middle Ages, vagabonds, adventurers,
and other new types of criminals compounded the crime problem. Grotesque
punishments shaped the response to crime. Because of the autocratic rule of the
sovereign, the public had no protection against political corruption or judicial
miscarriages. State criminal law, conceived in the blood of despotism, assumed
that revenge offered the only solution to the crime problem.

The Enlightenment reduced some of the horrors of the earlier periods. By
the end of the eighteenth century, the notion of bloody revenge had been replaced to a large extent by humanitarian ideals, deterrence by correction, arbitrariness and despotism by moderation and some guarantees of individual
freedom. By this time criminal justice had become entirely a state matter, and
all crime was held to be an act against the public interest. This was the age of the
"Italian Montesquieu" Gaetano Filangieri, an eminent advocate of criminal-law
reform; of Josef Sonnenfels, the Austrian proponent of radical change; of
Professors Claproth and Quistrop, enthusiastic German opponents of corporal
punishment; of John Howard, the unswerving prison reformer and true English
gentleman; and of Jeremy Bentham, the philosopher who linked morals and
legislation. It was an age of opposition to the older concept of criminal responsibility. Voltaire and the Encyclopedists prepared the foundation for the existing
reorientation of criminal law to the concept of the natural rights of man and
more humanistic goals propounded by the Italian Marchese de Beccaria.[3]

While safeguards for the rights of the individual against the arbitrariness of
the courts were introduced during this period, they did not take variations in
human conduct into account. Crime was conceived in purely legal terms; punishment was regarded as a just response to guilt, not as a corrective or rehabilitative
measure. This period made abstraction of the concept of crime a dominating
force and limited criminal justice to the mere interpretation of the written law.
The courts meted out punishment on the assumption that each violator acted
freely through his will, ignoring the intricate nature of the human beings and
their complex interactions, group characteristics, or social problems that were
the root causes of crime.

However, during this period such questions arose as: Is the will really free?
Is a person's will solely responsible for his unlawful conduct? In the search for
answers, it became apparent that other factors contribute to deviance. Whereas
in the eighteenth century the individualistic emphasis of criminal law held man
directly responsible for the antisocial acts he committed, and judged the harm
caused by the act, the emphasis in the nineteenth century was on judging the
criminal himself and searching for the factors responsible for his conduct. New
theories of crime, free of the ideas of revenge and deterrence, began to mitigate
some of the abuses apparent in the eighteenth and early nineteenth centuries.

Although this period is traditionally believed to have begun with the work of Cesare Lombroso in the 1870s, the scientific search for the causes of crime had in fact begun long before his work was published. Lombroso, the "great instigator" of ideas in criminology,[4] was not the first. Many before Lombroso had been fascinated by the concept of criminal predestination and by the notion that criminality could be predicted from a man's constitution. Others before Lombroso had attempted to relate crime to man's mental characteristics or physical appearance. Well into the nineteenth century the mentally unbalanced were treated as criminals. The sick mind, believed to be the product of an alliance with evil forces, was held to be an indication of future criminality.

The possible relationship between the shape of the individual's skull and his personality, including criminal behavior, attracted many early thinkers, among them even Aristotle, who was especially interested in the behavioral reflexes of the mind. Even before Aristotle, a Greek physiognomist who examined Socrates reportedly found in his skull and face indications of brutality and an inclination to be alcoholic.[5] The Roman physician Galen placed great emphasis on constitutional factors and their influence on behavior patterns. In the sixteenth century J. Baptiste della Porte, studying cadavers of criminals, founded the school of "human physiognomy." By the eighteenth century, physiognomy, the study of facial features, and phrenology, the study of the external conformations of the cranium, had developed as disciplines with the publication by the Swiss theologian Johann Caspar Lavater of a four-volume work on *Physiognomical Fragments.*[6] This was followed by work on "cranioscopy" by the Austrian anatomist Franz Joseph Gall and by Johann Gaspar Spurzheim in the first half of the nineteenth century. H. Lauvergne, prison doctor of the Toulon penitentiary, became a student of "peculiar faces," and the American Charles Caldwell wrote a textbook on this subject.[7] By the second half of the nineteenth century, phrenology was taken rather seriously.[8] The reports of the Eastern Penitentiary in Philadelphia from 1855 to 1865, for example, all contained phrenological profiles of the inmates.

Except by those who believed that mental illness was a factor in criminal behavior, criminality was held to be a product of demonic action or human cruelty. Only in the nineteenth century did some physicians begin to contribute to the development of criminal psychiatry. In England, James C. Pritchard's "new" pathology related "moral insanity" to criminal symptoms. In France, Britain, and Italy, Augustin Morel, Prosper Despine, Henry Maudsley, and Paul Broca, who in 1858 established the Société d'Anthropologie de Paris, approached the problem scientifically.

During this period, the science of statistics was organized. The Belgian astronomer and mathematician Adolphe Quetelet pioneered this effort. André Michel Guerry, Moreau de Jonnés, the Baltic theologian Alexander von Oettingen, the Belgian Edouard Ducpétiaux, the the German Georg von Mayr, together with Quetelet, were the leading proponents of measuring crime, anticipating many of the theories that arose in the middle of the nineteenth century and later.

The notion of social defense in criminology, a byproduct of the work of

Cesare Lombroso, Raffaele Garofalo, and Enrico Ferri, the "Holy Three of Criminology," revolutionalized the way of looking at the criminal. The seminal work of these three Italians made it clear that the era of religious explanations of crime was over and the age of scientific research had begun. Although Lombroso, Garofalo, and Ferri differed in the etiologies they proposed, the "enthusiastic doctor," the "sober anthropologist," and the "extremist sociologist," as they are sometimes respectively called, generally agreed that what was needed was a scientific treatment of the offender rather than a mere discussion of penalties. Each shifted in theoretical orientation from the criminal act to the criminal man. Although some of their ideas are often disparaged by modern students of criminology, the fruits of the seeds these men sowed a century ago are discernible even today.

Lombroso related psychic attitudes to physical characteristics. His studies of the lesions of the central nervous system, the crania, and the anthropometry of criminals culminated in his major book, *L'Uomo delinquente.*[9] The first edition contained 252 pages; the fifth and final edition, published twenty years later, 1,903 pages. This last work, which included not only modifications in his thoughts but thousands of new measurements, gained an enthusiastic reception and gave support to Lombroso's growing reputation.

Lombroso's general theory, crystallized in his mind after the post-mortem examination of the famous brigand Vilella, suggested that a criminal is an atavistic being, a biological throwback born "out of his own time" who possesses the ferocious and savage instincts of primitive man and the lower animals. Criminals, Lombroso proposed, can be distinguished from noncriminals by certain degenerative physical characteristics and physically inferior morphological features. Unable to adjust to modern civilization, the atavistic man clashes with his society and participates in crime. Such an offender, to use Ferri's term, is a "born criminal."

Garofalo contributed to the development of criminology through a discussion of many problems still vividly challenging today; for example, restitution to criminal victims, the "socialist superstition," and the need for international solidarity in combating crimes. His fame rests largely on his *Criminology,*[10] published when he was only twenty-eight years old. In it he made an effort to define the concept of "natural crime" on the basis of the criminal's lack of certain fundamental moral sentiments and moved toward a sociological notion of criminal conduct based on "injury to the society." Criminals, he believed, lacked pity and probity, which he saw as a reflection of the average moral sense of the community, and thus possessed a psychic or moral freedom to commit crime.

Ferri, a disciple of Lombroso, overshadowed his *spiritus rector* in many respects. A brilliant criminal lawyer, a member of the Italian parliament, editor of the socialist newspaper *Avanti,* a persuasive public lecturer and polemicist, a university professor, and a highly esteemed scholar, he was the leader of the so-called positivist school of criminal science, which attempted to explain crime "in its reality" without metaphysical speculations. At the age of twenty-one Ferri published *The Denial of Free Will and the Theory of Imputability,* which treated a problem even now neglected by students of crime. When he was only twenty-five, he became a professor at the University of Bologna, lecturing on the "new horizons" of criminal law (the title of one of his major works, later changed to Criminal Sociology).[11]

The core of Ferri's thought involved the replacement of the idea of moral responsibility with "social accountablity."[12] Because of the need for means of social protection other than punishment of the criminal, Ferri proposed "penal substitutes" (*sostituiti penali*), equivalent to penalties, which he reserved primarily for prevention. Repressive means, or, as he called them, "eliminative means," were to be applied to some crimes. He proposed the broadest possible correctional and penal system, ranging from social reform, socialization and reparative measures, repressive punishment, to the death penalty, the "last and most severe" intervention. In his program he gave support to radical social reforms yet he did not believe that social factors are the sole stimulants of crime. Nor did he concur with the Italian Napoleone Colajanni or with the renowned French sociologist Émile Durkheim in doubting the significance of individual organic factors in the development of deviance. Colajanni emphasized the economic factors of crime and the inability of the capitalist system to satisfy the wants of man and Durkheim contended that crime is an index of the strength of the collective conscience. Ferri took a multifactor approach to the criminal-deviance problem, seeing crime as a complex phenomenon with roots in both biological and physiosocial forces.

Cesare Lombroso's biological models of crime causation, Raffaele Garofalo's plea for a juristic understanding of crime, and Enrico Ferri's convincing stand for a sociological criminology in the last quarter of the nineteenth century marked significant departures from the notion of revenge and the beginning of attempts to theorize about the crime problem. Whereas the idea of revenge emphasized a return attack against the criminal, the idea of social defense emphasized understanding of the factors causing legal violations and transformation of the lawbreaker into a law-abiding individual.


## Crime Theories in Our Time

Three major orientations have emerged in the last hundred years from the long series of theoretical and empirical research efforts to understand crime. The *biological school* searches for the causes of crime in the physical and constitutional characteristics of the criminal himself. The *psychological school* seeks an answer to the problem of crime in man's mental processes. The *sociocultural school* locates the roots of criminality in the environment rather than in the individual and essentially supports Quetelet's thesis that "*tout le monde est*

*coupable du crime, exepté le criminel"* (everyone is guilty except the criminal).
Each of the three schools in addition includes suborientations that move in
different directions within the broader orientation of which they are a part. The
*compromissary school* strives to reconcile the propositions of these three approaches, viewing crime as a product of complex and multiple factors.

## The Biological School

The biological approach focuses on biological, somatological, or anthropological
models. This orientation, first established at the international criminal-anthropological congresses shortly before and after the turn of the century, holds basically that a criminal is biologically different from normal human beings. Because
he is partially or totally an abnormal organism, his conduct is likely to be somewhat deviant. His criminal conduct, in other words, originates in his somatic
abnormalities. The criminal should therefore be studied by criminal biologists or
anthropologists, as Ferri suggested, in anatomical or physiological laboratories.
The offender is criminal, according to this school, because his freedom of will is
subordinate to deterministic psychosomatic forces.

Hans Kurella, Lombroso's enthusiastic follower and friend, was one of those
who contended that criminality expresses itself "with an unavoidable necessity,
completely irrespective of social and individual life conditions." Others whose
work falls within this orientation are Hamilton D. Wey, who strongly believed in
somatic causes of crime; August Drähms, who collected a vast amount of data to
prove that man's biological makeup is responsible for crime; and Frances Kellor,
who investigated the physical characteristics of female offenders. The first
major criminal-anthropological study following Lombroso's work was completed
by Charles Buckman Goring, who claimed that he was "forced" to hypothesize
the existence of a characteristic in all men that he called "criminal diathesis": a
mental, moral, or physical proclivity to commit crime. Ernest A. Hooton,
although one of Goring's fiercest critics, eventually reached essentially similar
conclusions. At the end of a twelve-year anthropological study, he concluded
that criminals are organically inferior and that crime is the result of the impact
of the environment upon "low-grade human organisms."[13]

The so-called body type school, which includes some reference to the psychological aspects of crime, also belongs to the biological orientation. Among its
prominent supporters were Ernst Kretschmer, who classified men by specific
physical characteristics and related these characteristics to their temperamental
differences, and William H. Sheldon, who studied the connection between body
type and delinquent tendencies. A segment of this biological school of thought
also investigated the "destiny of twins." Johannes Lange, for example, concluded
from his research on twins that criminality is hereditary; Friedrich Stumpfl
related crime to the life career of twins; and A.J. Rosanoff and his collaborators

found a close relationship between identical twins in the etiology of childhood misbehavior, juvenile delinquency, and adult criminality.[14]

Still in the sphere of the biological theories but with a stronger leaning toward a psychological explanation are hypotheses that emphasize psychosomatic conditions as a cause of crime. Louis Vervaeck, who established in Belgium in 1907 what is believed to be the first criminal-biological clinic in the world, propounded a close relationship between the physical organism and personality tendencies. Adolf Lenz, founder of the criminal-biological observation institute at the University of Graz, argued the need to analyze the "whole life," physical and psychic, in order to understand the criminal personality. Karl Birnbaum proposed a theory of criminal psychopathology and the psychobiological study of criminals. M.G. Schlapp and E.H. Smith based their "new criminology" on the assumption that about a third of criminal offenders show glandular or toxic disturbances. Franz Exner contended that crime was due to inherited predispositions that are manifested under the pressure of an unfavorable social environment. In the past few years, abnormal distribution of human sex chromosomes, specifically the XYY carriers, has been mentioned as a causative factor within the framework of the biological theories.[15]

### The Psychological School

Although the biological, somatological, or anthropological orientations often touch upon psychic aspects, the psychological and psychiatric approaches to crime are clearly distinct from the biological ones. While the biological-somatic approaches stress constitutional characteristics and regard the psychic components as only supplementary elements, the psychological and psychiatric theories seek answers to the crime problem in mental processes, regardless of any physical stigmata or disorder. In this group of theories the criminal's psyche or mind is held responsible for his negative response to a legal command. Such deficiencies of psychic functioning are often conceived in terms of hereditary mental degeneration, mental illness, psychopathic disorders, and emotional disturbances. By the nineteenth century, psychiatry and psychology had broken loose from the type of thought that saw crime in terms of demons taking possession of individual minds and began to develop diverse explanations.

Probably the earliest explanation of crime linked it with hereditary mental degeneration, a kind of reversion to a lower type. Numerous "family trees" were constructed as evidence of the correlation between degenerate family life and antisocial conduct. Despine's Chrétien family, Aubry's Kéromgal family, Poeman's Zero family, McCullouch's Tribe of Ischmael, Blackmar's Smoky Pilgrims, and Davenport's Nam family are examples of a number of sordid family trees studied by criminologists, who explained crime and deviance among the members (somewhat questionably, owing to poor methodology) in terms of hereditary mental degeneration. The analysis of the descendants of Ada Juke, known as the "mother of criminals," by Richard Dugdale and Arthur Estabrook, and Henry Herbert Goddard's examination of the Kallikak family are among the best of these studies.[16]

Psychoses, defects of the central nervous system, neurasthenia, and inadequate mental ability have all at varying times been blamed for crime. But for some time the post popular explanation has involved analytic or dynamic psychiatry. Sigmund Freud's epoch-making contributions opened the way to an understanding of psychodynamics in the development of criminal conduct. Like Lombroso, Freud modified his basic hypothesis several times, paying increasing attention to societal factors. This suggests that, if he had lived longer, he might have become one of the outstanding early sociologists. However, most of his followers draw heavily upon his earliest doctrines,[17] ignoring his more sociological concepts. Such collaborators and disciples as Carl G. Jung, Alfred Adler, Otto Rank, Karen Horney, August Aichorn, Kate Friedlander, and Kurt R. Eissler have disagreed with certain aspects of Freud's original system and have since moved in different directions.

### The Sociological School

The sociological school, which contends that the criminal is a product of his society, can also be differentiated into suborientations. One of these focuses on man's surroundings, a concern traditionally referred to as criminal ecology. Gabriel Tarde's "laws of imitation," explaining crime in terms of "learned behavior," is one of the earliest ecological explanations. More recent criminal ecology theories attempt to anticipate these ecologically determined learning processes by searching for spatial influences on social life and deviant behavior. The pioneering efforts in this direction were made by Sophonisba Breckenridge and Edith Abbott, who in 1912 examined "delinquent neighborhoods" in Chicago.[18] Clifford R. Shaw, later joined by Henry D. McKay, also concentrated on the problems of juvenile delinquency. As a result of marking the residences of "official" delinquents on a map of Chicago and other cities they investigated, they coined the term "delinquency areas." Another "ecologist," Bernard Lander, studied Baltimore and argued against the concept of "ecological determinism"; he attributed high delinquency rates, rather, to anomic life situations.[19] Roland Chilton made an attempt to reconcile the findings of the various delinquency-area studies; his results did not support Lander's conclusions. The Englishman Terence Morris, who studied an English town and also analyzed many of the American and British efforts in this field, eventually questioned the methods generally used in the delinquency-area studies. Although many of the old beliefs concerning the influence of physical surroundings upon delinquency and crime can no longer be defended as valid, it can still be argued that the criminal man, as Hans von Hentig has noted, is a "puppet of time and space."[20]

A second subgroup within the sociological school sees criminal conduct as originating in abnormalities of the criminal's social existence or in society's behavior toward him. Criminality is a form of antisociality. Because the criminal is by definition socially distinct from the conventional members of a society, he is unaffected by the threat of traditional retributive punishment. According to the general argument of this school, the solution to the crime problem can be found only in an analysis of the criminal's relationship to his social environment, instead of in the physical aspects of the social surroundings.

This orientation itself includes numerous, sometimes overlapping, emphases, drawn from various sectors of the social sciences and even from other disciplines. Several of these orientations are only modifications of old theories of crime and delinquent behavior. Pitirim A. Sorkin, referring to theories and research in his time, correctly contended that the "main body of current research represents mainly a reiteration, variation, refinement and verification of the methods and theories developed by sociologists of the preceding period" and that "few of these improvements represent anything revolutionary or basically new."[21]

Some of these theories may be considered "offensive" from the point of view of the criminal in that they emphasize his "free will," which reacts to social injustice by causing him to attack society through crime. Others "blame" the society as a whole in that criminal conduct, they claim, is learned or acquired by the criminal as he operates within a social context. Still other theories lean in the direction of social psychology, focusing on crime as a product of socialization processes, or explain crime in terms of cultural differences, value or norm conflicts, or an imperfect or divided social structure.

The "offensive" approach to crime assumes that man freely decides whether or not to engage in criminal activity. Because the criminal believes that his aspirations cannot be realized in legitimate ways, he comes to regard society as unnecessarily constraining or unjust. To attain his aspirations, he therefore deliberately violates the legal norms that stand in his path. Cesare Beccaria is perhaps the classic exponent of this approach: his formalistic and essentially retributive theory has dominated criminal practice for 150 years.[22] Although they often deny it, most lawyers, courts, and penal systems continue to operate on this principle.

Although the "defensive" approaches to the crime problem do not deny the criminal's personal responsibility for his conduct, the interrelationship between the criminal and his environment remains the essential theoretical element. Crime is explained in terms of socially acquired conduct; it is a product of learning occurring within interpersonal relationships or of imperfect, misdirected, or undirected socialization. Thus, almost a hundred years before Cohen, Cloward and Ohlin, Miller, and other subcultural theorists of the 1950s and 1960s, Benoit Augustin Morel proposed that crime was learned and called attention to "moral contagion," Paul Aubry spoke of the "contagion of murder," and M.A. Vaccaro[23] similarly anticipated many contemporary learning theories. Gabriel Tarde gave the strongest voice to this viewpoint; it was he who identified interactional relationships that produce criminal patterns. The most outstanding American adherent of Tarde's theories was Edwin H. Sutherland, who drew on Tarde's work in his theory of "differential association," first stated in 1939 in the third edition of his *Principles of Criminology* and also in his penetrating analysis of the "professional thief."[24] Crime was described as socially acquired behavior in Edmund Mezger's *Legensfuhrungsschuld*, "responsibility for the life conduct," and in Ernst Seelig's *Lebensformen*, which refers to "forms of life" amenable to socialization processes.[25]

Another suborientation of the defensive-type sociological theories holds that cultural values, norms, and conflicts are responsible for the criminal's breaking of the law. Whereas the offensive approaches seem to advocate broad-scale cultural change, the defensive theories suggest a need for cultural correction. Adolphe Prins pioneered in this vein. More recently, Thorsten Sellin has described crime as a product of the conflict of conduct norms, as has Donald R. Taft.[26]

Sociological theories also include a group that finds crime to be a product of structural disturbances within the social system. While these theories generally contend that inconsistencies abound in the social structure and in the distribution of values, means, goals, and rewards, they do not typically recommend any radical change in the basic value system or in the economic or the general social construction of society. It is at this critical point that the social-existence theories differ from the work of Émile Durkheim, the French student of social organization who introduced the concept of anomie, the idea that the weakening or absence of rules and norms may lead to deviant behavior. Robert K. Merton was perhaps the first modern American sociologist to use this concept, relating it primarily to the American social structure. He contends that access to approved modes of acquiring success symbols is restricted or completely absent for a considerable portion of the population. Donald Cressey noted that this theory explains the overrepresentation of working-class members, young males, blacks, native white Americans, and urban dwellers in the American criminal population. Albert K. Cohen applied Merton's anomie theory in his study of delinquent boys, and Richard A. Cloward and Lloyd E. Ohlin in their study of delinquent gangs drew heavily upon Sutherland's differential association theory, from Durkheim's rich intellectual inventory, and from Merton's applications of anomie.[27]

A third group of sociological theories focuses on the economic conditions and structures of society and proposes changes in these elements in order to reduce crime. Economic conditions as a generating cause of crime engaged the attention of thinkers even before the rise of modern criminology. Xenophon, Plato, Aristotle, Virgil, and Horace all touched upon this subject; Thomas More in his *Utopia* commented on the economic conditions of England as they related to crime.[28] Although crime and delinquency are not confined to the poor, the close relationship between poverty and crime is impossible to ignore.

A Leipzig professor of criminal law, K.F. Hoemmel, in a lecture presented in April 1765 (a few months after Beccaria's work appeared), theorized that punishment is useless and ineffective so long as the misery that causes the criminal's action is uncorrected. In the nineteenth century, J.M. Charles Lucas also argued that crime originates in misery,[29] and even Morel and Lombroso made allowances within their markedly biological theories for poverty and misery as causes of crime. In fact, many theories of the nineteenth century refer to the role of economic conditions in criminality. The early statisticians Quetelet, Guerry, Ducpetiaux, von Mayr, Corne, Valentini, and Oettingen dealt with the relationship between economic conditions and crime. Although most of them did not recognize poverty as the principal cause, they believed it to be influential. A number of analysts, including Mittelstadt, Aschrott, Schmoller, Starke, Tugan-Baranowsky, and Rettich, extended the analysis from poverty to general economic conditions, mainly economic crises. The effect of economic conditions on criminality was especially emphasized by the so-called *terza scuola* (the "third school"), including Carnevale and Alimena, among others, which took a stand against the Lombrosian anthropological approach, arguing for a social and economic explanation of the crime problem. Perhaps E. Fornasari de Verce presented the most extensive nineteenth-century study of the relationship of economic conditions and crime.[30]

The twentieth-century Dutch lawyer and publicist Willem Adriaan Bonger, on the other hand, contended that the structure of capitalist society exerts varying pressures on the different social classes. (This calls to mind Radzinowicz's comment that Merton's notion of class vulnerability, a dimension he added to Durkheim's anomie theory, was "in some ways curiously reminiscent of Bonger.")[31] Bonger certainly was not the first to seek the answer to the problem of crime in the characteristics of capitalist economic systems. The historical understanding of economic conditions, the significance of the class struggle, the idea of surplus value, and other issues of Marxist ideology, toward which Bonger seemed to lean so strongly, were known in one form or another even before Karl Marx and Friedrich Engels united them into a single theory. Filippo Turati, in the second half of the nineteenth century, was probably the first to fully delineate a Marxist theory of crime and to propose that economic factors are virtually the only causes of criminality. This group also included Alfredo Niceforo, who pointed out the important role of class conflict; Max Nordau, who proposed a "new biological theory of crime" and in a Marxist fashion emphasized "human parasitism," an idea later adapted by the socialist criminal-law system of the Soviet Union; and Achille Loria, who heavily attacked the capitalist economic structure. Similarly, Bruno Battaglia took a Marxist stance, and Antonio Marro, in reviewing the characteristics of criminals, discovered that the desperate financial status of the proletariat produces a faulty nervous sytem which in turn leads to deviant behavior.[32]

A towering figure among the nineteenth-century criminal socialists was

Napoleone Colajanni, who identified himself closely with the Marxists, but without subscribing to all the original Marxist doctrines.[33] A milestone was reached
in the socialist perpsective of crime in 1899, when the law faculty of the University of Amsterdam offered a prize for a "systematic and critical review of the
literature concerning the influence of economic conditions on criminality."
Only students of the university submitted papers. Joseph van Kan won the gold
medal for a work published in 1903, and Willem Adriaan Bonger received honor-
able mention for his work, published in 1905. Both became fundamental
documents in the history of criminological thought. Although both men were
committed to economic collectivism and a socialist social order, neither sympa-
thized with any system of dictatorship.

What Turati, van Kan, and Bonger dreamed of was realized when the
Bolsheviks came to power in Russia in October 1917. The dethronement of
capitalism resulted in the establishment of a so-called supra-universalistic approach to the crime problem. This orientation tends to disregard individualistic
crime factors in favor of the primacy of its central ideological idea. Thus the
Soviet approach to crime emphasized broad social conditions, social cohesion,
and extensive social responsibility. However, its focus is not so much upon the
*universe* (that is, society as *is*) as upon the *supra-universe* (that is, the ideo-
logically viewed society as it *will be*). The victim of crime, therefore, is not a
person or a morality or the state but the governing ideology, which is itself
dominantly influenced by economic conditions and the economic structure of
the society.

### The Multifactor Approach (the Compromissary School)

The theoretical orientation referred to as the compromissary school represents a
multifactor approach to the crime problem; it attempts to synthesize the concerns of the biological, psychological, and sociological schools. Although this
theoretical stand emerged fully only after the first biological and psychological
explanations were developed, adherents of multiple causation proposed their
eclectic theories at the time of Enrico Ferri.

The pioneers of the modern multifactor approach were the Belgian Adolphe
Prins and the German Franz von Liszt, who, together with the Dutchman G.A.
van Hamel, established the International Association of Penal Law. Holding to
the basic assumption of multiple causation, they made efforts to rationalize the
discrepancies among the three major groups of monofactor theories.[34] Thus
Liszt conceived an approach which he called *Gesamte Strafrechtswissenschaft,*
the "global science of criminal law." On the American scene, at the beginning of
this century, William Healy led in multifactor development; a decade later in
England Cyril Burt formulated his multifactor explanation of crime. Walter C.
Reckless after World War II proposed a "containment theory" based on an attempt to combine crime factors, and Marvin E. Wolfgang and Franco Ferracuti

have recently attempted to reconcile the differing disciplines with the goal of developing an integrated theoretical understanding of crime.[35]

From this brief outline of the history of criminological thought it should be apparent that hypotheses regarding the causes of crime are legion. They may be differentiated in terms of those appearing from the publication of Lombroso's work in 1896 to the 1930s and those developed since that time. The first group consists of contemplative and philosophical works that are often vulnerable when subjected to empirical examination; the second is characterized by a lack of attention to past theoretical efforts and a strong dependence on empirical research and statistical methods. In this more recent period, many analyses and hypotheses have tended either to prejudge the issue or to ignore questions fundamental to the crime, delinquency, and deviance problem. Most theories of this second period merely skim the surface of the problem or propose only restatements of old theoretical concepts. When Sutherland put forth his "differential association" theory based on learning: Merton his concept of "anomie," indicating that all crimes are goal oriented; Cohen his "delinquent subculture," referring to contagion and also to a kind of subconscious class struggle; Cloward and Ohlin their "opportunity structures," calling attention to a characteristic feature of all capitalistic societies—all of these theorists offered a wealth of illuminating scholarship, yet they almost totally neglected such problems as the essence of law and the lawmaking processes, the changing nature of morality, questions of social power and social change, the political nature of the definition of crime and delinquency, and many other basic issues of the crime problem. They also ignored the fact that most of what they proposed had already been suggested a century earlier; there is hardly any new theory that does not carry the thoughts of the past, and hardly any that attempts to approach the fundamental questions of the crime problem, without which no empirical study can be truly fruitful. The history of criminological thought suggests not only that many so-called new theories are actually not new, but also that the crime problem is composed of many challenging mysteries.

## Notes

1. See Stephen Schafer, *Theories in Criminology: Past and Present Philosophies of the Crime Problem* (New York: 1969), pp. 97–110.

2. Donald R. Taft, *Criminology,* 3rd ed. (New York: 1956), p. 357.

3. See Cesare Bonesana, Marchese de Beccaria, *Trattato dei delitti e delle pene* (Tuscany: 1764).

4. Joseph van Kan, *Les causes economiques de la criminalité* (Paris: 1903), p. 59.

5. Reported in Havelock Ellis, *The Criminal,* 2nd ed. (New York: 1900), p. 27.

6. Johann Caspar Lavater, *Physiognomical Fragments* (Zurich: 1775).

7. Charles Caldwell, *Elements of Phrenology* (New York: 1824).

8. See Schafer, *Theories in Criminology,* and Richard D. Knudten, *Crime in a Complex Society* (Homewood, Ill.: 1970).

9. Cesare Lombroso, *L'Uomo delinquente* (Milan: 1876).

10. Raffaele Garofalo, *Criminology,* trans. by Robert Syness Millar (Boston: 1914); the first Italian edition appeared in 1885.

11. Enrico Ferri, *I Nuovi Orizzonti del Diritto e della Procedura Penale* (Turin: 1881); rev. 2nd ed. was published under the title *La Sociologia Criminale* (Turin: 1884); the English edition is entitled *Criminal Sociology,* trans. by Joseph I. Kelly and John Lisle (repr. New York: 1967).

12. Ibid. (English ed.), pp. 352–356.

13. Hans Kurella, *Naturgeschichte des Verbrechers: Grundzüge der Kriminellen Anthropologie und Kriminalpsychologie* (Stuttgart, 1893); Hamilton D. Wey, *Criminal Anthropology* (New York: 1890); August Drähms, *The Criminal: His Personnel and Environment* (New York: 1900); Frances Kellor, *Experimental Sociology* (New York: 1901); Charles B. Goring, *The English Convict: A Statistical Study* (London: 1913); and Ernest A. Hooton, *The American Criminal: An Anthropological Study* (Cambridge, Mass.: 1939), 1:309.

14. Ernst Kretschmer, *Physique and Character,* trans. by W.J.H. Sprott (London: 1925); William H. Sheldon, *Varieties of Delinquent Youth: An Introduction to Constitutional Psychiatry* (New York: 1949); Johannes Lange, *Crime and Destiny,* trans. by Charlotte Haldane (New York: 1930); Friedrich Stumpfl, "Kriminalbiologie," in Rudolf Sieverts, ed., *Handwörterbuch der Kriminologie,* 2nd ed. (Berlin, 1967–1968), 1:50; and A.J. Rosanoff, Leva M. Handy, and Isabel A. Rosanoff, "Etiology of Child Behavior Difficulties, Juvenile Delinquency, and Adult Criminality," *Psychiatric Monographs* (California Department of Institutions, 1941), no. 1.

15. Louis Vervaeck, *Syllabus du cours d'anthropologie criminelle donné à la prison de Forest* (Brussels: 1926); Adolf Lenz, *Grudriss der Kriminalbiologie* (Berlin: 1927); Karl Birnbaum, *Kriminal-psychopathologie und Psychobiologische Verbrecherkunde* (Berlin: 1931); M.G. Schlapp and E.H. Smith, *The New Criminology* (New York: 1928); Franz Exner, *Kriminologie* (Berlin: 1949); Patricia A. Jacobs and J.A. Strong, "A Case of Human Intersexuality Having a Possible XYY Sex-Determining Mechanism," *Nature* 183 (1959): 302; M.D. Casey et al., "YY Chromosomes and Antisocial Behavior," *Lancet* 2 (1966): 859; and a great number of studies in recent years.

16. Richard Louis Dugdale, *The Jukes: A Study in Crime, Pauperism, Disease and Heredity* (New York: 1895); Arthur Eastabrook, *The Jukes in 1915* (New York: 1916); and Henry Herbert Goddard, *The Kallikak Family: A Study in the Heredity of Feeble-mindedness* (New York: 1913).

17. Among the numerous well-known works of Sigmund Freud, see *A General Introduction to Psychoanalysis* (New York: 1920); *Das Ich und das Es* (Vienna: 1923); *Hemmung, Symptom und Angst* (Vienna: 1926); and *An Outline of Psychoanalysis* (New York: 1949).

18. Gabriel Tarde, *La Philosophie penale* (Paris: 1890); and Sophonisba P. Breckenridge and Edith Abbott, *The Delinquent Child and the Home* (New York: 1912).

19. Clifford R. Shaw, *Delinquency Areas* (Chicago: 1929); Shaw and Henry D. McKay, *Social Factors in Juvenile Delinquency* (Washington, D.C.: 1931); Shaw and McKay, *Juvenile Delinquency and Urban Areas: A Study of Rates of Delinquents in Relation to Different Characteristics of Local Communities in American Cities* (Chicago: 1942); and Bernard Lander, *Toward an Understanding of Juvenile Delinquency* (New York: 1954).

20. Roland J. Chilton, "Continuity in Delinquency Area Research: A Comparison of Studies for Baltimore, Detroit and Indianapolis," *American Sociological Review* 29 (February 1964): 71-83; Terence Morris, *The Criminal Area* (London: 1958); and Hans von Hentig, *Das Verbrechen: I. Der Kriminelle Mensch im Kraftespiel von Zeit und Raum* (Berlin: 1961).

21. Pitirim A. Sorokin, "Sociology of Yesterday, Today and Tomorrow," *American Sociological Review* 30 (December 1965): 834.

22. Beccaria, *Trattato dei delitti.*

23. Benoit Augustin Morel, *De la contagion morale: Du danger que presente pour la moralité et securité publique la relation des crimes donnée par les journaux* (Marseille: 1870); Paul Aubry, *La contagion de meurtre* (Paris: 1894); and M.A. Vaccaro, *Genesi e funzioni delle leggi penale* (Rome: 1889).

24. Tarde, *Philosophie penale,* and Edwin H. Sutherland, *Principles of Criminology,* 3rd ed. (New York: 1939).

25. Edmund Mezger, *Strafrecht* (Munich: 1948), and Ernst Seelig, "Die Gliederung der Verbrecher," in Ernst Seelig and Karl Weindler, eds., *Die Typen der Kriminellen* (Berlin: 1949).

26. Adolphe Prins, *Criminalité et repression* (Brussels: 1886); Thorsten Sellin, *Culture Conflict and Crime,* Social Science Research Council Bulletin 41 (New York, 1938); and Taft, *Criminology.*

27. Émile Durkheim, *De la division du travail social* (Paris: 1893); Durkheim, *Le suicide* (Paris: 1897); Robert K. Merton, "Social Structure and Anomie," *American Sociological Review* 3 (1938): 672-682; Donald R. Cressey, "Crime," in Robert K. Merton and Robert A. Nisbet, eds., *Contemporary Social Problems,* 2nd ed. (New York: 1966), p. 180; Albert K. Cohen, *Delinquent Boys: The Culture of the Gang* (New York: 1955); and Richard A. Cloward and Lloyd E. Ohlin, *Delinquency and Opportunity: A Theory of Delinquent Gangs* (Glencoe, Ill;: 1960).

28. Sir Thomas More, *De Optimo Reipublicae Statu Sive de Nova Insula Utopia.* The first edition was probably published in Louvain in 1516.

29. J.M. Charles Lucas, *Du système pénal et du système répressif en general, de la peine de mort en particulier* (Paris: 1827).

30. E. Fornasari de Verce, *La criminalita e le vicende economiche d'Italia dal 1873 al 1890 e osservazioni sommarie per il Regno Unito della Gran Bretagne e Irlanda (1840-1890) e per la Nova Galles del Sud (1882-1891)* (Turin: 1894).

31. Willem Adriaan Bonger, *Criminality and Economic Conditions,* trans. by Henry P. Horton (New York: 1967), and Leon Radzinowicz, *Ideology and Crime* (New York: 1966), p. 90.

32. Filippo Turati, *Il delitto e la questione sociale* (Milan: 1883); Alfredo Niceforo, "Criminalita e condizioni economiche in Sicilia," *Rivista di Scient di Diritto* (1897); Max Nordau, "Une nouvelle theorie biologique du crime," *La Revue* (1902); R. Beermann, "The Parasite Law in the Soviet Union," *The British Journal of Criminology* 3 (July 1962): 71–80; Achille Loria, *Les bases economiques de la constitution sociale* (Paris: 1894); Bruno Battaglia, *La dinamica del delitto* (Naples: 1886); and Antonio Marro, *I caratteri dei delinquenti* (Turin: 1887).

33. Napoleone Colajanni, *Sociologia criminale* (Catania, Sicily: 1889).

34. Prins, *Criminalité et repression*; Prins, *La defense sociale et les transformations du droit penal* (Brussels: 1910); Franz von Liszt, "Die determinsitischen Gegner der Zweckstrafe," an 1893 paper reprinted in his *Strafrechliche Aufsatze und Vortrage* (Berlin: 1905); Gegner der Zweckstrafe, and *Lehrbuch des deutschen Strafrechts* (Berlin: 1881).

35. William Healy, *The Individual Delinquent* (Boston: 1915); Cyril Burt, *The Young Delinquent* (London: 1925); Walter C. Reckless, *The Crime Problem,* 4th ed. (New York: 1967); Marvin E. Wolfgang and Franco Ferracuti, *The Subculture of Violence: Towards an Integrated Theory in Criminology* (London: 1967).

**Part I:
The Concept of Crime**

# Introduction: What is Crime?

The concept of crime has developed over centuries of philosophical debate, conflict, and legislation. From man's earliest days on earth, men have searched for answers to the problems of justice and social control. Plato suggested that justice was doing the greatest good for the greatest number. Others took his and other similar concepts and redirected this discussion to a concern for the victim and his criminal. As this occurred, many questions arose. Where does law flow from? From the Creator? From natural law? From a sovereign? From men who contract with the state to protect their interests even while they give up a portion of their independence?

As the questioning moved from an abstract inquiry into the nature of justice to a recognition that particular laws are created to achieve predetermined results, the definition of what constitutes a crime and who defines what is criminal became more exact. However, this definition varied according to the person making the judgment and the dominant pragmatic and philosophical concerns of the day. What was done with those who violated criminal law depended to a great extent upon the prevailing concept of crime that underlied criminal law, justice and the treatment of the violator.

Criminal law, which defines a given action as constituting a crime, grew out of the interaction of various individuals and groups in society. It is those who hold power who ultimately decide what acts shall be expected and endorsed or prohibited and punished. The concept of crime, therefore, nearly always reflects the value system of the controlling social power. Concepts of ethics and morality are rooted in beliefs in natural law, which flow from both theological and humanistic sources; the idea of crime, on the other hand, is fundamentally rooted in presuppositions concerning sovereignty, social power, and the rights of the group as opposed to those of the individual.

John Austin (1790–1859), an English jurist and legal writer who studied law under John Stuart Mill in the 1820s and who was a disciple of Jeremy Bentham, defines the idea of "positive law" as a body of rules created for intelligent beings by other intelligent beings who have political power over them. Every such law or rule is a command of the sovereign to engage in or restrain from particular behavior. Law is a rule created by one in power for those not in power and is law because of their relative positions. All laws are commands which have their meaning in the ability and authority of the commander to inflict pain or punishment upon those who disobey. The sovereign has no legal obligations or legal barriers. He does not have to observe principles of constitutional law. Men must respond to laws established by men in authority to govern other men who are their relative inferiors.

The late eighteenth-century English philosopher Jeremy Bentham (1748–1832), who criticized the belief that law is the will of the Creator as proposed by his former instructor William Blackstone (1723-1780), sees law as a product of a utilitarian response to the principles of pain and pleasure. The goal of every human pursuit is to add to the sum total of man's pleasures or to diminish the sum total of his pains. Law should, therefore, consider the happiness, security, or pleasure of the individuals who make up a community. In this sense, the legislator's task is utilitarian. The utility of the law can be measured by the extent to which it promotes the pleasure, goodness, and happiness of the people. The purpose of all legislation is the greatest happiness for the greatest number of citizens. The survival of the political community depends upon the obedience shown rulers by their subjects.

Rudolf Ihering, a genius of jurisprudence, took a slightly different tack in arguing in the late 1800s that law is the sum of the compulsory rules enforced within a state which has both organization and coercive force. The normative content of law is its inner side and coercion is its outer, but the law's power of political coercion is derived from the power of the state behind it. Although some persons are politically authorized to sustain the goals of every legal rule or political imperative, the use of coercion is not the right of an individual but rather the task of the state. Accordingly, crime is by definition an endangering social condition that can be eliminated legislatively only by the infliction of punishment.

Not all rules of conduct are laws. According to Edward Westermarck (1862-1939), a Finnish anthropologist and professor of sociology at the University of London, many customs influence or control the behavior of individuals without ever becoming laws. Law and custom are both rules of conduct, but custom has its basis in public opinion, whereas law, on the other hand, has its foundation in a definite legislative act by a sovereign person or body for a person or persons under its subjective control. All laws are presumed to be just in the sense that they are products of the sovereign power and have meaning as long as the social power prevails. Laws that are based upon customs express moral ideas. However, moral ideas are more extensively represented in customs. Punishment, which is an expression of the coercive power of the sovereign person or body, is an expression of societal indignation.

To the late nineteenth- and early twentieth-century Italian positivist jurist and Minister of Justice Raffaele Garofalo (1852-1934), a harmful and immoral act is not a crime in the eyes of public opinion unless it does injury to the fundamental moral "sentiments of pity or probity." When either of these sentiments is violated, the product is "natural crime." The criminal, Garofalo argues from a deterministic point of view, is a person with a lack, an eclipse, or a weakness in one or both of these sentiments. Society must eliminate criminals from civilized society by inflicting death, partial elimination (including imprisonment and transportation), or enforced reparation.

Although there are different kinds of crime, Émile Durkheim (1858-1917), the outstanding nineteenth-century French sociologist who contributed to the philosophy of law, finds a common element among them. Most laws defining a crime have a similar impact upon the moral conscience of nations and produce similar results; every written law seeks to prescribe obligations and to define sanctions. When a custom becomes a written and codified law, it represents a definitive solution to the problems of conduct. An act is criminal, Durkheim contends, "when it offends strong and defined states of the collective conscience." Repressive law originates in common beliefs and sentiments and is an index of the strength of the collective conscience. Criminal conduct is to be expected in any culture; crime is a necessary part of social life and is part of the normal processes of evolution in law and morality. Crime, then, has a functional existence apart from being designated a form of evil. Norms provide citizens with security even as they limit each person's aspirations. If individual social constraints break down or the line between cultural aspirations and social opportunities is lost, the anomic individual may engage in antisocial or deviant behavior. Durkheim's thought was later instrumental to the work of Merton and Cloward and Ohlin.

But the later American sociologist Edwin H. Sutherland, who leaned heavily on the work of Gabriel Tarde, argues that what makes a crime a crime is not the immorality, reprehensibility, or indecency of an act, but rather its prohibition by criminal law. Underlying the behavior of the courts, an agency which determines what the law is in a practical sense, is public opinion. Therefore the enforcement of law depends heavily on social attitudes at a particular point in history. The concept of crime ultimately involves three elements: (1) "a value which is appreciated by a group or part of a group that is politically important; (2) isolation of or cultural conflict in another part of this group so that its members do not appreciate the value or appreciate it less highly and consequently tend to endanger it; and (3) a pugnacious resort to coercion decently applied by those who appreciate the value to those who disregard the value." Criminal behavior is learned behavior and is determined through a process of association with criminals and isolation from noncriminal elements.

Stephen Schafer, the late Northeastern University (Boston) sociologist-criminologist who blended within his view point the heritage of both European and Western criminology, concurs that crime is fundamentally defined by law. However, because law is made by men, usually as a product of the complex interplay of individuals, groups, and conflicting values, it is in a constant state of flux. Even if behavior does not change, the legal understanding of that behavior may. Consequently, the idea of responsibility varies from decade to decade and from generation to generation. Law is created through the application of social power, which makes it possible for *a* law to become *the* law. As a social product, the law is administered by human beings, at times arbitrarily. "The irony of the man-committed crime," Schafer suggests, "is that it is so dependent upon the man-made law."

# 1

## Law as the Sovereign's Command

### John Austin

The matter of Jurisprudence is *positive law:* . . . law set by political superiors to political inferiors . . . .

A law, in the literal and proper sense of the word, may be defined as a rule laid down for the guidance of an intelligent being by an intelligent being having power over him. This definition seems to embrace all the objects to which the word can be applied without extension of its meaning by metaphor or analogy, and in this sense *law* comprises

Laws set by God to men, and

Laws set by men to men.

*Laws set by God to men.* To the whole portion of these has been sometimes applied the phrase, *Law of Nature,* or *Natural Law.* The phrase is also frequently applied to other objects which ought to be broadly distinguished. Rejecting it accordingly as ambiguous and misleading, I designate these laws, considered collectively, by the term *Law of God.*

*Laws set by men to men.* Of these . . . some are established by political superiors acting as such, and are marked by the name of *positive law*—the appropriate matter of jurisprudence; . . . others are set by men not political superiors, or not acting as such.

Closely analogous to human laws of this second class are a set of objects frequently but improperly termed laws, being rules set and enforced merely by the opinion of an indeterminate body of men; e.g., . . . "the law of honour," the "laws of fashion." . . .

There are numerous applications of the term *law* which rest upon a slender analogy, and are merely metaphorical. Such is the case when we talk of *laws* observed by the lower animals, of laws regulating the growth of vegetables, or determining the movements of inanimate bodies or masses. Intelligence is of the essence of law . . . .

---

From John Austin, *Lectures on Jurisprudence* (London: John Murray Publishers, 1875). Reprinted with permission.

The following table illustrates the division and relations between the several objects indicated:

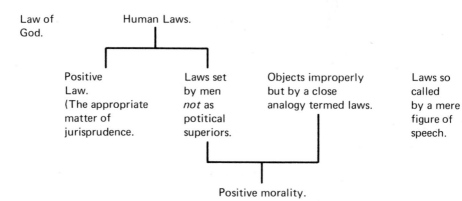

Laws properly so called, with laws improperly so called, may accordingly be divided into the following kinds.

1.  The divine laws, or the laws of God: that is to say, the laws which are set by God to his human creatures.
2.  Positive laws: that is to say, laws which are simply and strictly so called and which form the appropriate matter of general and particular jurisprudence.
3.  Positive morality, rules of positive morality, or positive moral rules.
4.  Laws metaphorical or figurative, or merely metaphorical or figurative.

\* \* \*

Every positive law, or every law strictly so called, is set by a sovereign person, or a sovereign body of persons, to a member or members of the independent political society wherein that person or body is sovereign or supreme.

\* \* \*

Every *law* or *rule* (taken with the largest signification which can be given to the term *properly*) is a *command.* Or, rather, laws or rules, properly so called, are a *species* of commands.

Now, since the term *command* comprises the term *law,* the first is the simpler as well as the larger of the two.

\* \* \*

Every positive law, or every law, simply and strictly so called, is set by a sovereign person or a sovereign body of persons, to a member or members of the independent political society wherein that person or body is sovereign or supreme.

* * *

Positive laws or laws *strictly* so called, are established *immediately* by monarchs or sovereign bodies, as supreme political superiors; by men in a state of subjection as subordinate political superiors; or by subjects as private persons in pursuance of legal rights. In each case they are set directly *or circuitously* by a monarch or sovereign body. They therefore flow from a *determinate* source and are laws properly so called.

* * *

Of laws properly so called which are set by subjects, some are set by subjects as subordinate political superiors; others by subjects as private persons . . . . Laws set by subjects as subordinate political superiors, are positive laws: they are clothed with legal sanctions, and impose legal duties. They are set circuitously or remotely by sovereigns or states in the character of political superiors. Of laws set by subjects as private persons, some are not established by sovereign or supreme authority—these are rules of positive morality; they are not clothed with legal sanctions; they are commands of sovereigns as political superiors, although they are set by sovereigns circuitously or remotely.

* * *

Every positive law, or every law simply and strictly so called, is set by a sovereign person, or a sovereign body of persons, to a member or members of the independent political society wherein that person or body is sovereign or supreme. In others words, it is set by a monarch, or sovereign number, to a person or persons in a state of subjection to its author.

* * *

In most or many of the societies whose supreme governments are monarchical, oligarchical, or aristocratical (in the specific meaning of the name), many of the sovereign powers are exercised by the sovereign directly. . . .

But in many of the societies whose supreme governments are popular, the sovereign or supreme body (or any numerous body forming a component part of it) exercises through representatives, whom it elects and appoints, the whole, or nearly the whole, of its sovereign or supreme powers. . . .

Where a sovereign body (or any smaller body forming a component part of it) exercises through representatives the whole of its sovereign powers, it may delegate its powers in either of two modes. (1) It may delegate them subject to a trust or trusts. (2) It may delegate them absolutely or unconditionally, so that the representative body, during the period for which it is elected and appointed, occupies completely the place of the electoral, and is invested completely with the sovereign character of the latter.

\* \* \*

The essential difference of a positive law may be put thus: it is set directly or circuitously by a monarch or sovereign member to a member or members of the independent political society wherein that person or body is sovereign or supreme.

It follows that the power of a monarch properly so called, or the power of a sovereign number in its collegiate and sovereign capacity, is incapable of *legal* limitation. For a monarch or sovereign number bound by a legal duty would be subject to a higher or superior sovereign: contrary to the hypothesis involved in the definition of the terms monarch and sovereign number.

And every political society must have a sovereign (one or a number) freed from *legal* restraints. For if the society is subject to a person or body not freed from legal restraints, that person or body must be subject to another person or body, and so on in a series of human authorities, which must terminate, and must therefore terminate in a person or body who *is* freed from legal restraint, and is sovereign.

Monarchs and sovereign bodies have attempted to oblige themselves or to oblige the successors to their sovereign powers. But, in spite of such attempts, the position that sovereign power is incapable of legal limits one holds without exception.

The author of a law of the kind, or any of the sovereign successors to that immediate author, may abrogate the law at pleasure. And if the law be not abrogated, the sovereign, for the time being, is not constrained to observe it by any legal sanction.

\* \* \*

When I affirm that the power of a sovereign is incapable of legal limitation, I always mean by a "sovereign," a monarch properly so called, or a sovereign number in its collegiate and sovereign capacity. Considered collectively, or considered in its corporate character, a sovereign number is sovereign and independent: but, considered severally, the individuals and smaller aggregates composing that sovereign number are subject to the supreme body of which they are component parts. Consequently, though the body is inevitably independent of legal or political duty, any of the individuals or aggregates whereof the body is composed may be legally bound by laws of which the body is the author. If a law set to the body by its members, even *as* members of the sovereign body, is clothed with a legal sanction, or the means of enforcing it judicially are provided by its author, it is properly a positive law. If it regards the constitution or structure of the given supreme government, a breach of the law, by the party to whom it is set, is not only *unconstitutional,* but is also *illegal.* The breach of the law is *unconstitutional,* inasmuch as the violated law regards the constitution of the state. The breach of the law is also *illegal,* inasmuch as the violated law may be enforced by judicial procedure.

\* \* \*

A sovereign government of one, or a sovereign government of a number in its collegiate and sovereign capacity, has no *legal rights* (in the proper acceptation of the term) *against its own subjects.*

Every legal right is the creature of a positive law; and it answers to a relative duty imposed by that positive law, and incumbent on a person other than the person or persons in whom the right resides. To every legal right, there are therefore three several parties: namely, a party bearing the right; a party burdened with the relative duty and a sovereign government setting the law through which the right and the duty are respectively conferred and imposed. A sovereign government cannot acquire right through laws set by itself to its own subjects. A man is no more able to confer a right on himself, than he is able to impose on himself a law or duty. Consequently, if a sovereign government had legal rights against its own subjects, those rights would be the creatures of positive laws set to its own subjects by a third person or body, who must, therefore, be sovereign over them. The community would therefore be subject to two different sovereigns, which is contrary to the definition of sovereignty.

But so far as they are bound by the law of God to obey their temporal sovereign, a sovereign government has *rights divine* against its own subjects: rights which are conferred upon itself, through duties which are laid upon its subjects, by laws of a common superior. And so far as the members of its own community are severally constrained to obey it by the opinion of the community at large, it has also *moral rights* against its own subjects severally considered: rights which are conferred upon itself by the opinion of the community at large, and which answer to relative moral duties.

The claim of the plaintiff against the sovereign defendant cannot be founded on a positive law. For then would the sovereign defendant be in a state of subjection—contrary to the definition of sovereignty. And the claim of the sovereign defendant cannot be founded on a positive law; for such a law must have been set by a third party to a member or members of the society wherein the defendant is supreme: or in other words, the society is subject to another sovereign—that is, to two sovereigns at once—contrary to the nature of sovereignty.

Though a sovereign government of one, or a sovereign government of a number in its collegiate and sovereign capacity, cannot have legal rights against its own subjects, it may have a legal right against a subject or subjects of another sovereign government. A law imposed by the other government upon its own subjects may create a right in favor of the first government. The possession of a legal or political right against a subject or subjects of another sovereign government consists, therefore, with that independence which is one of the essentials of sovereignty. . . .

The proper purpose or end of a sovereign political government, or the purpose or end for which it ought to exist, is the greatest possible advancement of human happiness.

Every positive law (or every law strictly and simply so called) is set, directly or circuitously, by a sovereign individual or body to a member or members of the independent political society wherein its author is supreme. In other words, it is set, directly or circuitously, by a monarch or sovereign number to a person or persons in a state of subjection to its author.

# 2

## The Utilitarian Approach to Crime

*Jeremy Bentham*

### Of the Principle of Utility

Nature has placed mankind under the governance of two sovereign masters, *pain* and *pleasure*. It is for them alone to point out what we ought to do, as well as to determine what we shall do. On the one hand the standard of right and wrong, on the other the chain of causes and effects, are fastened to their throne. . . .

The principle of utility is the foundation of the present work: it will be proper therefore at the outset to give an explicit and determinate account of what is meant by it. By the principle of utility is meant that principle which approves or disapproves of every action whatsoever, according to the tendency which it appears to have to augment or diminish the happiness of the party whose interest is in question: or, what is the same thing in other words, to promote or to oppose that happiness. I say of every action whatsoever; and therefore not only of every action of a private individual, but of every measure of government.

By utility is meant that property in any object, whereby it tends to produce benefit, advantage, pleasure, good, or happiness, (all this in the present case comes to the same thing) or (what comes again to the same thing) to prevent the happening of mischief, pain, evil, or unhappiness to the party whose interest is considered: if that party be the community in general, then the happiness of the community: if a particular individual, then the happiness of that individual.

The interest of the community is one of the most general expressions that can occur in the phraseology of morals: no wonder that the meaning of it is often lost. When it has a meaning, it is this. The community is a fictitious *body,* composed of the individual persons who are considered as constituting as it were its *members.* The interest of the community then is, what?—the sum of the interests of the several members who compose it.

It is vain to talk of the interest of the community, without understanding what is the interest of the individual. A thing is said to promote the interest, or to be *for* the interest, of an individual, when it tends to add to the sum total of

From Jeremy Bentham, *The Principles of Morals and Legislation* (New York: Macmillan Publishing Company, 1948). Reprinted with permission.

his pleasures: or, what comes to the same thing, to diminish the sum total of his pains.

An action then may be said to be conformable to the principle of utility, or, for shortness sake, to utility (meaning with respect to the community at large), when the tendency it has to augment the happiness of the community is greater than any it has to diminish it.

A measure of government (which is but a particular kind of action, performed by a particular person or persons) may be said to be conformable to or dictated by the principle of utility, when in like manner the tendency which it has to augment the happiness of the community is greater than any which it has to diminish it.

When an action, or in particular a measure of government, is supposed by a man to be conformable to the principle of utility, it may be convenient, for the purposes of discourse, to imagine a kind of law or dictate, called a law or dictate of utility: and to speak of the action in question, as being conformable to such law or dictate.

A man may be said to be a partisan of the principle of utility, when the approbation or disapprobation he annexes to any action, or to any measure, is determined by and proportioned to the tendency which he conceives it to have to augment or to diminish the happiness of the community: or in other words, to its conformity or unconformity to the laws or dictates of utility.

Of an action that is conformable to the principle of utility one may always say either that it is one that ought to be done, or at least that it is not one that ought not to be done. One may say also, that it is right it should be done; at least that it is not wrong it should be done; that it is a right action; at least that it is not a wrong action. When thus interpreted, the words *ought,* and *right* and *wrong,* and others of that stamp, have a meaning; when otherwise, they have none.

* * *

## Of the Four Sanctions or Sources of Pain and Pleasure

... The happiness of the individuals, of whom a community is composed, that is their pleasures and their security, is the end and the sole end which the legislator ought to have in view: the sole standard, in conformity to which each individual ought, as far as depends upon the legislator, to be *made* to fashion his behaviour. But whether it be this or anything else that is to be *done,* there is nothing by which a man can ultimately be *made* to do it, but either pain or pleasure. Having taken a general view of these two grand objects (vis. pleasure, and what comes to the same thing, immunity from pain) in the character of *final* causes; it will be necessary to take a view of pleasure and pain itself, in the character of *efficient* causes or means.

There are four distinguishable sources from which pleasure and pain are in use to flow: considered separately, they may be termed the *physical,* the *political,* the *moral,* and the *religious*: and inasmuch as the pleasures and pains belonging to each of them are capable of giving a binding force to any law or rule of conduct, they may all of them be termed *sanctions.*

If it be in the present life, and from the ordinary course of nature, not purposely modified by the interposition of the will of any human being, nor by any extraordinary interposition of any superior invisible being, that the pleasure or the pain takes place or is expected, it may be said to issue from or to belong to the *physical sanction.*

If at the hands of a *particular* person or set of persons in the community, who under names correspondent to that of *judge,* are chosen for the particular purpose of dispensing it, according to the will of the sovereign or supreme ruling power in the state, it may be said to issue from the *political sanction.*

If at the hands of such *chance* persons in the community, as the party in question may happen in the course of his life to have concerns with, according to each man's spontaneous disposition, and not according to any settled or concerted rule, it may be said to issue from the *moral* or *popular sanction.*

If from the immediate hand of a superior invisible being, either in the present life, or in a future, it may be said to issue from the *religious sanction.*

Pleasures and pains which may be expected to issue from the *physical, political,* or *moral* sanctions, must all of them be expected to be experienced, if ever, in the *present* life: those which may be expected to issue from the *religious* sanction, may be expected to be experienced either in the *present* life or in a *future.*

Those which can be experienced in the present life, can of course be no others than such as human nature in the course of the present life is susceptible of: and from each of these sources may flow all the pleasures or pains of which, in the course of the present life, human nature is susceptible.

\* \* \*

Pleasures then, and the avoidance of pains, are the *ends* which the legislator has in view: it behooves him therefore to understand their *value.* Pleasures and pains are the *instruments* he has to work with: it behooves him therefore to understand their force, which is again, in other words, their value.

To a person considered *by himself,* the value of a pleasure or pain considered *by itself,* will be greater or less, according to the four following circumstances:

1.   Its *intensity*
2.   Its *duration*
3.   Its *certainty* or *uncertainty*
4.   Its *propinquity* or *remoteness*

These are the circumstances which are to be considered in estimating a pleasure or a pain considered each of them by itself. But when the value of any pleasure or pain is considered for the purpose of estimating the tendency of any *act* by which it is produced, there are two other circumstances to be taken into the account; these are:

5.   Its *fecundity,* or the chance it has of being followed by sensations of the same kind: that is, pleasures, if it be a pleasure: pains, if it be a pain
6.   Its *purity,* or the chance it has of *not* being followed by sensations of the *opposite* kind: that is, pains, if it be a pleasure: pleasures, if it be a pain. . . .

To a number of persons, with reference to each of whom the value of a pleasure or a pain is considered, it will be greater or less, according to seven circumstances: to wit, the six preceding ones, vis:

1.   Its *intensity*
2.   Its *duration*
3.   Its *certainty* or *uncertainty*
4.   Its *propinquity* or *remoteness*
5.   Its *fecundity*
6.   Its *purity*
7.   Its *extent*; that is, the number of persons to whom it *extends*; or (in other words) who are affected by it.

* * *

**Pleasures and Pains, Their Kinds**

Having represented what belongs to all sorts of pleasures and pains alike, we come now to exhibit, each by itself, the several sorts of pains and pleasures. Pains and pleasures may be called by one general word, interesting perceptions. Interesting perceptions are either simple or complex. The simple ones are those which cannot any one of them be resolved into more: complex are those which are resolvable into divers simple ones. A complex interesting perception may accordingly be composed either (1) of pleasures alone; (2) of pains alone; or (3) of a pleasure or pleasures, and a pain or pains together. What determines a lot of pleasure, for example, to be regarded as one complex pleasure, rather than as divers simple ones, is the nature of the exciting cause. Whatever pleasures are excited all at once by the action of the same cause, are apt to be looked upon as constituting all together but one pleasure.

The several simple pleasures of which human nature is susceptible, seem to be as follows: (1) the pleasures of sense; (2) the pleasures of wealth; (3) the pleasures of skill; (4) the pleasures of amity; (5) the pleasures of a good name; (6) the pleasures of power; (7) the pleasures of piety; (8) the pleasures of benevolence; (9) the pleasures of malevolence; (10) the pleasures of memory; (11) the pleasures of imagination; (12) the pleasures of expectation; (13) the pleasures dependent on association; (14) the pleasures of relief.

The several simple pains seem to be as follows: (1) the pains of privation; (2) the pains of the senses; (3) the pains of awkwardness; (4) the pains of enmity; (5) the pains of an ill name; (6) the pains of piety; (7) the pains of benevolence; (8) the pains of malevolence; (9) the pains of the memory; (10) the pains of the imagination; (11) the pains of expectation; (12) the pains dependent on association.

* * *

Of all these several sorts of pleasures and pains, there is scarce any one which is not liable, on more accounts than one, to come under the consideration of the law. Is an offence committed? It is the tendency which it has to destroy, in such or such persons, some of these pleasures, or to produce some of these pains, that constitutes the mischief of it, and the ground for punishing it. It is the prospect of some of these pleasures, or of security from some of these pains, that constitutes the motive or temptation, it is the attainment of them that constitutes the profit of the offence. Is the offender to be punished? It can be only by the production of one or more of these pains that the punishment can be inflicted. . . .

# Law as a Means to an End

## Rudolf von Ihering

. . . The organization of social coercive force embraces two sides: the establishment of the external mechanism of force, and the setting up of principles to regulate its use. The form of solution of the first problem is the *State force,* that of the second is the *Law.* Both concepts stand in the relation of mutual dependence: the State force has need of the law, the law has need of the State force.

### State Force

The absolute requisite of the State force, demanded by the purpose of the State itself, is the possession of the highest force, superior to every other power within the jurisdiction of the State. Every other power of the individual or of the many, must be "under" it; and it must be "over" the other. . . . All other requirements of the State recede before this one. Before this is achieved all others are premature, for in order to fulfil them the State must exist first, and it does not exist until it has solved the question of power in the above sense. Powerlessness, impotence of the State force, is the capital sin of the State, from which there is no absolution; a sin which society neither forgives nor tolerates, it is an inner contradiction: *State force* without *force*!

\* \* \*

The firmness of the State depends upon the fact that the influence of the numerical element on the question of power is counteracted by two other factors: the organization of power in the hands of the State force, and the moral power which the idea of the State exerts.

The force of the State, as regards its substance, is nothing but a quantum of popular power—physical, spiritual, economic, collected for certain social purposes. And this power, too, as need scarcely be stated, is always much smaller than that which remains on the side of the people. Quantitatively, therefore, the

From Rudolf von Ihering, *Laws as a Means to an End* (Boston: The Boston Book Company, 1913).

natural bearer of the power, the people, is always superior to the official bearer thereof, the State. But this proportion of the two is essentially altered by the fact that the power of the people is raw substance, whereas that of the State is organized. . . .

The negative side of it consists of preventing the organization, dangerous to the State, of hostile elements; or since organization proceeds in the form of associations, in the use of the proper legal restrictions, and a careful administrative vigilance, for all associations. . . .

The State is the only competent as well as the sole owner of social coercive force—the right to coerce forms the *absolute monopoly* of the State. Every association that wishes to realize its claims upon its members by means of mechanical coercion is dependent upon the cooperation of the State, and the State has it in its power to fix the conditions under which it will grant such aid. But this means in other words that the State is the only source of law, for norms which cannot be enforced by him who lays them down are not *legal rules.* There is therefore no *association law* independent of the authority of the State, but only such as is derived therefrom. The State has therefore, as is involved in the concept of the supreme power, the primacy over all associations within its domain; and this applies to the Church also. If the State grants associations the right of coercion within their spheres, it holds good only as long as the State thinks this advisable. . . .

Law is the sum of the *compulsory rules* in force in a State. . . . The two elements which it contains are that of rule, and that of the realization of it through coercion. Only those rules laid down by society deserve the name of law which have coercion, or, since, as we have seen, the State alone possesses the monopoly of coercion, which have political coercion behind them. Hereby it is implicitly said that only the rules which are provided by the State with this function are legal rules; or that *the State is the only source of law.* . . .

The second element of the concept of law is norm; the latter contains the inner side of law, coercion the outer. The content of norm is an idea, a proposition (legal rule), but a proposition of a *practical* kind; i.e., a direction for human *conduct.* A norm is therefore a *rule* according to which we should direct ourselves. The rules of grammar come also under this concept. They are distinguished from norms by the fact that they do not concern *conduct.* Directions for conduct are contained also in propositions derived from experience concerning the element of purpose in conduct, viz., *maxims.* Norms are distinguished from the latter by the fact that they are of a *binding* nature. . . .

All coercion presupposes two parties: the one who coerces and the one who is coerced. To which one of these is the coercive norm of the State directed? The question has been raised by criminologists with special reference to criminal laws, and has received a three-fold answer from them; *the people, the judge, the State.*

\* \* \*

Every legal rule, every political imperative is characterized by the fact that some bearer of political force is entrusted with its practical realization. Coercion against the private person, though it belongs to it, is an unsafe criterion of law; coercion which any political authority exercises either within, downward or outward is an absolutely safe one; provided that the imperative is equal to the requirements which the government expects of it.

* * *

No matter how variable the extent of crime may be, the concept is always the same. It always represents to us, on the part of the criminal, an attack on the conditions of social life; on the part of society, it represents its conviction, expressed in the form of law, that it can ward it off only by means of punishment. *Crime is that which endangers the conditions of social life, and of which legislation is convinced that it can be removed only by punishment.*

The standard by which the legislator measures this character of crime is not the *concrete* danger of the *particular* act, but the *abstract* danger of the whole *category* of acts. The punishment of a particular act is only the necessary consequence of the threat of punishment once it is made, for without it the latter would be ineffective. Whether the particular act endangers society or not is quite indifferent, and there is no error more serious in criminal law than to substitute the standpoint of the *execution* of punishment for that of the *threat* thereof. . . .

The criminal law shows us everywhere a gradation of punishment according to the nature of the crime. It will be granted that a definition of crime which gives the key for the explanation of this fact, and at the same time supplies the standard for the gravity of the penalty, is to be preferred to every other that cannot do this. I believe I can claim this for my definition. The standpoint of endangering the conditions of social life embraces two elements that are capable of gradation, and should therefore be considered in the legislative estimation of punishment. They are, the *conditions of life*—not all are equally important, some are more essential than others: and the *danger* accruing to them—not every injury to the conditions endangers society equally.

The higher a good stands, the more thought we take to make it secure. Society does the same thing with its conditions of life (I shall call them social goods) in so far as the legal protection is concerned which it summons for their security. The higher the good, the higher the punishment. *The list of penalties gives the standard of values for social goods.* What price is for business, that punishment is for criminal law. If you put the social goods on one side and the penalties on the other, you have the scale of social values. . . .

In addition to the *objective* element of the threatened *good* on the part of society, there is the *subjective* element, on the part of the criminal, arising from his disposition and the manner in which the crime was carried out, which constitutes him a danger to society. Not every criminal who commits the same crime endangers society in the same degree. Society has more to fear from the relapsing or habitual criminal than from the novice in crime; it has more to fear from a conspiracy or band than from a single individual. Cunning threatens greater dangers than passion; design than negligence. . . .

# 4

## The Morality of Crime

*Edward Westermarck*

Custom has proved stronger than law and religion combined. . . . The laws themselves, in fact, command obedience more as customs than as laws. A rule of conduct which, from one point of view, is a law, is in most cases, from another
point of view, a custom; for, as Hegel remarks, "the valid laws of a nation,
when written and collected, do not cease to be customs."[1] There are instances
of laws that were never published, the knowledge and administration of which
belonged to a privileged class, and which nevertheless were respected and
obeyed.[2] And among ourselves the ordinary citizen stands in no need of studying the laws under which he lives, custom being generally the safe guiding star of
his conduct. . . .

Many laws were customs before they became laws. Ancient customs lie at
the foundation of all Aryan law books. . . . The transformation of customs into
laws was not a mere ceremony. Law, like custom, is a rule of conduct, but, while
custom is established by usage and obtains, in a more or less indefinite way, its
binding force from public opinion, a law originates in a definite legislative act,
being set, as Austin says, by a sovereign person, or a sovereign body of persons,
to a person or persons in a state of subjection to its author.[3] By becoming laws,
then, the customs were expressly formulated, and were enforced by a more
definite sanction. It seems that the process in question arose both from considerations of social utility and from a sense of justice. . . . There are customs which
are too indefinite to assume the stereotyped shape of law.[4] There are others, the
breach of which excites too little public indignation, or which are of too little
importance for the public welfare, to be proper objects of legislation. And there
are others which may be said to exist unconsciously; that is, which are universally observed as a matter of course, and which, never being transgressed, are
never thought of.

Laws which are based on customs naturally express moral ideas prevalent at
the time when they are established. On the other hand, though still in existence,
they are not necessarily faithful representatives of the ideas of a later age. Law

From Edward Westermarck, *The Origin and Development of the Moral Ideas* (Hampshire,
England: Macmillan Company, 1912). Reprinted by permission of Macmillan London and
Basingstoke.

may be even more conservative than custom. Though the latter exercises a very preservative influence on public opinion, it *eo ipso* changes when public opinion changes. . . .

The moral ideas of a people are less extensively represented in its laws than in its customs. This is a corollary of the fact that there are always a great number of customs which never become laws. Moreover, whilst law, like custom, directly expresses only what is obligatory, it hardly ever deals with merit, even indirectly. . . .

Law, like custom, only deals with overt acts, or omissions, and cares nothing for the mental side of conduct, unless the law be transgressed. Yet, as will be seen subsequently, though this constitutes an essential difference between law and the enlightened moral consciousness, it throws considerable light on the moral judgments of the unreflecting mind.

Being a general, and at the same time a strictly defined, rule of conduct, a law can even less than a custom make special provision for every case so as to satisfy the demand of justice. This disadvantage, however, was hardly felt in early periods of legislation, when little account was taken of what was behind the overt act; and at later stages of development, the difficulty was overcome by leaving greater discretion to the judge. . . .

Laws which represent public opinion are no more than customs safe exponents of the moral ideas held by particular members of the society. But on the other hand, there are cases in which a law, unlike a custom, may express the ideas, or simply the will, of a few, or even of a single individual; that is, of the sovereign power only. It is obvious that laws imposed upon a barbarous people by civilised legislators may differ widely from the people's own ideas of right and wrong. . . . At the same time, however, it should be remembered that the moral consciousness of a people may gradually be brought into harmony with a law originally foreign to it. . . .

Finally, a law may enjoin or forbid acts which by themselves are regarded as indifferent from a moral point of view. . . .

A law expresses a rule of duty by making an act or omission which is regarded as wrong a crime, that is, by forbidding it under pain of punishment. Law does not in all cases directly threaten[5] with punishment—I say directly, since all law is coercive, and all coercion at some stage involves the possibility of punishment.[6] Sanctions, or the consequences by which the sovereign political authority threatens to enforce the laws set by it, may have in view either the indemnification of the injured party, or the suffering of the injurer. . . . Punishment, in all its forms, is essentially an expression of indignation in the society which inflicts it. . . .

**Notes**

1. Hegel, *Philosophie des Rechts,* §211, p. 199.
2. Rein, *Japan,* p. 314.

3. Austin, *Lectures on Jurisprudence,* i. 87, 181ff.

4. Cf. Aristotle, *Ethica Nicomachea,* v. 10. 6.

5. "Not every sovereign can make sure of enforcing his commands; and sometimes laws are made without even any great intention of enforcing them" (Pollock, *Essays in Jurisprudence and Ethics,* p. 9 *sq.*).

6. Cf. Stephen, *History of the Criminal Law of England,* i. 2.

# 5

## Natural Crime

### Raffaele Garofalo

[The] element of immorality requisite before a harmful act can be regarded as criminal by public opinion, is the injury to so much of the moral sense as is represented by one or the other of the elementary altruistic sentiments of *pity* and *probity*. The injury must wound these sentiments not in their superior and finer degrees, but in the average measure in which they are possessed by a community—a measure which is indispensable for the adaptation of the individual to society. Given such a violation of either of these sentiments, and we have what may properly be called *natural crime*. The foregoing is not a complete definition, but it furnishes a determinant which I believe to be of the highest importance. I have sought to show the futility of saying in the usual fashion that crime is an act at once immoral and harmful. It is something more: it is a determinate species of immorality. Hundreds of deeds might be mentioned which are both harmful and immoral and still not considered as crimes. And this is so, because the element of immorality which they contain is neither cruelty nor improbity. If, for example, immorality *in general* be spoken of, we are obliged to recognize that this element in some degree exists in every voluntary disobedience to law. But it is nevertheless true that there is a host of acts which are misdemeanors and even crimes in the eye of the law and yet do not tend to lower their authors in the estimation of their friends. . . .

Offenses against chastity are rendered criminal by the interference with individual liberty—the violation of the sentiment of benevolence or pity—and this even if the offense is accomplished by seduction unattended with force, because of the moral suffering, shame, and other harmful consequences suffered by the victim. But when the woman has submitted of her own free will and no element of seduction is involved, the unchaste act of itself is a matter of indifference. The same reason equally prevents us from classing as crimes certain acts of sexual perversion, although the laws of some countries still endeavor to repress such offenses by means of physical punishments ("peines afflictives"). . . .

It is [the] universality of pity within the family which renders criminal

---

From Baron Raffaele Garofalo *Criminology* (Boston: Little, Brown and Company, 1914). Reprinted with permission of Patterson-Smith Company, New Jersey, 1968.

certain acts in relation to our parents and children, which if committed against outsiders would not be given a criminal character. On the other hand, the idea of the family community—a traditional idea which persists in spite of the laws—denies a criminal character to certain attacks upon property within the family circle, as, for example, larceny between father and son, husband and wife, or brother and sister. And this is not because the sentiment of probity is overborne by the sentiment of family, but simply because the idea of a common ownership diminishes the degree of improbity or renders its existence doubtful.

Disobedience to the paternal authority has long since ceased to be classed as a crime, but adultery continues to be so regarded.

* * *

The subject of political crimes presents difficulties of a most serious character. . . . There is here a clear-cut distinction. One may, to be sure, speak of *political crime,* but the word "crime," standing alone, has nothing to do with the present class of acts. . . .

Still, there are certain crimes commonly called political which, nevertheless, properly come under our definition. Such, for example, are attacks upon the life of the head of the State or other public officers, the use of bombs and dynamite to further revolutionary propaganda, and similar acts of violence. In these cases it is of little moment what the political object may be, if the sentiment of humanity is wounded. Has there been killing or an attempt to kill, not in the course of war or in the exercise of lawful self-defense? If so, the author, by that fact alone, is a criminal. His degree of criminality may be greater or less, according to the intent and the surrounding circumstances—a matter to which we shall later refer. But if crime arises from the single fact of a serious violation of pity, there must be at least an attempt to commit it. This is so, because we cannot admit that any crime exists before some step has been taken in its accomplishment, even if the design has been fully formed in the author's mind. It may be that public policy, in cases of this character, will treat as a punishable attempt that which is not an attempt in the ordinary sense; here we have a true political crime. The cases to which we have reference, however, are those in which there has been murder, incendiarism, or dynamiting, actual or attempted. In such cases the crime exists independently of the passion which has provoked it. It exists because of the willful intent to destroy human lives. Only when the act of the fanatic or revolutionary exhibits no such cruelty or carelessness of human life can we distinguish the true political crime, and say that it inherently differs from the natural crime. But the act which is normally a political crime may become a natural crime when a society suddenly returns to a condition in which the collective existence is threatened. . . . We need only repeat that for public opinion there can be neither crime nor criminal in the absence of injury to the universal moral sense. . . .

For us, all crime falls into two extensive categories, according as offense is principally occasioned to the one or the other of the two primordial altruistic sentiments. . . .

1. *Offense to the Sentiment of Pity.* The first category—offense to the sentiment of pity or humanity—includes: (a) attacks upon human life and all manner of acts tending to produce physical harm to human beings, such as the deliberate infliction of physical torture ("sévices"), mayhem ("mutilations"), the maltreatment of the weak and infirm, the voluntary causing of illness, the imposition upon children of excessive labor or such work as tends to injure their health or stunt their physical development; (b) physical acts which produce suffering at once physical and moral, such as the violation of personal liberty in an egoistic end, whether for carnal pleasure or pecuniary gain—abduction of a female or kidnapping for ransom may be cited as types; and (c) acts which directly produce moral suffering. Defamation ("diffamation"), false accusation ("calomnie"), and seduction under promise of marriage are of this last character.

2. *Offense to the Sentiment of Probity.* In the second category—offense to the elementary sentiment of probity—are comprised: (a) attacks upon property involving violence, viz.: robbery, extortion by threats, malicious mischief ("devastation"), arson, and the like; (b) attacks unaccompanied by violence, but involving breach of trust: obtaining money by false pretenses; embezzlement; the conveyance of property in fraud of creditors ("insolvabilite volontaire"), bankruptcy occurring through negligence or fraud ("banqueroute"), the revelation of professional secrets, the misappropriation of literary property ("plagiat"), and all the various forms of counterfeiting tending to injure the rights of inventors and manufacturers; and (c) all indirect injuries to a person's property or civil rights occasioned by false statements or entries made in some formal or solemn manner, among which may be mentioned perjury, the forgery or spoliation of official documents and records ("faux dans les actes authentiques"), the substitution of children, and the suppression of civil status ("suppression d'état civil").

## Offenses Excluded

It will be noted that we thus exclude from the field of criminality: (a) acts which menace the State as a governmental organization. Of this type are such deeds as may involve one nation in hostilities with another, unauthorized military enlistments, political rioting, meetings to conspire against the government, the utterance of seditious outcries, seditious offenses of the press, affiliation with revolutionary sects or anti-constitutional parties, inciting to civil war, etc.; (b) acts which attack the social power but without a political object. Among these would be: resistance to officers of the law (except when involving murder or the infliction of bodily injury), the usurpation of titles, dignities, or public functions, without purpose of unlawful pecuniary gain, the refusal to perform a service owed to the States, smuggling, etc.; (c) acts resulting in injury to the public peace, the political rights of citizens or the respect due to religion, or causing offense to public decency. In this division would fall the unlawful invasion of private dwellings ("violation de domicile"),[1] the exercise of a right by force instead of by legal means, the spreading of false news tending to alarm the public, the act of aiding or abetting the escape of prisoners, election intrigues, offenses against religion or worship, illegal arrests, acts of sexual perversion of which no innocent person has been made the victim; and (d) acts which contravene the local or special legislation of a given country, e.g., gambling, the unlawful carrying of arms, clandestine prostitution, and infringements of laws relating to railroads, telegraphs, sanitation, the customs, hunting, fishing, forests, and watercourses, and the civil status of citizens, as well as violations of many kinds of municipal regulations, etc. . . .

I am firmly convinced that the two sentiments [of pity and probity] are entirely distinct, and that one may be wounded without the other being affected, although it may frequently happen that both are wounded by a single act. . . .

It will very probably ensue that many facts today regarded as indifferent will come to be viewed as immoral, and that others simply immoral will be vested with a criminal character. . . .

It is easily understood, however, that the sentiments wounded by the crimes of the future will be the same sentiments with which we have dealt, but these sentiments in their higher and more refined development—a state which the efflux of time will have rendered much more common than at the present day. It is wholly impossible to suppose crimes of a different character, or to suppose that offenses to other sentiments can ever become crimes. . . .

The sole object of my concept of crime is to distinguish among the punishable facts, those which are governed by the same natural laws, because revealing certain individual anomalies, principally the lack of a part of the moral sense or, in other words, a deficiency in the sentiments which, as the basis of morality, are constantly undergoing development in the progress of civilized nations. . . . What I have done has been to select from among all these natural facts, a certain class of offenses which exhibit the distinctive character of a special immorality, and these I have termed "natural crimes," to denote that, at the present day, they are universally such, irrespective of laws and governments.

* * *

A distinction thus exists . . . between two classes of harmful acts: on the one hand, acts which place their author in a condition of social inferiority, and are known in the popular language as crimes; and on the other, acts which are characterized by revolt against the State or disobedience to the laws, without any implication that the agent is lacking in the elements of morality which contemporary society deems essential.

* * *

The necessities of scientific study have required us to isolate the natural crime. No such study would be possible if we were obliged to deal with all the punishable acts heterogeneously assembled into the codes. So, too, the legal notion of crime must be laid aside as valueless for our purposes. Consequently, our first step has been to disregard all facts not wounding the altruistic sentiments; such facts it is absolutely impossible to conceive as crimes. Next, we have reduced the altruistic sentiments to two distinct types. And lastly, we have fixed the average measure in which these sentiments are possessed by civilized mankind; their nicer development, being present only in a small minority, does not enter into the question.

In a word, it is not upon the violation of rights but upon the violation of sentiments that the concept of natural crime must be based. In this, the principle for which we contend is totally different from that of the jurists. Nor is there any reason to fear that this principle will tend to bring into the field of criminality acts which merely reveal immoral inclinations, and which have never been and never will be of a punishable character. Our fixation of the necessary measure of the altruistic sentiments stands in the way. With this as a criterion we are effectually prevented from regarding as crimes, acts which, despite their harmfulness, cannot properly be made the subject of punishment. . . .

Since crime consists in an act which is at once harmful to society and violative of one or both of the most elementary sentiments of pity and probity, the criminal is necessarily a man in whom there is an absence, eclipse, or weakness of these sentiments, one or both. This is evident, because if he had possessed the elementary altruistic sentiments in a sufficient degree, any *real* violation of them on his part would have been impossible. Possession of them is perhaps not inconsistent with an *apparent* violation, but in this case the crime is not really a crime.

The sentiments in question being the substratum of all morality, their absence renders the deficient person incompatible with society. If average and relative morality consists of the individual's adaptation to society, this adaptation becomes impossible when the sentiments lacking are precisely those which the environment regards as indispensable. The same thing happens in a narrower circle where a higher sense of morality is requisite, and where refinement, the maintenance of a high standard of honor, and extreme politeness are the rule. There the absence of these qualities implies the inadaptability of the individual to his environment. Thus, in those associations whose morality is based upon sentiments of religion or patriotism, violation of these sentiments is a mortal offense. Society at large is contented with little: it demands that the individual refrain from offending the slender measure of morality of which we have spoken—it insists on keeping inviolate that most elementary and least refined degree of morality which is vital to its existence. Only when this is trampled under foot does society protest that a crime has been committed.

It is now plain what classes of crimes are to engage our attention. To these classes, as we shall find, there correspond, beyond question, two psychic varieties of the race, two distinct types—on the one hand, men devoid of the sentiment of pity in its average measure, on the other, men devoid of the average sentiment of probity. These we must study directly, and ascertain the cases in which, because of the criminal's insusceptibility to the sentiment which he has violated, the anomaly is irreducible. . . .

Other cases exist in which the anomaly may perhaps be lessened, because there is not a total absence, but merely a weakness, of the moral sense. Here the defect renders impossible the adaptation of the criminal so long as his surroundings remain unchanged, but permits such adaptation when he is withdrawn from his deleterious surroundings and subjected to new conditions of existence.

**Note**

1. ["Violation de domicile" is of two kinds. One comprises unlawful domiciliary visitations by the police or other public officers. The other consists of the act of a private person in effecting an entrance to a dwelling house, against the will of the owner, by the use of force or threats, and for an unlawful purpose, not necessarily that of theft.—Transl.]

# 6

## Crime as Normal Behavior

## *Émile Durkheim*

The link of social solidarity to which repressive law corresponds is the one whose break constitutes a crime. By this name we call every act which, in any degree whatever, invokes against its author the characteristic reaction which we term punishment. To seek the nature of this link is to inquire into the cause of punishment, or, more precisely, to inquire what crime essentially consists of.

Surely there are crimes of different kinds; but among all these kinds, there is, no less surely, a common element. The proof of this is that the reaction which crimes call forth from society, in respect of punishment, is, save for differences of degree, always and ever the same. The unity of effect shows the unity of cause. Not only among the types of crime provided for legally in the same society, but even among those which have been or are recognized and punished in different social systems, essential resemblances assuredly exist. As different as they appear at first glance, they must have a common foundation, for they everywhere affect the moral conscience of nations in the same way and produce the same result. They are all crimes; that is to say, acts reprised by definite punishments. The essential properties of a thing are those which one observes universally wherever that thing exists and which pertain to it alone. If, then, we wish to know what crime essentially is, we must extract the elements of crimes which are found similar in all criminological varieties in different social systems. None must be neglected. The juridical conceptions of the most inferior societies are no less significant than those of the most elevated societies; they are not less instructive. To omit any would expose us to the error of finding the essence of crime where it is not. . . .

The method of finding this permanent and pervasive element is surely not by enumerating the acts that at all times and in every place have been termed crimes, observing, thus, the characters that they present. For if, as it may be, they are actions which have universally been regarded as criminal, they are the smallest minority, and, consequently, such a method would give us a very mistaken notion, since it would be applied only to exceptions.[1] These variations of repressive law prove at the same time that the constant characteristic could

not be found among the intrinsic properties of acts imposed or prohibited by
penal rules, since they present such diversity, but rather in the relations that
they sustain with some condition external to them. . . .

[It] has been said that penal rules announce the fundamental conditions
of collective life for each social type. Their authority thus derives from their
necessity. Moreover, as these necessities vary with societies, the variability of
repressive law would thus be explained. But we have already made ourselves
explicit on this point. Besides the fact that such a theory accords too large a
part in the direction of social evolution to calculation and reflection, there
are many acts which have been and still are regarded as criminal without in
themselves being harmful to society. . . .

Even when a criminal act is certainly harmful to society, it is not true that
the amount of harm that it does is regularly related to the intensity of the
repression which it calls forth. In the penal law of the most civilized people,
murder is universally regarded as the greatest of crimes. However, an economic
crisis, a stockmarket crash, even a failure, can disorganize the social body more
severely than an isolated homicide.

* * *

Every written law has a double object: to prescribe certain obligations, and
to define the sanctions which are attached to them. In civil law, and more
generally in every type of law with restitutive sanctions, the legislator takes up
and solves the two questions separately. He first determines the obligation with
all possible precision, and it is only later that he stipulates the manner in which
it should be sanctioned. . . . When a law of custom becomes written and is
codified, it is because questions of litigation demand a more definite solution.
If the custom continues to function silently, without raising any discussion
or difficulties, there is no reason for transforming it. Since penal law is codified
only to establish a graduated scale of punishments, it is thus the scale alone
which can lend itself to doubt. Inversely, if rules whose violation is punished
do not need a juridical expression, it is because they are the object of no
contest, because everybody feels their authority.

* * *

[We] have not defined crime when we say that it consists in an offense
to collective sentiments, for there are some among these which can be offended
without there being a crime. The collective sentiments to which crime corresponds must, therefore, singularize themselves from others by some distinctive
property; they must have a certain average intensity. Not only are they engraven
in all consciences, but they are strongly engraven. They are not hesitant and
superficial desires, but emotions and tendencies which are strongly ingrained

in us. The proof of this is the extreme slowness with which penal law evolves. Not only is it modified more slowly than custom, but it is the part of the positive law most refractory to change. . . .

If, in general, the sentiments which purely moral sanctions protect, that is to say, diffuse sanctions, are less intense and less solidly organized than those which punishment, properly called, protects, nevertheless there are exceptions. Thus, there is no reason for believing that the average filial piety or even the elementary forms of compassion for the most apparent evils today consist of sentiments more superficial than those concerning property or public authority. The wayward son, however, and even the most hardened egotist are not treated as criminals. It is not sufficient, then, that the sentiments be strong; they must be precise. In effect, each of them is relative to a very definite practice. . . .

The totality of beliefs and sentiments common to average citizens of the same society forms a determinate system which has its own life; one may call it the *collective* or *common conscience.* No doubt, it has not a specific organ as a substratum; it is, by definition, diffuse in every reach of society. Nevertheless, it has specific characteristics which make it a distinct reality. It is, in effect, independent of the particular conditions in which individuals are placed; they pass on and it remains. . . . Moreover, it does not change with each generation, but, on the contrary, it connects successive generations with one another. It is, thus, an entirely different thing from particular consciences, although it can be realized only through them. . . . We can . . . say that an act is criminal when it offends strong and defined states of the collective conscience.[2] . . .

We must not say that an action shocks the common conscience because it is criminal, but rather that it is criminal because it shocks the common conscience. We do not reprove it because it is a crime, but it is a crime because we reprove it. As for the intrinsic nature of these sentiments, it is impossible to specify them. They have the most diverse objects and cannot be encompassed in a single formula. We can say that they relate neither to vital interests of society nor to a minimum of justice. All these definitions are inadequate. By this alone can we recognize it: a sentiment, whatever its origin and end, is found in all consciences with a certain degree of force and precision, and every action which violates it is a crime. . . .

[Once] a governmental power is instituted it has, by itself, enough to attach a penal sanction spontaneously to certain rules of conduct. It is capable, by its own action, of creating certain delicts or of increasing the criminological value of certain others.

* * *

Crime is not simply the disruption even of serious interests; it is an offense against an authority in some way transcendent. But, from experience, there is no moral force superior to the individual save collective force. . . .

What characterizes crime is that it determines punishment. . . . [Punishment] consists of a passionate reaction. This character is especially apparent in less cultivated societies. . . .

But today, it is said, punishment has changed its character; it is no longer to avenge itself that society punishes, it is to defend itself. The pain which it inflicts is in its hands no longer anything but a methodical means or protection. It punishes, not because chastisement offers it any satisfaction for itself, but so that the fear of punishment may paralyze those who contemplate evil.

* * *

Punishment [however] remains for us what it was for our fathers. It is still an act of vengeance since it is an expiation. What we avenge, what the criminal expiates, is the outrage to morality.

* * *

Everybody knows that it is society that punishes, but it might be held that this is not by design. What puts beyond doubt the social character of punishment is that, once pronounced, it cannot be lifted except by the government in the name of society.

* * *

When we think of penal law as it functions in our own societies, we consider it as a code where very definite punishments are attached to equally definite crimes. The judge is given a certain latitude in the application to each particular case of these general dispositions, but in its essential lineaments, punishment is predetermined for each category of delictuous acts. This planned organization does not, however, constitute punishment, for there are societies where punishment exists without being fixed in advance. . . .

Punishment consists, then, essentially in a passionate reaction of graduated intensity that society exercises through the medium of a body acting upon those of its members who have violated certain rules of conduct.

* * *

[At] the bottom of the notion of expiation there is the idea of a satisfaction accorded to some power, real or ideal, which is superior to us. When we desire the repression of crime, it is not we that we desire to avenge personally, but to avenge something sacred which we feel more or less confusedly outside and above us. This something we conceive of in different ways according to the time and the place. Sometimes it is a simple idea, as morality, duty; most often we represent it in the form of one or several concrete beings: ancestors, divinity. That is why penal law is not alone essentially religious in origin, but indeed always retains a certain religious stamp. It is because the acts that it punishes appear to be attacks upon something transcendent, whether being or concept. It is for this very reason that we explain to ourselves the need for a sanction superior to a simple reparation which would content us in the order of purely human interests.

Assuredly, this representation is illusory. It is ourselves that we, in a sense, avenge, ourselves that we satisfy, since it is within us and in us alone that the offended sentiments are found. But this illusion is necessary. Since these settlements have exceptional force because of their collective origin, their universality, their permanence, and their intrinsic intensity, they separate themselves radically from the rest of our conscience whose states are much more feeble. They dominate us; they are, so to speak, something superhuman, and, at the same time, they bind us to objects which are outside of our temporal life. They appear to us an echo in us of a force which is foreign to us, and which is superior to that which we are. We are thus forced to project them outside ourselves, to attribute what concerns them to some exterior object. We know today how partial alienations of personality thus come about. This mirage is so inevitable that, under one form or another, it will grow until a repressive system appears. For, if this did not follow, we would not need collective sentiments of more than mediocre intensity, and in that case there would no longer be such a thing as punishment. . . . Since these sentiments are collective it is not us they represent in use, but society. Thus, in avenging them, it is surely society and not ourselves that we avenge, and, moreover, it is something superior to the individual. It is thus wrong for us to seize upon this quasi-religious character of expiation and consider it as a sort of parasitic hypostatization. It is, on the contrary, an integral element of punishment. No doubt, it expresses its nature in a somewhat metaphorical manner, but the metaphor is not without truth.

Moreover, we know that the penal reaction is not uniform in all cases since the emotions which determine it are not always the same. They are, in effect, more or less lively according to the vivacity of the offended sentiment, and also according to the gravity of the offense suffered. A strong state reacts more than a feeble state, and two states of the same intensity react unequally according as they are more or less violently opposed. These variations are produced of necessity, and, moreover, they have their uses, since it is right that the appeal of forces be related to the importance of the danger.

* * *

Crime brings together upright consciences and concentrates them. . . . The sentiments . . . in question derive all their force from the fact that they are common to everybody. They are strong because they are uncontested. What

adds the peculiar respect of which they are the object is that they are universally respected. But crime is possible only if this respect is not truly universal.
Consequently, it implies that they are not absolutely collective. Crime thus
damages this unanimity which is the source of their authority. If, then, when it
is committed, the consciences which it offends do not unite themselves to give
mutual evidence of their communion, and recognize that the case is anomalous,
they would be permanently unsettled. They must re-enforce themselves by
mutual assurances that they are always agreed. The only means for this is action
in common. In short, since it is the common conscience which is attacked, it
must be that which resists, and accordingly the resistance must be collective.

\* \* \*

There are in us two consciences: one contains states which are personal
to each of us and which characterize us, while the states which comprehend
the other are common to all society.[3] The first represent only our individual
personality and constitute it; the second represent the collective type and,
consequently, society, without which it would not exist. When it is one of the
elements of this latter which determines our conduct, it is not in view of our
personal interest that we act, but we pursue collective ends. Although distinct,
these two consciences are linked one to the other, since, in sum, they are only
one, having one and the same organic substratum. They are thus solidary. From
this results a solidarity *sui generis,* which, born of resemblances, directly links
the individual with society. . . .

It is this solidarity which repressive law expresses, at least whatever there
is vital in it. The acts that it prohibits and qualifies as crimes are of two sorts.
Either they directly manifest very violent dissemblance between the agent who
accomplishes them and the collective type, or else they offend the organ of the
common conscience. . . .

We thus explain why acts have been so often reputed criminal and punished
as such without, in themselves, being evil for society.

\* \* \*

We can thus say without paradox that punishment is above all designed
to act upon upright people, for, since it serves to heal the wounds made upon
collective sentiments, it can fill this role only where these sentiments exist, and
commensurately with their vivacity. . . .

[There] exists a social solidarity which comes from a certain number of
states of conscience which are common to all the members of the same society.
This is what repressive law materially represents, at least in so far as it is essential.
The part that it plays in the general integration of society evidently depends
upon the greater or lesser extent of the social life which the common conscience

embraces and regulates. The greater the diversity of relations wherein the latter makes its action felt, the more also it creates links which attach the individual to the group; the more, consequently, social cohesion derives completely from this source and bears its mark. But the number of these relations is itself proportional to that of the repressive rules. In determining what fraction of the juridical system penal law represents, we, at the same time, measure the relative importance of this solidarity. It is true that in such a procedure we do not take into account certain elements of the collective conscience which, because of their smaller power or their indeterminateness, remain foreign to repressive law while contributing to the assurance of social harmony. These are the ones protected by punishments which are merely diffuse. But the same is the case with other parts of law. There is not one of them which is not complemented by custom, and as there is no reason for supposing that the relation of law and custom is not the same in these different spheres, this elimination is not made at the risk of having to alter the results of our comparison.

## Notes

1. It is this method which Garofalo has followed.

2. We shall not consider the question whether the collective conscience is a conscience as is that of the individual. By this term, we simply signify the totality of social likenesses, without prejudging the category by which this system of phenomena ought to be defined.

3. To simplify the exposition, we hold that the individual appears only in one society. In fact, we take part in several groups and there are in us several collective consciences; but this complication changes nothing with regard to the relation that we are now establishing.

# 7

## Crime in a Sociological Mirror

### Edwin H. Sutherland

Criminal behavior is behavior in violation of the criminal law. No matter what the degree of immorality, reprehensibility, or indecency of an act, it is not a crime unless it is prohibited by the criminal law. The criminal law, in turn, is defined conventionally as a body of specific rules regarding human conduct which have been promulgated by political authority, which apply uniformly to all members of the classes to which the rules refer, and which are enforced by punishment administered by the state. The characteristics which distinguish this body of rules regarding human conduct from other rules are, therefore, *politicality, specificity, uniformity,* and *penal sanction.* However, these are characteristics of an ideal, completely rational system of criminal law; in practice the differences between the criminal law and other bodies of rules for human conduct are not clear cut. Also, the ideal characteristics of the criminal law are not always features of the criminal law in action.

### Characteristics of the Criminal Law

The vast majority of the rules which define certain behavior as crime are found in constitutions, treaties, common law, enactments by the legislatures of the state and its subdivisions, and in judicial and administrative regulations. However, the criminal law is not merely a collection of written proscriptions. The agency of enforcement of law is the court, and thus it is the court rather than the legislature which determines what the law is. According to one school of thought, courts merely "apply" the law in an even-handed manner to all persons who come before them. However, both the techniques used by the court in interpreting and applying the statutes and the body of ideals held by the court are a part of the law in action, as truly as are the written statutes. The court decision in one controversy becomes a part of the body of rules used in making decisions in other controversies. . . . [Behind] the behavior of courts is public opinion. Also, between the courts and the legislature are intermediate agencies,

From *Criminology* by Edwin H. Sutherland and Donald R. Cressey. Reprinted by permission of the publishers, J.B. Lippincott. Copyright © 1966.

such as the police, which affect the enforcement and administration of the law. Many statutes are never enforced; some are enforced only on rare occasions; others are enforced with a striking disregard for uniformity. These enforcement and administrative agencies, also, are affected by public opinion, and a leader in the field of jurisprudence concluded that law in action is determined chiefly by public opinion.[1] Consequently, the law does not consist in the statutes alone and may change while the statutes remain constant.

*Politicality* is regarded almost universally as a necessary element in criminal law. The rules of the trade union, the church, or the family are not regarded as criminal law, nor are violations of these rules regarded as crimes. Only violations of rules made by the state are crimes. This distinction between the state and other groups is not only arbitrary but also is difficult to maintain when attention is turned to societies where patriarchal power, private self-help, popular justice, and other forerunners of legislative justice are found. . . .

*Specificity* is included as an element in the definition of criminal law because of the contrast in this respect between criminal law and civil law. The civil law may be general. . . . The criminal law, on the other hand, generally gives a strict definition of a specific act, and when there is doubt as to whether a definition describes the behavior of a defendant the judge is obligated to decide in favor of the defendant. . . .

*Uniformity* or regularity is included in the conventional definition of criminal law because law attempts to provide even-handed justice without respect to persons. This means that no exceptions are made to criminal liability because of a person's social status; an act described as a crime is crime, no matter who perpetrates it. Also, uniformity means that the law-enforcement process shall be administered without regard for the status of the persons who have committed crimes or are accused of committing crimes. This ideal, however, has varied widely in practice. . . .

*Penal sanction,* as one of the elements in the orthodox definition of law, refers to the notion that violators will be punished or, at least, threatened with punishment by the state. Punishment under the law differs from that imposed by a mob in that it is applied dispassionately by representatives of the state in such a manner that it may win the approval of the cool judgment of impartial observers. A law which does not provide a penalty that will cause suffering is regarded as quite impotent and in fact no criminal law at all.

* * *

### Nature of Criminal Law from the Genetic Point of View

Many theories of the origin of the criminal law as an agency of social control have been developed. First, in the classical theory the criminal law was regarded as originating in torts, or wrongs to individuals. According to this theory, all wrongs produced efforts at self-redress in the injured parties and were therefore treated as injuries to particular individuals; and later, by a series of transitions, the group took charge of the treatment, and the wrongs came to be regarded as injuries to the group or to the state. . . .

A second theory is that the criminal law originated in the rational process of a unified society. When wrongs occurred, the society took action and made a regulation to prevent a repetition of such wrongs. An alternative interpretation is that the enactment of a statute is an expression of emotion. . . .

A third theory is that the criminal law originated in and is a crystallization of the mores. Customs developed with little or no rational analysis, but after persisting for a time they achieved an ethical foundation. Infraction of such customs produced antagonistic reactions of the group, which were expressed in the form of criminal law with penal sanctions. . . .

A fourth theory is that criminal law originated in conflict of interests of different groups. When an interest group secures the enactment of a law, it secures the assistance of the state in a conflict with a rival interest group; the opposition of the rival group thus becomes criminal. . . .

No positive conclusion can be reached about the comparative efficiency of the various theories concerning the origin of criminal law. . . .

Ideally, behavior would not be called crime unless all seven differentiae were present. The following brief description of the differentiae is greatly simplified.

*First,* before behavior can be called crime there must be certain external consequences or "harm." A crime has a harmful impact on social interests; a "mental" or emotional state is not enough. Even if one decides to commit a crime but changes his mind before he does anything about it, he has committed no crime. The intention is not taken for the deed.

*Second,* the harm must be legally forbidden, must have been proscribed in penal law. Anti-social behavior is not crime unless it is prohibited by law. . . .

*Third,* there must be "conduct"; that is, there must be an intentional or reckless action or inaction which brings the harmful consequences about. . . .

*Fourth,* "criminal intent" or *mens rea* must be present. . . .

*Fifth,* there must be a fusion or concurrence of *mens rea* and conduct. This means, for example, that a policeman who goes into a house to make an arrest and who then commits a crime after making the arrest while still in the house, cannot be considered a trespasser from the beginning. The criminal intent and the conduct do not fuse or concur.

*Sixth,* there must be a "causal" relation between the legally forbidden harm and the voluntary misconduct. The "conduct" of one who fails to file an income tax return is his failure to take pen and ink, fill out the form, etc.; the "harm" is the absence of a return in the collector's office. . . .

*Seventh,* there must be legally prescribed punishment. Not only must the harm be proscribed by law but, as indicated above, the proscription must carry a threat of punishment to violators. The voluntary conduct must be punishable by law.

* * *

### Nature of Crime from the Social Point of View

. . . Crime may be considered . . . to involve three elements: a value which is appreciated by a group or a part of a group which is politically important; isolation of or cultural conflict in another part of this group so that its members do not appreciate the value or appreciate it less highly and consequently tend to endanger it; and a pugnacious resort to coercion decently applied by those who appreciate the value to those who disregard the value. When a crime is committed, these relationships are involved. Crime is this set of relationships when viewed from the point of view of the group rather than of the individual. This conception of the social nature of crime, as well as the preceding definitions, is suggestive and may be developed into a fundamental definition, but at present certainly lacks precision.

### The Relativity of Crime

Crime is relative from the legal point of view and also from the social point of view. The criminal law has had a constantly changing content. Many of the early crimes were primarily religious offenses, and these remained important until recent times; now few religious offenses are included in the penal codes. . . .

Laws differ, also, from one jurisdiction to another at a particular time. . . . In a particular jurisdiction at a particular time there are wide variations in the interpretation and implementation of the law. These variations are related to the specific characteristics of the crimes and to the status of the offenders. . . .

### Classification of Crimes

Since crime is not a homogeneous type of behavior, efforts have been made to classify crimes. They are frequently classified in respect to atrocity as felonies and misdemeanors. The more serious are called felonies and are usually punishable by death or by confinement in a state prison; the less serious are called misdemeanors and are usually punishable by confinement in a local prison or by fines. . . .

The greatest objection to the classification of crimes as felonies and misdemeanors is that it is used also as a classification of criminals. The individual who commits a felony is a felon; the individual who commits a misdemeanor is a misdemeanant. It is assumed that misdemeanants are less dangerous and more susceptible to rehabilitative measures than felons. But it is quite fallacious to judge the danger to the group or the probability of reformation from one act, for an individual may commit a misdemeanor one week, a felony the second week, and a misdemeanor the third. The acts do not represent changes in his character or changes in the danger to the group.

* * *

In a classification of crimes for theoretical purposes each class should be a sociological entity, differentiated from the other classes by variations in causal processes. Professional crime, for instance, would be a class, or more likely a combination of classes, differentiated from other crimes by the regularity of this behavior, the development of techniques, and the association among offenders and the consequent development of a group culture. Within this class might be included some cases of murder, arson, burglary, robbery, and theft, but not all of the cases in any of those legal categories. Similarly, specific criteria for describing cases as "criminal violation of financial trust" have been developed, with the result that some, but not all, cases of embezzlement, confidence game, forgery, larceny by bailee, and other crimes are included. The new classification avoided the error of extending a legal concept beyond its legal meaning, e.g., calling all the behavior "embezzlement," and at the same time it provided a rigorous definition of the beahvior being studied. . . .

## The Criminal

Who is a criminal? An answer consistent with the previous discussion is: A person who commits a crime. However, in the democratic legal tradition even one who admits to having committed a crime is not designated a criminal until his criminality has been *proven* by means of the accepted court procedures. . . .

## Note

1. Roscoe Pound, *Criminal Justice in America* (New York: Holt, 1930), p. 120.

# 8 Dual Responsibility

*Stephen Schafer*

What constitutes a criminological theory and what is its appropriate scope are extremely difficult questions. The delimitation of theories in criminology is no less difficult than in general philosophy, and any attempt at delimiting cannot avoid considerable arbitrariness. Criminology, like the other social sciences, is primarily a research-oriented discipline and therefore its theories are accepted as valid only if verified by existing data. Even the law, which objectively defines the necessary conditions of crime, and which seems to be abstract before applied practically, is increasingly predicated on observation. In criminology a "pure theory" cannot be profitably employed unless, as a last resort, purely abstract thinking aids in the understanding of the empirical material.

However, if verification is fundamental to any theory and proof is as rigorously interpreted as it is in the natural sciences, hardly any current set of propositions in criminology could correctly be labeled a theory. The vision of most theorists is not always based on mathematical-statistical evidence, a fate also true of almost every social science theory. No criminological theory has established the "truth" or shown us the causes of crime. This is not a matter of judgment, but a statistical fact: a panoramic study and appraisal of criminological theories and related action programs clearly demonstrates that crime rates have not dropped and criminal recidivism has not been reduced. A cynical judgment may be that these ideas are hypotheses rather than theories.

It may be that no criminological theory can ever be verified fully; most criminological truths have a transitional character. Crimes and criminals change in definition, by time and place; what is a crime today may not be a crime tomorrow. . . .

We are faced with a curious duality in criminological theories. There are theories that attempt to explain the causes of criminal behavior and independent propositions dealing with the rehabilitation of criminals and the efficiency of the penal system. Theories of causes are coupled with "theories" of treatment. . . . There is an increasing number of those who respond to crime with recommendations for what can be done with the criminals, rather than seeking an explanation of why criminals violate the law. Much relief may come from therapies, correctional methods, operational decisions and actions; perhaps the only barrier

47

between them and the criminological theories is that the treatment propositions want to treat something that is not known and is yet to be found by the theories.

## Crime and Responsibility

When Xerxes, son of the great Darius, caned the furious waves for their disobedience, he was not entirely correct. A case could have been made for holding them responsible and punishing them for their rebellious lack of response to his order; but he should have paid closer attention to the nature of their resistance. Most criminological theories approach crime in a reverse direction of thinking; they try to explicate criminal conduct but pay little attention to why certain acts are defined as crimes and why criminal responsibility is attached to some actions. Actually, the crime problem presents two interconnected elements: the types of behavior defined in the law as crimes and the forces that impel some people to engage in conduct labeled criminal by the law. Both pose the problem of responsibility, but from two different angles.

The former deals with the responsibility of individuals who have engaged in certain acts and are thereby threatened with punishment under the law. Misappropriation or misapplication of money entrusted to one's care may involve his being held responsible for embezzlement. A person who willfully or maliciously burns something, even without the intent to defraud, may be responsible for arson. The law threatens anyone who takes anything of value from a person by force or violence with the responsibility for the crime of robbery. Lawmakers select, define, and imbue these and other acts with responsibility. Penal sanctions remain only abstract threats so long as the law is respected.

The other type of responsibility involves the forces that motivate one's conduct against the law. Why does a person become an embezzler, an arsonist, or a robber? What factors are responsible for his disrespect for the legal threat of punishment? Is it his biological makeup, his psychiatric condition, his social or economic environment that is responsible for his criminal conduct? Or did he simply "want" to engage in a crime and, in a sense, accepted responsibility by his "free will"?

Who can be made responsible for what, and who is responsible and why—these are the two crucial issues in criminological thought. The answer to both issues is certainly ever changing, mirroring the values of the social, cultural, and political conditions of the given era. Both responsibilities are changing.

The concept of responsibility as used here is not the individual legal accountability or culpability for having engaged in punishable conduct. This responsibility may be classified as "answerability," for it involves the lawmaker defining crime and the individual reacting to the law by breaking it—both are elements of a single continuum.[1] Crime factors cannot be understood without an intimate knowledge of the law. Criminal law similarly cannot be fully comprehended without some understanding of the etiology of crime. Without this dual under-standing of responsibility, crime may remain unknown.

The two responsibilities are interrelated and cannot be disconnected. This twofold concept seems to be the heart of the crime problem; its crux is the drama between the threatening responsibility and the counterresponsibility. Without the former we would have a lawless and, necessarily, a "crimeless" society; with it we may only hope for some miraculous disappearance of crime. Changes in the law are not inevitably followed by changes in human conduct. A new law requires adjustment in individual behavior, but this may not always be made by all members of the society. Changes in law are variables of a composite and complicated relationship. Two variables are almost never perfectly corre-lated; in the case of extremely complex phenomena, such as the law and criminal behavior, any number of contributory, contingent, and alternative conditions may sharply affect the relationship between the two. Yet, in crude generaliza-tion, the criminal conduct may be viewed as the dependent variable. Crime is committed by man, but crime is defined by law; the supreme tragedy of the drama is that the law, too, is made by man.

Since no one has yet invented a system of absolute justice, every society has produced its own unique system of control. But the systems are continually changing. A constant and eternal natural law would be possible only if all social phenomena, and all lawmaking powers, recurred with unchanging uniformity. Thus, an accurate description of the causes of crime could be determined only if an immutable natural law existed. Raffaele Garofalo's exciting pursuit of "nat-ural" crime is never ultimately convincing.[2] In most criminological analyses the question of causes—in other words, the "responsibility" for the criminal con-duct—has become so central that it is easy to lose sight of the changing criminal law.

Because the law is in a constant state of flux, an individual's frame of refer-ence cannot be "naturally" consistent with his society's demands. His conduct has to be adjusted to changes in the system of control. Even if the laws of two different control systems seem to resemble one another, invariably differ in the interpretation and application of the law, largely because of variation in the use of the lawmaking powers. The concept of responsibility fluctuates bewilderingly from society to society and from one generation to the next. In all periods of human history man has been aware of its inconsistencies, for herein lies the dis-tinction between conformists and criminals. . . .

Responsibility is determined by an ever changing formula. It might be said that crime does not change but responsibility does. Some individuals may enjoy a lifetime without being frustrated by significant changes of law, while others may be exposed to painful changes in the system of responsibilities that require severe changes in their behavior. The reason for changes in law is inherent in the reason for the law itself. A system of law might be understood without reference to crime, but the meaning of crime can hardly be perceived without understanding its relationship with the responsibility-making law.

## Responsibility and Law

The source of responsibility-making law is "social power." Only support for such power makes it possible for a law to become "the law." Inversely, from the law we can discover its source; a given concept of responsibility usually reflects the lawmaking power. John Austin contended that the law is the "command of the sovereign."[3] Gustav Radbruch, in a sense, extended Austin's statement by contending that absolute justice is undiscoverable.[4] A combination of Austin's dictate with Radbruchian relativism would imply that lawmaking power is not necessarily in the hands of a king or a dictator. Any group or particular individual may, at a given moment of time, acquire such power. . . . [The] law will never, so long as it is administered by human beings, be free from arbitrary will and brute force. And this is probably true for all of human history, regardless of the form of the sovereign authority or social power that designed the concept of responsibility.

Edward Westermarck, after reviewing and analyzing the origin and development of the moral ideas, finally concluded that the simple historical fact is that the "law expresses a rule of duty by making an act or omission which is regarded as wrong a crime."[5] All laws are formulated on the assumption that they are just. They are "just" at least insofar as they are defined by the ruling social power and so long as the existing social power prevails. This social power knows what is right and wrong, and in the form of the commands raises the law to the level of "truth." . . .

In his somewhat naturalist search for the morality of law, Lon Fuller contended, "There is no doubt that a legal system derives its ultimate support from a sense of being 'right.'"[6] But, understandably, his stand is based on what he or we think is "right." Dennis Lloyd, another modern philosopher of law, suggests that whoever requires the obedience of others should be entitled to do so.[7] In other words, he seems to opt for a law to enable the lawmaker to make the law. Perhaps Herbert Hart came closest to the truth when, in one of his generalizing "issues," he proposed that a penal statute declaring certain conduct as criminal and specifying the punishment to which the criminal is liable "may appear to be the gunman situation writ large."[8] Certainly the lawmaker cannot be identified with a gunman simply by virtue of having the coercive power of making others obey his commands, yet there are intrinsic similarities between the two situations. The death penalty and the first-degree murder differ only in their legality, as determined by conventional society.

Although from the Justinian law to our time many laws were born in dictatorial situations, the gunman circumstances are not typical in the responsibility-making processes. The lawmaker is not necessarily a gunman, but he may be. . . . In both variations of the origin of law, John Austin's claim, that in the last analysis the law is the command of the sovereign, may well be a terrifying truth. Austin, a disciple of Jeremy Bentham, may have oversimplified the essence of the lawmaking, but his tenet offers little shelter for those who abandon the real world for the comfort of illusions. Indeed, there is much more involved in the idea of law than sheer obedience, but the factor of obedience is nevertheless a crucial one. Usually a rich and complex interplay between individuals, groups, and conflicting values takes place before a law is created. Questions as to who has this sovereign power, what legalities or formalities must be observed, and what behavior is demanded, do not alter the fundamental structure of lawmaking. Hans Kelsen's theory on the identity of state and law[9] would be closer to John Austin's thinking if the state were equated with power.

One may assume that the puzzle of what power exists, and the related questions of "legitimacy" of this power, leads inevitably to the problem of the "rightness" of law. Perhaps the greatest obstacle to settling this apparently interminable argument is our reluctance to accept the fact that what we think of as right does not necessarily represent the only correct view. We tend to think in terms of a single immutable truth and conclude that therefore there is only one possible system of justice. The claim that the law is moral or ethical rests upon the dubious hypothesis that there is only one moral or ethical code. The law makes objective rather than absolute judgments; it is right or wrong only in the way it interprets actions. The social power of the group defines values to be learned; it defines the rightness or wrongness of some modes of human conduct. Whatever is defined by this social power as right or wrong must be accepted by those who are required to obey so long as the power is a "power." . . .

Changes take different form and speed in different cultures and under the rule of different "sovereigns." It is inherent in the dynamics of totalitarian powers that changes in the law are generally faster and more abrupt than in democracies. But it is difficult to agree with Rudolf Stammler, who, in his quest for a "just" law expressing a "social ideal," hypothesized despotic control systems where the commands of the rulers were not binding on the rulers.[10] Most dictatorships make no less effort to maintain the continuity of law than do democracies. Whether the rulers are bound by their own commands is hardly a distinguishing characteristic of authoritarian systems. Even in democracies, where the supreme legal authority is the constitution itself, behind legitimacy lies authority, and behind authority, power. It is not true that the continuity of law is preserved simply because a constitution is written. The English are constitutionalists and therefore have a constitution, even though it is an unwritten one; "certain other peoples have written constitutions but are not constitutionalists."[11]

Clearly legislative apparatus and lawmaking in totalitarian systems differ from those in democracies. Dictatorial powers monopolize lawmaking; in democracies, there is a great variety of interactions between social evolution and legal change. However distinct the two lawmaking processes are, it does seem that essentially both remain "commands of the sovereign." . . .

The lawmaking power may be a single man or many men; it may be a despotic dictator or a democratic parliament; "The source of authority may be . . . the words of a prophet or a saint."[12] But man makes the law and defines responsibility, and thus they vary with changing ideas and transfers in power. The idea of the continuity of law seems weakened by the discontinuity in the source of law. The inevitable changes in the participants of the lawmaking process alone account for unavoidable changes in the definition of crimes and punishments. *Lex posterior derogat priori*; the law of yesterday may not be the law of today if it is no longer supported by the ultimate power in the society. The later law derogates earlier ones. Sometimes the "continuity" of the law involves a legal code of great stability with only minor changes; but upon examination this continuity is proved a fiction. It is therefore impossible to speak about "causes" of crime or crime "in general" without an awareness of the forces that create and enforce the law and the manner in which the forces themselves change.

The test of a man is how he responds to the system of control in his society that aims to establish or fortify an ideal social order. Studying "criminal" behavior relative to the changing law may lead to a balanced assessment of the crime problem. It is a highly complex relationship, and the correlation between legal prohibition and criminal action is much too intricate to be measured by conventional methods; the frame of reference the observer is using is vital to the judgment. Yet a balanced perspective seems to be the cornerstone of any meaningful etiology of crime. The correlation between making people responsible for engaging in crime and the factors that produce noncompliance largely determines the relative significance of crime and the success of the social order. The irony of the man-committed crime is that it is so dependent upon the man-made law.

## Notes

1. H.L.A. Hart in his *Punishment and Responsibility* (Oxford: 1968), pp. 211-212, called attention to the wide range of ideas covered by the term "responsibility" in and out of the law. Hart distinguished among role responsibility, causal responsibility, liability responsibility, and capacity responsibility. In the present context, liability responsibility is the one charged by the lawmaking power (it is role responsibility only in its moral sense as a general obligation of all members of the society), and causal responsibility refers to crime factors. Capacity responsibility, as concrete accountability, is merely a legal and often technical question and thus outside the scope of the present topic.

2. Raffaele Garofalo, *Criminology,* trans. by Robert Wyness Millar (Boston: 1914).

3. John Austin, *Lectures on Jurisprudence or the Philosophy of Positive Law* (London: 1861). Austin's first six lectures were published in his lifetime under the title *The Province of Jurisprudence Determined* (1832); the rest were published with the assistance of his widow.

4. Gustav Radbruch, *Rechtsphilosophie,* 3rd ed. (Berlin: 1932).

5. Edward Westermarck, *The Origin and Development of the Moral Ideas,* vol. 1, 2nd ed. (London: 1912), p. 168.

6. Lon L. Fuller, *The Morality of Law* (New Haven and London: 1964), p. 138.

7. Dennis Lloyd, *The Idea of Law* (Baltimore: 1964), pp. 27-28.

8. H.L.A. Hart, *The Concept of Law* (Oxford: 1961), pp. 6-7.

9. Hans Kelsen, *Allgemeine Staatslehr* (Berlin: 1925).

10. Rudolf Stammler, *Wirtschaft und Recht nach der materialistischen Geschichtsanfassung,* 5th ed. (Leipzig: 1924).

11. Alfred de Grazia, *The Elements of Political Science* 2 (London and New York, 1965), p. 49.

12. Karl Mannheim, *Systematic Sociology: An Introduction to the Study of Society,* ed. J.S. Erös and W.A.C. Stewart (New York: 1957), p. 126.

**Part II**
**Biological Factors in Crime**

# Introduction

Modern biological-criminological theory has its origins in the polar arguments of what are now known as the classical and positivist schools. The classical position, enunciated in the progressive and yet retributive thought of Cesare Beccaria, an eighteenth-century Italian lawyer (1738–1794) influenced by Montesquieu, Hume, Bacon, Helvetius, and Rousseau, presupposed that the Italian crimino-legal system of the late 1700s was not only abusive but also arbitrary in its processing of offenders. Consequently, criminal law, Beccaria argued, should be reoriented and punishment be applied in direct proportion to the seriousness of the crime committed and not in relationship to the judge's variable use of his sentencing power. The function of the law is to order society and to coordinate the activities of individual members; each person contracts with the society at large for the maintenance of order and permits punishment as a means of secur-ing individual conformity to societal ideals. Punishment, however, is legitimate, Beccaria believed, only when it is used to defend political sovereignty against the acts of individuals who would undermine it. The goal of punishment, he main-tained, is to deter future and current criminal offenders from endangering the stability of the society. However, the pleasure of crime is such that the criminal can be discouraged only by certain and painful punishment. The free will of each person anticipating punishment will keep each potential offender from com-mitting criminal acts.

The Italian criminologist-physician Cesare Lombroso (1835–1909), at the opposite extreme, rejected the legal definition of crime as he reacted more than seventy-five years later to Beccaria's thesis and adapted Darwin's ideas concern-ing the species to the person who commits the criminal act. A proponent of a positivist criminology, he posited a "born criminal," a term used by Enrico Ferri, offender type, characterized by a particular malformation of the skull and skeletal bones, especially revealed in peculiar cranial and facial asymmetry. The born criminal, Lombroso concluded, has either an under- or an oversized brain, high cheekbones, big ears, minimal facial hair, a projecting or a receding jaw, and overdeveloped arms. The congenital or born criminal reflects an atavistic or degenerative human type. A second major group of criminals includes the sub-categories of pseudo-criminals, criminaloids, those who commit crimes of passion, habitual criminals, and the criminally insane. Criminals, Lombroso con-cluded, are commonly reversions to a primitive or subhuman type, as is even-tually revealed by their inferior morphological features. Because they are degen-erative, they oppose the rules and expectations of their societies. Their violation of criminal law is a natural byproduct of their biological condition. The criminal is a throwback to an earlier stage of human evolution and is a person who is un-able to adjust to modern civilization. Therefore, criminals should be dealt with in social rather than legal terms. Emphasis should be placed upon the person of the criminal, his needs and his eventual treatment rather than his violation of a legal statute. While stigmata disclose who may be the criminal, they alone do not make the person a lawbreaker.

Other theorists have in varying degrees either supported or challenged these polar positions. Swiss theologian, J.K. Lavater (1741-1801) accepted a phrenological explanation of crime, holding that exterior skull shape, unusual cranial protuberances, and other structural brain abnormalities are closely related to criminal tendencies. Franz Joseph Gall (1758-1828) accepted a smiliar premise which was later amplified by his student and collaborator John Gaspar Spurzheim (1776-1853). Spurzheim maintained that criminal tendencies are biologically inherited and are revealed in skull conformations, especially the size of the ear lobes and skull protuberances. The phrenology of Gall and Spurzheim assumed that the exterior of the skull conforms to the shape of the brain; the so-called mind is a composite of multiple faculties or functions; and these faculties are related to specific areas of the brain and skull. The German psychiatrist Ernst Kretschmer, following Emil Kraepelin's (1856-1926) fundamental distinction between two general mental types, finally related criminal tendencies to basic body types, the asthenic, athletic, pyknic, and mixed or unclassifiable types, classified on the basis of body build, height, muscular construction, limb characteristics, and similar factors. Kretschmer suggested that abnormal persons fluctuate between mental health and mental disorder and carried the original concern for anthropological causes of crime to a new level of theorizing.

At the same time that Kretschmer was presenting his ideas, the colorful Italian criminologist and criminal lawyer Enrico Ferri (1856-1929), a disciple of Lombroso, suggested in overshadowing his mentor that crime is a product of individual ("anthropological"), physical and social factors, which, while interrelated, are yet distinct. Among the *anthropological* factors are the criminal's sex, age, occupation, civil status, social class and residence; *physical* factors of importance include climate, race, human fertility, distribution of soil, annual temperature, and the like; among the *social* factors are customs, religion, family characteristics, political forms, education and welfare. Criminals, Ferri hypothesized, can be classified into five basic groups: born or instinctive, insane, occasional, passionate and habitual criminals. The concept of free will should be rejected as the basis of criminal responsibility; man's acts, Ferri argued, are socially determined and the offender is not actually responsible for his crime, although he is held responsible for his criminal conduct by society. The function of criminal justice, according to Ferri, is not to measure the moral guilt of an offender, but rather to determine whether a criminal act was carried out and whether it violated social prohibitions. The goal of criminal justice is, in effect, "social defense." Crime should be understood in its reality in scientific terms. Traditional punishments are of limited value in combating crime. As with Lombroso, Ferri believed that criminals are not ordinary men.

Given this backdrop, it is easy to see the development of biological explanations of crime as presented in part II. Franz Joseph Gall (1758–1828), a late eighteenth- and early nineteenth-century Austrian phrenologist-anatomist who provided the foundation for Spurzheim's work, distinguished between voluntary and involuntary criminal acts and recognized that imbecility, depending upon degree, does not permit a man to act in a moral manner. A partially or generally handicapped (alienated) person may retain several moral qualities and intellectual faculties, for moral and intellectual dispositions, Gall suggests, as a result of his research in prisons and lunatic asylums, are innate: their manifestation depends upon organization. The brain has twenty-seven faculties or functions, including combativeness, secretiveness, and acquisitiveness, which presuppose a person to criminal conduct.

The surgeon Charles Caldwell (1772–1853), the leading American proponent of phrenology, defends his support of a scientific phrenology against an attack by David M. Reiss, arguing the need for a less subjective and a more scientific method for studying personality. Caldwell believes that a propensity to destructiveness may lead to murder, combativeness to assault, and acquisitiveness to theft or robbery. However, a person can inhibit his biological propensity to crime with the development of higher sentiments and intelligence under the right social conditions. Caldwell contends the phrenological method, despite its imprecision, represents a scientific advance over the earlier biological-psychological explanations of deviant conduct.

The late nineteenth-, early twentieth-century sociologist-novelist Max Nordau, who broke loose from the phrenological school and proposed a "new biological theory of crime" (later to be incorporated into the legal philosophy of the socialist system of criminal law in the U.S.S.R.), suggests that instincts may degenerate and undermine the unity of society. If degenerative creatures attempt to appease their desires in a manner detrimental to society, they should be suppressed and not be permitted to express their individuality in crime. Human parasitism, a product of social maladjustment, often leads to crime as some men seek to live off the labor of others without compensation. Parasites treat other men as raw material which they use to satisfy their needs and wants.

The nineteenth-century positivist Cesare Lombroso suggests that the nature and distribution of certain crimes can be explained in terms of atavism. In the second article in part II (here translated for the first time from the first edition), Lombroso not only suggests that crime is necessary to a society, but also that criminals are most frequently persons who have not kept pace with the development of the human race. While the social order needs crime to progress (crime is a byproduct of social change), it also needs defense against crime in the form of punishment.

But prison medical officer Charles Goring (1870–1919), an antagonist of Lombroso's idea of the born criminal, contends that it is impossible to state categorically whether a criminal is born or made. As a result of his studies of some 3,000 English recidivist offenders and a control group of Oxford and Cambridge students, British soldiers and hospital patients, Goring suggests the possibility that both constitutional and environmental factors are instrumental in the production of criminality, that there may exist a criminal diasthesis—a mental, moral, or physical proclivity which leads some individuals toward a criminal career and eventual imprisonment. A distinct anthropological criminal type has no existence in fact, but certain physical, mental and moral types of moral persons tend to be convicted of crime. The fates of men and the fortunes of society depend upon the forces of heredity, circumstance, and chance. The criminal personality is determined by a defective state of mind combined with a poor physical condition, often expressed through heredity. The criminal is somewhat shorter and lighter than members of the regular population; violent criminals are frequently taller and heavier, however.

The twentieth-century American anthropologist Ernest Hooton, a critic of Goring's unscientific methods and bias, finds as the result of his metric and morphological studies of a sample of American criminals and noncriminals in the 1930s that tatooing is more common among criminals than among civilians, that criminals probably have less facial and bodily hair, more head hair and a higher proportion of red-brown hair than civilians, and that criminals are deficient in very dark and very light shades of eye color. Overall, the physical features of the criminal population tend to be more or less uniform, although variations may exist among offenders. The primary cause of crime, Hooton, the Harvard anthropologist, maintains, is biological inferiority. Criminals are organically inferior, and crime is a product of environmental impact upon low-grade human organisms. For the most part, criminals are constitutionally inferior persons. Crime can only be eliminated if the morally, physically, and mentally unfit are either segregated or extirpated from society.

The German Ernst Kretschmer, writing in 1921, is even more precise as he links criminal deviance to three principal physic types: asthenic, athletic and pyknic. Each body type not only possesses its own descriptive characteristics, but each group shares some degree of propensity toward schizophrenia. The asthenic and athletic types tend to schizophrenia and the pyknic to the manic depressive state. Dysplastic or mixed types do not show the same overriding temperamental pattern.

William H. Sheldon, who improved upon Kretschmer's theory during the 1930s–1940s, explores the three body types of endomorph, mesomorph, and ectomorph, which correspond respectively to Kretschmer's three body types of pyknic, athletic, and asthenic. Each constitutional type has its counterpart in temperament, and both body type and temperament have a direct relationship to the kinds of conduct a person engages in. The endomorph loves comfort and food and is sociable, calm, and slow acting. The mesomorph has well developed muscles and is characteristically aggressive, direct, and combative. The ectomorph is often introverted, private, cool to others, and self-restrained.

On the basis of the first major study of thirty pairs of twins (thirteen identical and seventeen fraternal) that had one member in a Bavarian prison, Johannes Lange (1891- ), a German physician-reformer, concludes from his work at the beginning of this century that crime is not a "purely biological phenomenon which ceases with the criminal." It also presents a social picture and as such must always have a basis in culture and environment. Heredity, he notes, cannot be the exclusive cause of criminality and yet criminal tendencies may be inherited.

Genetic researcher W.M. Court-Brown, a modern contemporary, writing in 1967, rather optimistically suggests that certain kinds of sex chromosomes complement abnormality and have an important relationship to criminal conduct. Preliminary evidence shows, Court-Brown believes, that XYY chromosome males may be disproportionately included within the ordinary prison population, a position that has been challenged by more recent data.

Contemporary American sociologist Robert K. Merton and anthropologist M.F. Ashley-Montagu, criticizing the anthropological methodology used by Ernest Hooton, hold that Hooton fails to support scientifically his conclusion that criminals are oganically inferior and anticipate that similar problems may be found in almost any form of biological-psychological research. Hooton's preoccupation with biological determinism, they contend, undermines his attempt to interpret the extensive statistical data which he had gathered.

# 9 The Origin of Moral Qualities

*Franz Joseph Gall*

Application of my principles to illegal actions that are the consequence of a particular feebleness of the intellectual faculties:

I here use the expression "a particular feebleness of intellectual faculties" because I treat only actions that are the consequence of more or less imbecility of spirit; I will not speak of acts derived from total and general stupidity of spirit. These acts, being purely involuntary or automatic, do not have the same bearing on moral liberty and can by no means be the object of my research. . . .

Man should be considered in two respects: first as having common qualities with the lower animals, then as being endowed with the character of humanity of the qualities of a superior order. . . . By means of his superior qualities, man is in a position to control and direct the inclinations of his inferior self. But if the qualities of the superior order are suppressed in an extraordinary manner, to the point that they cannot be expressed action, whereas those of the inferior order are very active, then the criminal part of man dominates, and the flesh or the brutal desires hold in subjection the spirit or the dispositions of the superior properties, which are barely outlines. The same thing happens with such an organization for the functions of the soul . . . as in an organ whose development is defective—that is, it results in a relative imbecility and, by consequence, an incapacity to act morally. . . . Such an individual finds it an absolute necessity to act uniquely, according to the strength of the inclination that dominates him, and his drives often make him less able to restrain himself than is a well-organized animal. This imbecility does not always exclude other very active properties that are common to animals, such as that of craftiness; so that this same individual, in completely abandoning himself to a guilty and irresistible inclination, seems to act in this relationship with reflection and deliberation. Thus the most stupid idiots often find the most skillful means of satisfying their brutal lasciviousness or their fatal desires. . . . Although there is nothing to hope for in these imbeciles, it does not follow that there is nothing to dread. It often happens, on the contrary, that they are very dangerous, above all when they have the in-

From Franz Joseph Gall, *Sur Les Fonctions du Curveau et sur Celles de Chacune de Ses Parties* (Paris: J.B. Baillere & Fil's, 1825). Reprinted with permission.

63

clination toward sex and the inclination to kill to a high degree, so that the slightest cause puts these inclinations in action. . . . Such examples prove that talents can exist separately; that an inclination or a particular talent results in the particular activity of an organ, and that the activity of an organ can very well take place, whereas in relationship to the other organs, there is a true imbecility.

Moreover, this condition having several degrees, one can only affirm that for beings who are also poorly organized, all methods of correction would be equally fruitless. . . . It would be impossible to explain partial and incomplete imbecility if one did not recognize that the diverse properties of the soul and the spirit possess each one of the different organs and that the manifestations of these properties depend on organization.

Although these partially imbecilic individuals are not moral beings, nor by consequence punishable, the tasks of their surveillance nevertheless belongs to the detective force. It is essential to keep distant from social commerce all imbeciles in whom one observes sufficiently strong indications of an evil character.

Application of my principles to illegal actions that are the consequence of mental alienation:

Mental alienation is either *general,* as when the functions of all the faculties of the soul and spirit are troubled; or *partial,* as when this derangement takes place only in one or several organs. Mental alienation, be it general or partial, continuous or permanent, manifests itself in a manner so clear that one cannot be mistaken about its existence. Hence, one does not run the risk of regarding actions committed in this condition as if they were done with a moral liberty, and of holding their author responsible for them. . . .

Permanent general alienation cannot be mistaken. But it is completely otherwise when the general alienation is periodic . . . or when the alienation affects only certain qualities—above all, when this partial alienation disappears entirely from time to time and comes back sometimes irregularly, sometimes periodically. Several moral qualities or intellectual faculties suffer no derangement during the onset of partial alienation; just as in intermittent general alienation, no trace of deviation can be perceived in the lucid intervals. Partial alienation is not, also, always a consequence of the derangement of intellectual faculties; often the inclinations or the moral sentiments suffer alone, and the spirit of the intellectual faculties stays perfectly healthy. These diverse rapports make it very difficult to judge the innocence or the guilt of equivocal actions.

## On the Functions of the Brain

Research on the measure of intelligence in man and animals has found that the brains of animals are more simple or more complex according to the simplicity and complexity of their instincts, their inclinations, and their faculties; that the diverse regions of the brain are assigned to different categories of functions; that, finally, the brain of each type of animal, and consequently also that of man, comprises so many particular organs that there is in man or in animal essentially different moral qualities and intellectual faculties.

Moral and intellectual dispositions are innate; their manifestation depends on organization; the brain is exclusively the organ of the soul; the brain is composed of as many particular and independent organs as there are fundamental forces of the soul: these are four incontestible principles which form the base of all the physiology of the brain. . . .

# 10 Phrenology Vindicated

*Charles Caldwell*

## Reese's Humbug

It was my intention before I had seen the work, to give, in this "Vindication," a brief analysis accompanied by an argumentative refutation, of an attack on Phrenology, in the "Humbugs of New-York," by "David Meredity Reese, M.D.," of that city. A glance at the production however has dissuaded me from my purpose. I cannot descend to the level of such publication, and reply to it with argument, or in any other way that might imply toward it the slightest degree of respect; or which might give it even imaginary weight. . . .

If the author of the "New-York Humbugs" either possesses now, or aims at possessing hereafter, the slightest standing in science and letters, it is surprising that even folly itself, however rank and wanton, should have permitted in him an act so irrevocably suicidal to his reputation, as that he has perpetrated by his attack on Phrenology. . . .

Our author commences "Chapter III" with an untruth, in asserting that Phrenology and Animal Magnetism are similar in character; that the same forms of mind are particularly prone to a belief in both; and that these forms are necessarily *imaginative,* fanatical, and inclined to the marvellous. The following are his words.

This "science, falsely so called (Phrenology), is among the *prevalent* and *prevailing* humbugs of the day, and it is placed next to animal magnetism, in the present volume, because of its claiming to be of similar antiquity, and of kindred character to; since both *profess to be eminently philosophical. The same individuals who embrace the one, very frequently become the willing disciples of the other.*"

This I say is untrue. There are few, if any, persons living who seriously profess the "*philosophy*" of Animal Magnetism. The number of those who even practise the *art* of it is very small; and respecting the *philosophy* or *reason* of it, nearly all, I believe, are silent; or, stronger still, acknowledge their *ig-*

From Charles Caldwell, *Phrenology Vindicated, and Anti-Phrenology Unmasked* (New York: S. Colman, 1838).

*norance.* Assuredly I have never heard an individual attempting to explain it, except by attributing it to *action on the imagination;* which comes much nearer to a confession of ignorance, than to a profession of philosophy. Nor do I know of any respectable publication on the subject. No one, as far as I am informed, has ever pretended to say, either verbally or in print, why, or how any magnetic or galvanic influence is excited by the process pursued; or why or how, if it even were excited, it could produce the effects ascribed to the art. And, that "the same individuals who embrace Phrenology are more prone than others to a belief in Animal Magnetism," is a position as unfounded as imagination can conceive. It is an empty and groundless assertion of our author, made for the purpose of carrying a point, under a recklessness whether it be true or false.

As far as my information extends, Spurzheim was the only distinguished Phrenologist who has expressed a belief in Animal Magnetism. And his belief in it was exceedingly limited. It was a good-natured friendliness toward it, and nothing more. . . .

Gall, on the contrary, was no Animal Magnetist. Nor was he in any degree an *imaginative* man. Onthe contrary, he was more sternly a votary of *facts* and fair inferences, than almost any other man I have ever known. . . .

Were it admissible in me to speak of myself, I might correctly say, that, within the last eighteen years, I have been instrumental in making several thousand converts to Phrenology. And I am inclined to believe, that there was not an Animal Magnetist in the number.

Let it not be understood, however, from these remarks, that I am a positive condemner of Animal Magnetism. Far from it. I have not hitherto studied the subject with sufficient closeness, and to a sufficient extent, to have matured my opinion, and prepared myself to pronounce on it. . . . Had the author of the "*Humbugs*" acted with like caution, fairness, and justice, that "clap-trap" work would have been yet unwritten.

Speaking of Gall's discovery of the organ of Language, our author asserts that the illustrious German "located that organ *in the eyes,*" and deemed its strength and perfection to correspond to the *size* and *structure* of *those orbs.* "All phrenologists," says he again, "agree in attributing the *faculty of speech,* and the power of articulating sounds, to the *eyes.*"

An untruth more deliberate and flagitious than this has never been uttered. That Dr. Gall discovered and pronounced that . . . great linguists had prominent eyes is true. But it is equally so that he also pronounced that the organ or source of language was *not* in the eyes but in that portion of the brain which lies behind and a little above them. That point, therefore, if unusually developed, necessarily protruded the eyes forward, and somewhat downward. Hence their prominence, which Gall declared to be an external manifestation of the internal *cerebral* organ. But, with neither the "size" nor "structure" of the eye has the discoverer alleged the power of language to have the shadow of connexion, as far as cause and effect are concerned. . . .

In his attempt to arraign phrenology before the public on the odious and fatal charge of *immorality* and *irreligion,* Dr. Reese is guilty of as unprincipled and nefarious a distortion of facts, and perversion of argument, as ever disgraced the lips of a false witness or accuser, or unveiled the turpitude of a *venal informer.*

Did not other considerations forbid the measure, neither time nor space permits me at present to reply to the charges of materialism and fatalism, immorality and impiety, preferred against Phrenology, by those who are ignorant of it, or hostile to it through the influence of sinister motives. For the science has but two classes of opponents; those who have never studied it, and do not therefore understand it; and those who feel themselves in some way personally interested in its refutation and overthrow. And they have been already scores of times answered to the satisfaction of all such as are actuated by candour, amenable to reason, and the possessors of common sense. To repeat the arguments, therefore, in defence of the science, on the present occasion, would be altogether superfluous in me.

Let not the author of the "Humbugs" however, imagine that I have any disposition to decline a contest, of a becoming and beneficial character, in behalf of Phrenology, should any thing occur to render it necessary. Though no professed knight-errant in the cause, yet on *one condition* I will cheerfully break a lance with any writer, whose name and standing entitle him to a meeting. And the condition, which is an honourable one, is as follows: The champion must deport himself with knightly courtesy, bear TRUTH on his banner, and present in the tourney some new ground of challenge—I mean some new charge against the soundness and merits of the science. In that case he shall be met in a corresponding style of courtesy and respectfulness. Not otherwise. To no charge or challenge, stained with untruth, stale and trashy in its character, or dictated by a spirit of bigotry or fanaticism, invective or abuse, will an answer be returned. And of such unmanly and unchristian description is every imputation, by which phrenology has been hitherto assailed. By neither justice nor truth, magnanimity nor decency, nor by the slightest discoverable wish to benefit science, or promote the true interests of the human family, has even one of them been characterized. Nor has any of the assaults which Phrenology has sustained, committed a more profligate outrage on truth and manliness, morality and religion, than Dr. Reese's Humbug.

# 11

## Degeneration as a Cause of Crime

*Max Nordau*

## Degeneration

To allow one's self to be carried away by instincts is . . . to make unconscious life the master of consciousness, to subordinate the highest nervous centres to the inferior centres. But all progress rests on this, that the highest centres assume more and more authority over the entire organism, that judgement and will control and direct ever more strictly the instincts and passions, that consciousness encroaches ever further on the domain of the unconscious, and continually annexes new portions of the latter. Of course, instinct expresses a directly felt need, the satisfaction of which procures a direct pleasure. But this need is often that of a single organ, and its satisfaction, however agreeable to the organ which demands it, may be pernicious, and even fatal to the total organism. Then there are antisocial instincts, the gratification of which is not directly injurious to the organism itself, it is true, but makes life in common with the race difficult or impossible, worsening consequently its vital conditions, and preparing its ruin indirectly. Judgement alone is fitted to oppose these instincts by the representation of the needs of the collective organism and of the race and the will has the task of ensuring the victory over suicidal instinct to the rational representation. Judgement may be deceived, for it is the result of the work of a highly differentiated and delicate instrument, which, like all fine and complicated machinery, gets out of order more easily than a simpler and rougher tool. Instinct, the inherited and organized experience of the race, is as a rule more sure and reliable. This must certainly be admitted. But what harm is done if judgement does make a mistake for once in the opposition which it offers to instinct? The organism is, as a rule, only deprived of a momentary feeling of pleasure; it suffers therefore at most a negative loss; the will, on the other hand, will have made an effort, and acquired strength by the exercise, and this is for the organism a positive gain, which nearly always at least balances those negative losses.

From Max Nordau, *Degeneration* (New York: J. Appleton and Company, 1895). Reprinted with permission of Prentice-Hall, Inc.

And then all these considerations take for granted the perfect health of
the organism, for in such a one only does the unconscious work as normally
as consciousness. But we have seen above that the unconscious itself is subject
to disease; it may be stupid, obtuse and mad, like consciousness; it then ceases
completely to be dependable; then the instincts are as worthless guides as are
the blind or drunken; then the organism, if it gives itself up to them, must
stagger to ruin and death. The only thing which can sometimes save it in this
case is the constant, anxious, tense vigilance of the judgement, and as the latter
is never capable, by its own resources of resisting a strong flood of revolted and
riotous instincts, it must demand reinforcements from the judgement of the
race, i.e., from some law, from some recognized morality.

Such is the foolish aberration of the "cultivators of the 'I'." They fall into
the same errors as the shallow psychologists of the eighteenth century, who
only recognized reason; they only see one portion of man's mental life, i.e., his
unconscious life; they wish to receive their law only from instinct, but wholly
neglect to notice that instinct may become degenerate, diseased, exhausted, and
thereby be rendered as useless for legislative purposes as a raving lunatic or an
idiot. . . .

The dipsomaniac and clastomaniac are sincere when they respectively drink
or break everything within reach. We do not, however, acknowledge their right
to satisfy their desire. We prevent them by force. We put them under guardian-
ship, although their drunkenness and destructiveness may perhaps be injurious
to no one but themselves. And still more decidedly does society oppose itself
to the satisfaction of those cravings which cannot be appeased without violently
acting upon others. The new science of criminal anthropology admits without
dispute that homicidal maniacs, certain incendiaries, many thieves and vagabonds, act under an impulsion; that through their crimes they satisfy an organic
craving; that they outrage, kill, burn, idle, as others sit down to dinner, simply
because they hunger to do so; but in spite of this and because of this, it demands
that the appeasing of the sincere longings of these degenerate creatures be
prevented by all means, and, if needs be, by their complete suppression. It
never occurs to us to permit the criminal by organic disposition to "expand"
his individuality in crime, and just as little can it be expected of us to permit
the degenerate artist to expand his individuality in immoral works of art. The
artist who complacently represents what is reprehensible, vicious, criminal, approves of it, perhaps glorifies it, differs not in kind, but only in degree, from
the criminal who actually commits it. It is a question of the intensity of the
impulsion and the resisting power of the judgement, perhaps also of courage and
cowardice; nothing else. If the actual law does not treat the criminal by intention so rigorously as the criminal in act, it is because the criminal law pursues the
deed, and not the purpose; the objective phenomenon, not its subjective roots.
The Middle Ages had places of sanctuary where criminals could not be molested

for their misdemeanors. Modern law has done away with this institution. Ought art to be or present the last asylum to which criminals may fly to escape punishment? Are they to be able to satisfy, in the so-called "temple" of art, instincts which the policeman prevents them from appeasing in the street? I do not see how a privilege so inimical to society can be willingly defended.

# 12 On Atavism

*Cesare Lombroso*

Many of the characteristics found in primitives, among the coloured races, are also to be found in habitual delinquents. They have in common, for example, thinning hair, lack of strength and weight, low cranial capacity, receding foreheads, highly evolved frontal protuberances, a high ratio of medio-frontal sutures, precocious synosteosis, particularly frontal, protrusion of the curved line of the temporal, simplicity of the sutures, considerable thickness of the cranial bone, enormous enlargement of the jaws and the zygomata, sloping of the orbits, darker skin, thicker and curly hair, broad or handle-shaped ears, similarity between the two sexes, less pronounced genetic activity, lower sensitivity to pain, total moral insensibility, indolence, lack of remorse, recklessness sometimes giving the appearance of courage, and courage alternating with base cowardice, great vanity, ready superstition, magnified impressibility of the ego, and finally moral relativism.

Similarities extend to minor details which could hardly be foreseen—e.g., an abundance of metaphor and onomatopoeia in speech, extemporized laws in partnerships, the strangely personal authority of the chiefs, the custom of tattooing, a literature recalling times when crime was extolled and writing and speech tended to take a rhythmical, rhymed form.

This atavism explains the essence and distribution of specific crimes. It would be difficult to explain pederasty and infanticide, which gained a hold over whole societies, if we neglected the periods of the Romans and the Greeks, when not only these were not considered crimes but were frequently a moral custom; and this possibly suggests an interpretation for the common association of aesthetic tastes with pederasts, as was the case with the Greeks.

Extending the atavistic analogies still further, even beyond race, we can interpret certain other phenomena of the criminal environment that would otherwise seem inexplicable, even to the expert in psychiatry; e.g., the frequency of the welding over the atlas with the occiput which is duplicated in certain fossilized cetacea, and that of the median occipital depression and its excep-

From Cesare Lombroso, *Crime, Its Causes and Remedies* (Boston: Little, Brown and Company, 1911). Reprinted with permission of Patterson-Smith Company, 1976.

tional development, precisely as in the lemurs and rodents; the inclination
toward cannibalism, even without feelings of revenge, and furthermore toward
that form of bloody savagery mixed with lust . . . which recalls the time
when copulation in man, as in the case of animals, was preceded by and
associated with fierce and bloody struggles, both to overcome the resistance
of the female and also to vanquish opponents in love. In many tribes in
Australia, the lover is accustomed to awaiting his wife behind a bush, striking
her senseless with a blow from his club, and carrying her unconscious into the
marital abode. Vestiges of these traditions persist in the marriage rites in
many of our valleys, and in the dreadful celebrations of the Jagraate and in the
Roman bacchanals where anyone, including males, offering any opposition to
raping was cut into such small pieces that the corpse could not be found. And
a trace even remains among ourselves.

The first and foremost writer on nature, Lucretius, observed how even in
the most common cases mating there may be discovered a germ of savagery
against the woman, inciting us on to injure anyone hindering our satisfaction.
I know of a distinguished poet who no sooner sees a calf shot or even its bleeding
carcass hanging than he is seized with lust; and another who experiences ejacula-
tions merely by strangling a fowl or a pigeon. . . .

These instances clearly prove that the most dreadful and inhuman crimes
still have a point of departure that is physiological and atavistic, that is located
in those animal instincts which, held in check for a time by man's upbringing,
his environment, and his fear of punishment, quickly emerge under the influence
of certain circumstances, such as sickness, atmospheric phenomena, imitation,
spermatic inebriation as a result of excessive continence, so that it is always
found in early puberty, in paretics or uncivilized individuals or those forced to
lead a celibate or solitary life, such as priests, shepherds, and soldiers.

Since it is known that specific disease conditions such as cranial injuries,
meningitis, alcoholism, and other types of chronic intoxication and particular
physiological conditions such as old age cause development of the nervous
centers to stop and accordingly cause atavistic regression, we can estimate how
they must contribute to the tendency toward crime.

Realizing that the delinquent is not far removed from the uncouth and
the barbarian, and that on occasion the distance between them disappears
altogether, we can appreciate why men from the lower orders, even if not immoral, so often have a predilection for crime . . . and why convicts in turn inter-
mingle so easily with savages, adopting their habits entirely, even their cannibalism, as happens in Australia and Guyana.

Observing how our children, before they are educated, are unable to dis-
criminate between vice and virtue, and steal, fight, and lie without the least
remorse, we can comprehend why so many abandoned children, orphans, and
foundlings surrender to bad habits.

Atavism also helps to understand the ineffectiveness of punishment and

the constant, periodic repetition of a given number of crimes; the variations
in the number of crimes against the person did not surpass one-twenty-fifth
and in the case of those against property, one-fiftieth; we find for given months
a given category of crimes predominates in equal proportions, e.g., lechery in
July and June, poisoning and vagrancy in May, theft and forgery in January,
according to given variations in the thermometer or the cost of food. We are
ruled by silent laws, but ones that never fall into disuse, administering society
more surely than the laws contained in the statutes.

In short, crime would appear, both from statistics and from anthropological
investigation, to be a natural phenomenon—some philosophers would even say
a necessary phenomenon, like birth, death, and conception. This idea of the
necessity of crime, presumptuous though it may seem, is neither new nor so
revolutionary as one might think at first glance. . . .

If we compare the various pursuits by the statutes, we discover that the
lawmaker never succeeds in fixing the theory of responsibility and finding a
clear definition for it. All agree as to what is a good or a bad action, but it is
difficult if not impossible to discern whether the depraved act was committed
with complete or incomplete consciousness of the wrong. . . . There are men
who suffer from incipient madness or have such an inclination thereto that
they can redress to it at the slightest encouragement, while others are driven
by heredity to peculiar behavior and immoral extravagance. Knowledge of the
fact, with an investigation of the body and the mind before and after the fact,
are inadequate to solve the question of responsibility; rather, we need to know
the life of the criminal, beginning with the cradle and ending with the anatomical
table. . . .

Scientific knowledge is not at odds with social practice and order, but
forms a bridge to them and a support for them . . . there is need for scientific
knowledge for defense and hence for punishment. Punishment will thus acquire
a much less barbaric character, and also one that is less contradictory, and certainly more effective.

# 13 Criminal Diathesis

*Charles Goring*

. . . The Criminal is a legal fact: but it is difficult to understand the suggestion that he should be considered simply and solely in this light, nor are we able to reconcile that injunction with the spirit of unbiased investigation. For the proposition which denies the necessity of any presumption with regard to the mental constitution of the criminal does not represent, as it would claim to do, a complete detachment from theory. On the contrary, it presumes that there is no constitutional factor determining, either wholly, or in part, a criminal career; it presupposes that, innately, all men are mentally and morally equal, and that the criminal must be explained, not by reference to what he does (as the classical school premised), nor by reference to what he is (as Lombroso declared), but by reference, solely and entirely, to the circumstances in which he is placed. This proposition has, however, been chiefly employed not as a theory of criminality, but as an artifice by which to steer clear of the dangers of those picturesque conceptions which have loomed too high in the passage of criminological pioneers. But the necessity for forming *some* conception is not to be evaded by the mere negation of those fallacious ideas whose development has been as inevitable in the past as it has been logical and true to one common guiding principle; in fact, that all men are innately, morally equal.

We have traced the starting point of the "criminality" idea to the evolution of the criminal law, when the criminal was regarded as an outcase from the spiritual world. Innately, all men were mentally and morally equal: by deliberate choice the criminal had enlisted away from the side of the angels. It was against this first notion, and against the severity of the punishments it engendered, that the classical school protested: all men were mentally and morally equal, but crime very often was the result, not of the criminal's deliberate selection of evil, but of his misdirected choice. Next came the Lombrosian notion. All normal men were mentally and morally equal: therefore the criminal's abnormal choice of evil was a proof of disease. Finally, the latest a priori development of the notion of criminality yields the same refrain. All healthy men are mentally and morally equal, and consequently, the criminal must either be morally insane, or he must be solely and entirely the product of an adverse environment. . . .

From Charles Goring, *The English Conflict* (London: Her Majesty's Stationery Office, 1913).

We wish to approach the present inquiry with an open mind regarding the theory of original equality, which hitherto has been regarded as beyond question: and, in so doing, we must assert that, in view of the intricate nature of the mind of man, and of the mutability and complexity of environmental influences, it is impossible to state dogmatically, on a priori grounds, whether the criminal is born or made; and to what extent criminality results from a constitutional quality of moral fibre; or to what extent this condition is a purely traditional acquirement. All we can assume, and what we must assume, is the *possibility* that *constitutional,* as well as *environmental* factors, play a part in the production of criminality. In other words, we are forced to an hypothesis of the possible existence of a character in all men which, in the absence of a better term, we call "the criminal diathesis."

Using the word "criminal," not necessarily in description of moral defectiveness, but merely to designate, in legal terminology, the fact that an individual has been imprisoned—using "criminal" in this sense, the term "diathesis" implies a hypothetical character of some kind, a constitutional proclivity, either mental, moral or physical, present to a certain degree in all individuals, but so potent in some, as to determine for them, eventually, the fate of imprisonment. Direct evidence of the existence of a criminal diathesis cannot, of course, be given. The criminal diathesis, like the tubercular diathesis, if existent, would not be visible to the senses. Direct experience of the existence of either is impossible. But, just as we are compelled to assume that the existence of a tubercular diathesis is revealed by the phenomenon of tubercular diseases, so are we compelled to assume the possible existence of a criminal diathesis from the phenomenon of crime. We make no presumption as to what qualities constitute this diathesis: but unless the committing of crime, and the apprehension and conviction following it, be regarded as a series of absolutely fortuitous catastrophies—unless the criminal in the dock is chosen as much at random as is the juryman in the box— we do not see how the conclusion can be evaded that the criminal diathesis, although present in greater average intensity among the lawless, is a certain constitutional fact, common to the whole of humanity. In fine, however, criminality may be analyzed, or crimes may be classified, however the penal record of the criminal may be accounted for, we must presume that, determining his fate, there may be, within the criminal himself, some quality or combination of qualities, some constitutional tendency of stupidity, perhaps, or of lack of control, or, as the cynic might suggest, of unfortunate *naïveté,* which leads to his being found out, while his more acute fellow scoundrel escapes—something in him, we must presume, there may be, which, as we have stated, is a character proper to mankind. . . .

The ends of Criminological Science, of all Social Science, must be approached across facts, and facts only. The collecting of opinion, the exercising of dialectical ingenuity, the referring to authority, the quoting of illustrative cases— these uncharted ways of the old descriptive sociologists have led only to confusion, dogma and superstition: they must be abandoned. The discoveries of the explorer cannot be recognized until he produces a verifiable map of his journey; if the goal, professed to have been reached by the sociological pioneer, is to be accepted, he must show that the path he has pursued is one which others may follow.

Now, the road we have attempted to shape, during the past eight years, is paved with statistical facts; each of which within the limits of our search, we believe to be indestructible by controversy. The credentials of our every statement will be found in the scheduled data, in the tables of analyzed data, in the figures resulting from these analyzed data; and by their aid, our path may be retraced step by step, its bearings tested, and its direction criticized. If we have gone astray anywhere, the fault can be logically demonstrated by the critic pointing the error in our data, or in the analysis of these data, or in their interpretation. But he must not dismiss our results because they may be opposed to his opinion, or to current opinion: he must enforce any condemnation he may make by the production of statistics more representative than ours, and related to a more exhaustive and accurate observation.

Let us resume our results. . . .

In the first place, we were confronted with the notion of a distinct anthropological criminal type: with the idea of the criminal being such in consequences of an hereditary element in his psychic organization, and of certain physical and mental peculiarities, which stigmatized him as predestined to evil, and which differentiated him from the morally well-conditioned person. In accordance with this notion, every individual criminal is an anomaly among mankind, by inheritance and can be detected by his physical malformation, and mental eccentricities: the inevitable deduction being that any attempt at his reform must prove vain.

The preliminary conclusion reached by our inquiry is that this anthropological monster has no existence in fact. The physical and mental constitution of both criminal and law-abiding persons, of the same age, stature, class, and intelligence, are identical. There is no such thing as an anthropological criminal type. But, despite this negation, and upon the evidence of our statistics, it appears to be an equally indisputable fact that there is a physical, mental, and moral type of normal person who tends to be convicted of crime: that is to say, our evidence conclusively shows that, on the average, the criminal of English prisons is markedly differentiated by defective physique—as measured by stature and body weight: by defective mental capacity—as measured by general intelligence; and by an increased possession of willful antisocial proclivities—as measured, apart from intelligence, by length of sentence to imprisonment. . . .

The second conclusion resulting from our inquiry defines the relative importance of constitutional and environmental factors in the etiology of crime. The criminal anthropologists assert that the chief source of crime lies in the personal constitution. His physical and mental stigmata, they argue, while showing the anomalous biological origin of the law-breaker, prove also the existence in him of a peculiar constitutional psychic quality: by reason of which he is destined from birth to do evil, and will become criminal, however favourable or unfavourable his circumstances may be. On the other hand, the criminal sociologists say that the source of crime must be sought, not in the constitution of the malefactor, but in his adverse social and economic environment. He is not born, but is made, criminal, it is contended: his physical, mental, and moral characteristics, and the ultimate fate of imprisonment these entail, are products of unfavourable circumstances; in the absence of which, even inborn criminal tendencies will fail to develop.

We have traced and measured the relations of conviction for crime in a variety of constitutional and environmental conditions: and while, with many of the former, high degrees of associaton have been revealed, with practically none of the latter do we discover any definite degree of relationship. Thus, as already stated, we find close bonds of association with defective physique and intelligence; and, to a less intimate extent, with moral defectiveness, or willful antisocial proclivities—as demonstrated by the fact that it is the most intelligent recidivists who are guilty of the most serious acquisitive offenses. We find, also, that crimes of violence are associated with the finer physiques, health, and muscular development, with the more marked degrees of ungovernable temper, obstinacy of purpose, and inebriety, and with the greater amount of insane and suicidal proclivity, of persons convicted of these offenses; and that tall persons are relatively immune from conviction for rape; and that fraudulent offenders are relatively free from the constitutional determinants which appear to conduce to other forms of crime. Alcoholism also, and all diseases associated with alcoholism; venereal diseases, and all conditions associated with venereal diseases; epilepsy, and insanity—appear to be constitutional determinants of crime: although, upon the evidence of our data, it would seem that these conditions, in their relation to conviction, are mainly accidental associations, depending upon the high degree of relationship between defective intelligence and crime. On the other hand, between a variety of environmental conditions examined, such as literacy, parental neglect, lack of employment, the stress of poverty, etc., including the states of a healthy, delicate, or morbid constitution per se, and even the situation induced by the approach of death[a]—between these conditions and the committing of crime, we find no evidence of any significant relationship. Our second conclusion, then, is this: that, relatively to its origin in the constitution of the malefactor, and especially in his mentally defective constitution, crime is only to a trifling extent (if to any) the product of social inequalities, of adverse environment, or of other manifestation of what may be comprehensively termed the force of circumstances.

---

[a]At all ages of life up to fifty-five the death rates of prisoners are practically identical with the general population rates.

Our third conclusion refers to the influence of imprisonment upon the physical and mental well-being of prisoners. We find that imprisonment, on the whole, has no apparent effect upon physique, as measured by body weight, or upon mentality, as measured by intelligence; and that mortality from accidental negligence is pronouncedly diminished, and the prevalency of infectious fevers due to defective sanitation—taking enteric as a type—is lessened, by prison environment; on the other hand, mortality from suicide, and from conditions involving major surgical interference amongst prisoners, greatly exceeds the general population standard. . . .

We find, moreover, that long terms of imprisonment militate against the regularity of a convict's employment when he is free from prison, but tend to increase the standard of his scholastic education; and that frequency of incarceration leads to a diminution of the fertility of the convict, owing to the circumstance that, after a certain period of continually interrupted married life, habitual criminals are deserted by their wives, or by the women with whom they have lived.

Our fourth conclusion disposes of the current allegation that "criminals share in the relative sterility of all degenerate stocks." Upon the evidence of our statistics, we find the criminal to be unquestionably a product of the most prolific stocks in the general community: and that his own apparent diminution of fertility is not due to physiological sterility, but to the definite, psychological, human reaction we have just affirmed.

The fact that conviction for crime is associated, as our figures have shown, mainly with constitutional, and scarcely to any appreciable extent with circumstantial, conditions, would make the hypothesis a plausible one that the force of heredity plays some part in determining the fate of imprisonment. . . .

Our family histories of convicts bear testimony to this truth; and the fifth and final conclusion emerging from our biometric inquiry is as follows: that the criminal diathesis, revealed by the tendency to be convicted and imprisoned for crime, is influenced by the force of heredity in much the same way, and to much the same extent, as are physical and mental qualities and conditions in man.

The scientist, and, in so far as he would be guided by the word of science, the legislator, have to reckon with three natural forces, upon which the fates of men, and the fortunes of society, depend: the forces of heredity, circumstance, and chance. . . .

Our own statement is that degrees of the criminal tendency possessed, to some degree, by all people, are inherited in the same way as other conditions and tendencies in men are inherited: which is to say that, in regard to constitutional qualities—feeble-mindedness, inebriety, ungovernable temper, etc.—tending to affect conviction for crime, there is a degree of parental resemblance of much the same intensity as there is between parents and offspring in regard to their tendency to become diseased, or to develop, under the influence of a common environment, to a certain grade of stature. But this fact of resemblance does not argue absence of the influence of environment in the development of human beings. It is absurd to say that, because criminal tendency is heritable, a man's conviction for crime cannot be influenced by education, as it would be to assert that, because mathematical ability is heritable, accomplishment in mathematics is independent of instruction; or that, because stature is heritable, growth is independent of nutriment and exercise. Our correlations tell us that, despite education, heritable constitutional conditions prevail in the making of criminals; but they contain no pronouncement upon the extent to which the general standard of morality may have been raised by education. We know that to make a law-abiding citizen, two things are needed—capacity and training. Within dwells the potentiality for growth; but without stands the natural right of each child born into the world—the right to possess every opportunity of growing to his full height. . . .

# 14

## The Anthropological Approach to Crime

*Ernest A. Hooton*

This survey began with a study of some 2,000 county jail prisoners of Massachusetts, carried out under the aegis of the State Department of Mental Diseases.
It was then extended to the adult male inmates of Massachusetts prisons and
reformatories, and to those of the states of North Carolina, Tennessee, Kentucky, Wisconsin, Missouri, Texas, Colorado, Arizona, and New Mexico. The
choice of states was dictated partially by the ambition to secure adequate
samples of criminals of every race and nationality represented in the country,
and was limited to some extent by the impermeability of certain states to the
type of investigation undertaken. . . .

The totals of subjects measured and observed in the survey were: prison and
reformatory inmates 10,953; county jail prisoners 2,004; criminal insane 743;
defective delinquents 173; insane civilians 1,227; sane civilians 1,976. The grand
total was 17,680, but of these some 604 were omitted in analysis, largely because of unknown parentage or because they belonged to racial and ethnic
groups too small in the prison population to furnish samples adequate for study.

Some twenty-two standard anthropometric measurements on head and
body were taken in the case of each individual, and from these measurements
were calculated thirteen indices or percental relations of one measurement to
another, such as the relation of head breadth to head length.

\* \* \*

### Metric and Indicial Differences

Now in the first and most positive category of unanimous and truly significant
differences are seven measurements, or 21.1 per cent of those taken. Criminals
are deficient in age to the extent of 3.80 years, in weight to the amount of 11.7
pounds, and also in chest breadth, head circumference, upper face height, nose

height, and ear length. Of almost certain validity also are five criminal deviations in which all three comparisons agree on direction, and the total comparison difference and that one of the two state comparisons attain statistical significance. . . . Similarly, in shoulder breadth and chest depth all three comparisons agree, but in one state the criminal inferiority is insignificant. In this same category fall the nasal index, in which criminals show an elevation indicating a relatively shorter nose, and the zygo-frontal index, in which the criminals show a greater forehead breadth relative to the total breadth of the face across the cheek bones. Differences of this class, amounting to virtually certain validity, occur in five metric features or 15.15 of the total. Finally, there is a third category in which the total comparison difference between criminals and civilians is significant, and both of the state comparisons agree in direction but fail to attain statistical validity. The one measurement in this category is total face height in which criminals are inferior to civilians in the total comparison by 1.5 mm., which is 5.56 times the probable error. . . .

Altogether we have 39.39 per cent of differences in metric features between civilians and criminals which seem to be of general validity. . . . Only one of the thirteen metric features in which differences between criminals and civilians were validated on the basis of sampling error and state agreement is possibly affected by disparity of age composition. This is head breadth. While we cannot be sure that the difference between criminals and civilians is due to an age factor, yet the counsel of caution bids us to discard head breadth as a differentiated feature. Hence, for the moment, we are left with twelve metric differences between criminals and civilians: criminal deficiency in age, weight, stature, shoulder breadth, chest depth, chest breadth, total face height and nose height, criminal excesses of the nasal index (indicating shorter noses with respect to their breadth) and of the zygo-frontal index (meaning that the criminal forehead is broader relative to face breadth than that of the civilian), a deficiency in the facial index of criminals (who thus have relatively shorter, broader faces), and finally in criminals a slight elevation of sitting height expressed as a percentage of stature.

## Morphological Differences

However, before we can discuss the meaning of these metric differences between criminals and civilians, we must tackle the vastly more difficult task of appraising the number, significance, and validity of the morphological judgment of the field observer. . . .

Tattooing, a practice of stupid and ignorant persons, is commoner among criminals than among civilians, but in this group of criminals it occurs infrequently, in about one of seven prisoners. . . .

Probably criminals have less beard and body hair and more head hair than civilians, apart from differences which may be due to age, but the data on these points are somewhat conflicting and unsatisfactory. . . . Criminals have much higher proportions of red-brown hair than civilians, and the latter have excesses of gray and white hair, but the difference is probably attributable in large measure to the fact that the criminals in our series are, on the average, considerably younger than the civilians of the check sample. . . . Criminals (always as compared with our check sample of civilians) are deficient in the very dark and very light shades of eye color (browns and blues) and include an unduly large proportion of men with mixed eyes. . . .

The entire pigmentation of the body—hair, skin, and eyes—seems to me to present, in general, little of criminological importance, except in so far as pigment types assist us to separate various racial elements in a mixed population. . . . Quite apart from complicating influences, criminals seem to have more eye folds of the upper eyelid than do our civilians, especially the fold across the inner corner of the eye which is often called the Mongoloid fold, but is likely to happen in the best of our supposedly non-Mongoloid families. . . .

Our materials substantiate the findings of the Lombrosian School that criminals display more low and sloping foreheads than do civilians, but the personal equations of observers cast some little doubt upon the complete validity of this result. . . . In addition to its diminished length and relatively slightly greater breadth, the nose of the criminal tends to be higher in the root and in the bridge, and more frequently undulating or concavo-convex than in our sample of civilians. The septum of the nose (the partition between the nostrils) is prevailingly inclined upward and is more frequently skewed to one side or the other than in the civilian noses. . . . [Our] criminals are younger than our civilians, and have lost fewer teeth than their law-abiding elders. Consequently, these thin criminal lips go contrary to the expected age difference. . . . The hinder angles of the jaws in our criminals are oftener compressed and less often prominent than among our comparable civilians. Compressed jaw angles often accompany poor facial development. . . .

Our data do not confirm the Lombrosian contention that criminals manifest a higher percentage of atavistic and degenerative features of the ear than civilians, except in the following details: The rim of the ear, or the helix, is more frequently unrolled, or almost so, in criminals than in civilians. . . .

Finally, this series of native born American criminals of native parentage is distinguished among the civilian check sample by the inclusion among the delinquents of many more individuals with long, thin necks and with sloping shoulders, features associated with the prevailingly weedy build of the criminals.

Thus, the physical contrast between the criminal and his civilian mate emphasizes the smaller size of the felon, his inferior weight and poorer body build, his smaller head, straighter hair, absolutely shorter and relatively broader face, with the prominent but short and often snubbed nose, his narrow jaws and his rather small and relatively broad, ears. . . .

[Our] criminals tend to present a more or less uniform array of physical differences from civilians, irrespective of the nature of the offense of which the prisoners have been convicted. . . .

Criminal behavior is capable of considerable diversification in the manner and kind of the overt act, but that, whatever the crime may be, it ordinarily arises from a deteriorated organism which, so far as we now know, manifests its inferiority in comparatively few and uniform ways.

You may say that this is tantamount to a declaration that the primary cause of crime is biological inferiority—and that is exactly what I mean. . . .

# 15 On Body Types

*Ernst Kretschmer*

## Method

Investigation into the build of the body must be made an exact branch of medical science. For it is one of the master-keys to the problem of the constitution—that is to say, to the fundamental question of medical and psychiatric and clinical work. . . . And not only must we do this in a few interesting cases, but we must take hundreds of observations, using every patient we can get hold of, and for each we must make out the same complete scheme.

\* \* \*

We place in our schema the optical description of the measurement first, for both should be obtained as far as possible independently of each other, and the eye must not find an asses' bridge already prepared for it in the shape of accurate measurements. Everything depends on a complete, artistic, and sure schooling of our eyes, for a scholarly list of single measurements without any idea or intuition of the general structure will not bring us much further. The tape-measure sees nothing: it never leads us to a grasp of the biological types which are our object. But if we have learnt to see, then we shall notice that the calipers bring us exact statements and numerical formulations, and also in some places important corrections of what we have discovered with our eyes. Certain conditions which are not prepared for in this schema will emerge here and there, and may then be written in; occasionally at certain points a much fuller and more distinct description of the aesthetic impression is required. . . .

The measurements given in our schema give the majority of those measureable body-proportions which are of importance for us, and they also, particularly in the circumference-measurements of the stomach and extremities, provide certain complex points of vantage from which we can study the development of the fat, bone, and muscle.

\* \* \*

From Ernst Kretschmer, *Physique and Character* (New York: Harcourt Brace Jovanovich, 1925). Reprinted with permission of Routledge & Kegan Paul Ltd., London.

Only those characteristics which become strongly marked in the average values are described as "typical." We must not believe that it only requires careful observation to discover such a type clearly delineated and that we can do without wearisome practice of our eyes on our material; we find, on the contrary, in concrete cases, the typical elements always veiled by the concrete cases, the typical elements always veiled by heterogeneous "individual" characteristics, and, in many respects, blurred. It is the same here as in clinical medicine, or in botany or zoology. The "classic" cases, almost free from any mixture, and endowed with all the essential characteristics of a perfect example of some form of disease, or a zoological race-type, are more or less lucky finds, which we cannot produce every day. From this it follows, that our description of types, such as will be found in what follows, refers not to the most frequent cases, but to ideal cases, to such cases as bring most clearly to view common characteristics which in the majority of instances appear only blurred, but which, all the same, can be empirically demonstrated. The same applies to the description of psychological types in the second part.

**Types of Physique**

With the methods we have described, three everrecurring principal types of physique have emerged from our clinical material, which we will call "asthenic," "athletic," and "pyknic." They are to be found among men and women, only on account of the fact that the female body is less strikingly morphologically differentiated, the most pregnant forms are less often found among women. The way, however, in which these three types are correlated with the schizophrene and circular categories, is very varied and remarkable. Among healthy people we come across these types on every side, they have no foundation in disease, but they form certain normal biological bases of which only a small proportion comes to pathological culmination—whether in the region of psychiatry or in certain established internal diseases. . . . In general we must emphasize the fact that the morphology of the physique must be studied first always in the case of men and not women. The female physique is far less "significant" on the average, particularly with regard to the form of the face, and the development of the muscles and fat. We find, therefore, among women, many more indefinite and atypical forms. . . .

*Asthenic Type*

The essential characteristic of the type of the male asthenic is . . . *a deficiency in thickness combined with an average unlessened length.* This deficiency in the thickness development is present in all parts of the body—face, neck, trunk, extremities, and in all the tissues—skin, fat, muscle, bone, and vascular system throughout. On this account we find the average weight, as well as the total circumference and breadth measurements, below the general value for males.

We have, therefore, in the clearest cases the following general impression . . . a lean narrowly-built man, who looks taller than he is, with a skin poor in secretion and blood, with narrow shoulders, from which hang lean arms with thin muscles, and delicately boned hands; a long, narrow, flat chest, on which we can count the ribs, with a sharp rib-angle. A thin stomach, devoid of fat, and lower limbs which are just like the upper ones in character. In the average values for the measurement in males, the way the weight of the body lags behind the length (50 · 5):(164 · 4), and the chest measurement behind the hip measurement (84 · 1):(84 · 7) stands out clearly. . . .

Often we find a variety of the asthenic type distinguished by stronger or weaker manifestation of symptoms of the dysgenital group—of infantilism (akromicria), of feminism (waist, enlarged buttock-circumference, enlarged hip measurements, feminine arrangement of puberty hair), and particularly a streak of eunochoidism with abnormal height and abnormal length of extremities. We shall return to this later in the account.

A favourite form of variation is a mixture between asthenic and athletic types, where we find either asthenic and athletic characteristics standing immediately next to one another (e.g., long, narrow chests, with coarse extremities, an incongruity between face and physique, etc.), or else a middle-type of slim muscular figure, which, again, may tend more towards the gracile thin side, or more towards the strong muscular side.

If we observe the asthenic type over a long period of development, it seems to be fairly constant in its fundamental peculiarities through all ages. Already, as children, these people are often characterized as weakly and frail; at puberty they often rapidly shoop up their narrow forms, and when grown-up and in old age they show not the least tendency to inordinate muscle or fat. . . .

In one class of asthenics their premature aging strikes us as an important biological stigma. In extreme cases, I found men of ages between thirty-five and forty, already quite senile, with wrinkled fallen-in skin, which was completely dry, flabby, and sallow, and well-marked protruding veins on the temples. . . . One often finds in such cases, in spite of a normal mode of life, often a quite astounding degree of general atrophy of fat and muscle, which points to extreme chronic disturbances of the metabolism.

\* \* \*

*Athletic Type*

The male athletic type is recognized by the strong development of the skeleton, the musculature and also the skin.

The rough impression of the best example of this species is as follows:

A middle-sized to tall man, with particularly wide projecting shoulders, a superb chest, a firm stomach, and a trunk which tapers in its lower region, so that the pelvis, and the magnificent legs, sometimes seem almost graceful compared with the size of the upper limbs and particularly the hypertrophied shoulders.

The solid long head is carried upright on a free neck, so that the sloping linear contour of the firm trapezius, looked at from in front, gives that part of the shoulder which is nearest the neck, its peculiar shape.

The outlines and shadings of the body are determined by the swelling of the muscles of the good or hypertrophied musculature which stands out plastically as muscle-relief. The bone-relief is specially prominent in the shape of the face. The coarse boning throughout is to be seen particularly in the collar-bones, the hand and foot joints, and the hands. Next to the shoulders the trophic accent often lies on the extremities, which in some cases are reminiscent of acromegaly. The largest hand circumference among our material reached the very remarkable figure of 25 cm., that is to say, a measurement which oversteps the male average value of about 20 cm. by 5 cm. Hand circumferences of 23 cm. are quite common. Besides the hand circumference, the width of the shoulders is with this type specially remarkable, which, in two cases, reached the astonishingly high figure of 42.5 cm., which defeats the average figure of our people of roughly 37.5 to 38 cm. by about 5 cm. The length of the extremities is rather long than short. By the side of bone and muscle the skin has its share of the general hypertrophy. It has a very good, firm, elastic turgor, and, particularly in the face, it looks solid, thick, and often pasty. In contradistinction to all this tissue, the fat is relatively only moderately developed, and, speaking absolutely, is more or less normal. It is on this account, above all, that the distinctive muscle-relief is conditioned, since the over-developed musculature stands out through only a thin sheath of fat.

The height lies above the average, length measurements of over 180 cm. are not rare, the tallest athletic of our material measured 186 cm. At the other end of the scale the boundary cannot be fixed, because the morphological transition stages between the athletic type, and the type of hypoplastic broad shoulders (see below) cannot be defined. At the tall end we must notice transitions to certain gigantic types which are to be described later.

* * *

The athletic type among women, as far as it is recognizable, corresponds to the male form, with certain characteristic deviations. The development of fat, especially, is often not restricted with women, but rich; in any case it is in good proportion to the rest of the tissue, particularly to the bones and muscle, and is, anyway, in the cases of our material, not electively abnormal as with pyknics. . . .

## Pyknic Type

The pyknic type, in the height of its perfection in middle-age, is characterized by the pronounced peripheral development of the body cavities (head, breast, and stomach), and a tendency to a distribution of fat about the trunk, with a more graceful construction of the motor apparatus (shoulders and extremities).

The rough impression in well-developed cases is very distinctive: middle height, rounded figure, a soft broad face on a short massive neck, sitting between the shoulders; the magnificent fat paunch protrudes from the deep *vaulted* chest which broadens out towards the lower part of the body.

If we look at the limbs, we find them soft, rounded, and displaying little muscle-relief, or bone-relief, often quite delicate, the hands soft, rather short and wide. The joints of the hands in particular and the clavicle are often slim and almost elegantly formed. The shoulders are not broad and projecting as with the athletics, but (especially among older people) are rounded, rather high, and pushed forwards together, and they are often set down against the breast with a characteristically sharp depression on the inner deltoid curve. It seems then as if the whole mass of the shoulders were slipping downwards and inwards over the swelling chest; and the head also plays a part in this static displacement: it sinks forward between the shoulders, so that the short thick neck seems almost to disappear, and the upper portion of the spinal column takes on a slight kyphotic bend. In profile the neck no longer seems, as is the case with the other types, a slim round column, which carries the chin like a sharply cut-off, widely projecting capital, but in well-developed cases of middle-age and over, the point of the chin is directly joined with the upper forehead without any definite bends by a sloping line. . . .

The breast-shoulder-neck proportion is, apart from the shape of the head and face, and the manner of the disposition of the fat, the most characteristic mark of the pyknic character. The ratio of the moderate-sized breadth of shoulder to the large-sized breast circumference—$(36 \cdot 9):(94 \cdot 5)$—stands out strongly by the side of the characteristic proportions of the athletic, where the chest circumference is completely dominated by the huge breadth of the shoulders—$(39 \cdot 1):(91 \cdot 7)$. While the athletic torso seems especially broad, the pyknic appears deep; in the former the trophic accent lies on the shoulders and extremities, in the latter on the width of the trunk, or the bowl-shaped chest which widens towards the lower region of the body, and on the fat abdomen. The extremities are on an average rather short than long.

The pyknics tend emphatically to a covering of fat. And besides this the manner in which the fat is disposed is characteristic and must be accurately distinguished, not in comparison with the asthenics and athletics, which have absolutely no noticeable tendency to fat, so much as in comparison with certain purely dysplastic special types (see below). The obesity of the pyknic is restricted for the most part within *moderate* limits, and is primarily an obesity of the trunk, the fat deposit in the case of the male results usually in a compact fat belly. All the other body-forms are soft and rounded through diffuse covering of fat, but not disguised and disfigured. Thus the face is to be distinguished by its round, soft lines, and the hips, and often (but not always) the calves share in the increased covering of fat. The forearm and hands, and the lateral parts of the shoulders, on the other hand, are often only moderately provided. The legs also in the case of older pyknic males can be astoundingly thin.

The skin is neither loose, as in the case of the asthenic, nor tight as with the athletic, but smooth, well-fitting, of moderate thickness, and following strongly marked contours, as, for example, over the cheek-bones, and well-rounded over the outer side of the upper arm. The muscles are of moderate strength but of a soft consistency.

The average height of the pyknic males is a moderate one (167 · 8). The characteristically strong covering of fat comes thus to view, so that, contrary to the other types, and even to the athletic types, the weight of the pyknic over-steps the last two figures of the height (68 · 0). Weights of one to two hundred-weight have been found in certain phases of the lives of isolated cases; as the maximum weight we found among our material 107 kg. with 171 height. On the other hand we do find, especially among older people, occasionally remarkable cases of underweight (in one case the ratio was 163:49) as a result of strong in-volution. Pyknics not seldom show striking and at times abrupt changes in weight, particularly in connection with the life periods and the psychotic changes of phase. In the above-mentioned cases there began from about the thirtieth year onwards a rapid increase in weight, which in middle-age, with numerous significant vacillations, reached the height of 107 kg., to fall rapidly at the age of sixty, coincident with psychic depression, to 76 kg., and after that, even when the depression was removed, no more to rise. Small undersized fig-ures are very common among the pyknics of our folk, but there is only one single instance of our material below 160 cm. while outstanding height is rare; only two cases, both strongly mixed with elements of the athletic constitution, over-step the limit of 180 with 181 and 182.

The pyknic type is very regular, and contains no very strongly marked vari-ants. We must notice that it is clearly distinguished by the build of the skeleton, especially the skeletal proportions of the skull, face, and hand, apart from the overlay of fat, and often by the breast, shoulder, and neck proportions, and that an outstanding overlay of fat is not necessary to its diagnosis. The rough peri-pheral form of the body is outwardly very varied, according as the fat stomach and the thick neck give it the characteristic appearance or not. When one thinks that with the majority of hard workers . . . and also the majority of young people under 35 to 40 years of age the compact pyknic overlay of fat is absent, one will realize how many errors in diagnosis will occur, if one limits oneself to this symptom, which, however, striking and important, is not an unvarying criterion. Strongly alleged instances . . . can, at first sight, remind one of nothing

remotely connected with the pyknic average form, and yet, after careful observation and measurement, typical pyknic components will be discovered. Mixture with athletic elements is not rare, in which case the shoulders are wider, and
the limbs solider, and more bony. Asthenic-pyknic interference in structure one
finds in, e.g., the following arrangement: small fat stomach, long thorax, long
thin extremities, and, in addition, in the shape of the face and skull, a slight form
of "tower-skull" over a pyknically soft and wide cheek and jaw formation; we
could reel off here, and with other types, innumerable mixtures of such a kind:
there is absolutely no single criterion which cannot be varied and combined with
marks of another type.

The morphological differences between single life periods is among pyknics
far greater than among other types. The pyknic type reaches its most typical
form usually early in the riper years between thirty and forty, and after the
sixtieth year can become again somewhat disguised by strong involutionary
processes. These differences have in the first place to do with the layer of fat, and
the changes in the thorax which are induced secondarily on this account. There
are cases where the pyknic fat belly and the broadening of the lower thorax
aperture which grows parallel with it makes its appearance shortly after the
twentieth year. This is, however, an exception. We generally find among young
pyknics between twenty and thirty the following characteristics. . . . The broad
soft face with good moderate height proportions, and the characteristic under-
jaw are already fairly clear, the neck is short, rather thick, but not strikingly
depressed, and is well set away from the under side of the chin. The coming-
together of the neck and shoulder proportions above the blown-out thorax has
not yet made its appearance, and no kyphosis, and no depression of the head
forwards between the raised shoulders is visible. Thus the young pyknic at first
sight can easily be confused with the athletic. . . .

Even the young pyknics stand well at the head with their head, chest, and
stomach measurements and thereby betray their tendency to breadth and rotund-
ity. And particularly we notice again the ratio—so important for diagnosis—
between shoulder-breadth and chest: for the pyknics stand below the athletic on
an average, while he stands above him in chest measurement. The depression of
the shoulder on the inner deltoid curve is usually already observable among quite
young pyknics.

The tendency to fat is more diffuse among young pyknics and is particularly
observable in the face, and in the smooth modelling of the trunk and extremities, which show but little muscle-relief.

In old age the pot-belly is usually still in evidence, but it has often to a
certain extent fallen in, so that the chest is not pushed up so much. The skin is
loose and flabby. The principal bodily criteria of the type remain, however, as
they were.

The bodily characteristics of the pyknics are slightly modified when we
come to deal with women, in accordance with their sexual characteristics. We

find here as before that the main covering of fat is round the trunk, but more strongly concentrated over the breast and hips. The ratio of chest to shoulder is the same as in the male. With regard to chest and hip measurements the pyknic women do not absolutely exceed the athletic but only relatively when the height is taken into consideration. All this hangs together with the greater covering of fat among the athletic women, and the fact that the pyknic women are relatively smaller than the pyknic men. Remarkably small stature, under 150 cm., is not seldom found among them. The smallest of our material measured 145 cm. Very young pyknic women, who so far show no marked covering of fat, can at first glance, on account of the grace of their bodies, be confused with asthenics. The accurate observation of the measurement ratios, the shape of the face, the vaso-motor system (see below), and the body-forms, which are already noticeably full and round, will guard against this mistake. Young pyknic men can look, at first sight, very athletic, when they have good musculature, and fresh skin. Where the shape of the face and the breast-shoulder ratio are typical they cannot be confused. Otherwise in isolated cases the diagnosis may be very uncertain.

When we look at the photographs of old circulars when they were young, it is particularly remarkable that certain men and women exhibited quite atypical bodies, longish faces, and a narrow build in their twenties, while later on they have developed along distinctly pyknic lines. When dealing with young circulars, therefore, one must be very careful in one's negative judgments in this respect, because from the state of the body before it is forty years old, one cannot say for certain that there are not, at any rate, pyknic components present. These episodically appearing pyknic components play an important part when we come to the question of change of dominance. . . .

There are only two quite young circulars under the age of seventeen among our material. They both show, with their well-formed, rounded bodies and limbs, clear retardation in their development. Whether there is some law lying behind this, we cannot say for lack of sufficient evidence.


*Distribution of the Body-Types among the*
*Schizophrene and Circular Classes*

Before we go on to a more detailed account of the diagnosis of the type by means of the head and periphery, and to the description of the smaller special types, let us first give a bird's-eye view of the numerical distribution of the body-types over the area covered by the circular and schizophrene classes.

It must be noticed here that a sharp line can obviously not be drawn between the individual types, and that therefore the distribution of borderline cases can never be exact. Among the circulars we have underlined the number of cases with indubitably strong preponderance of pyknic structural elements (58). Fourteen others are cases of mixture, which show clear pyknic body symptoms, but by their side, equally well-marked heterogeneous streaks, e.g., pyknic-athletic (five cases), and pyknic-asthenic (three cases), all mixed forms.

Among the schizophrenes also the asthenico-athletic forms are very prevalent. Among a large number of "pure cases" we shall, of course, be able to establish smaller traits in physique, indicative of alien types; they must be very carefully observed in each single case, and are often very interesting in connection with questions of heredity characterology, and the development of psychotic symptoms. They may, however, be ignored in the bird's-eye view of the statistics of the whole. . . .

In the case of *circulars,* among a number of mixed and indefinite forms, we find a marked preponderance of the pyknic bodily type on the one hand, and a comparatively weak distribution of the classical asthenic, athletic, and dysplastic forms on the other.

In the case of *schizophrenes* on the contrary, among a number of heterogeneously mixed and indefinite forms we find a marked preponderance of asthenic, athletic and dysplastic types (with their mixtures) on the one hand, and a surprisingly weak distribution of typical cases of the pyknic bodily type on the other.

Thus we can formulate our results straight away:

1.  There is a clear biological affinity between the psychic disposition of the manic depressives and the pyknic body type.
2.  There is a clear biological affinity between the psychic disposition of the schizophrenes and the bodily disposition characteristic of the asthenics, athletics, and certain dysplastics.
3.  And vice versa, there is only a weak affinity between schizophrene and pyknic on the one hand, and between circulars and asthenics, athletics, and dysplastics on the other.

# 16

## On Somatotypes

### *William H. Sheldon*

## Structural Concepts

*CONSTITUTION:* The organizational or underlying pattern. Literally, the way a thing stands together. The whole aggregate of the relatively fixed and deep-seated structural and behavioral characteristics that collectively differentiate a personality. Perhaps the most satisfactory way to start an examination of the constitutional pattern of a human being is photographically, although this is only a beginning and offers but an anchorage or frame of reference for constitutional description. Behind the objective and overt aspects of morphology lie individual differences first in those aspects of morphology which are not outwardly revealed, such as the structure, dyplasias, and *t* component of internal organs, of the nervous system, of the endocrine glands, and so on; and further, individual differences in physiology and chemistry. All of these differences contributes to and make up what is referred to as personality. The term constitution implies only a certain relatedness and orderliness or patterning with respect to the underlying aspects of personality. In so far as the student of constitution addresses his energies to the study of external morphology he is but trying to anchor (to something taxonomically describable) an approach to personality as a whole, in its physiological and immunological and psychological as well as morphological aspects.

    *THE SOMATOTYPE:* A quantification of the primary components determining the morphological structure of an individual. In practice the somatotype is a series of three numerals, each expressing the approximate strength of one of the primary components in a physique. The first numeral always refers to endomorphy, the second to mesomorphy, the third to ectomorphy. When a 7-point scale is used the somatotype 7-1-1 is the most extreme endomorph, the 1-7-1 is the most extreme mesomorph, and the 1-1-7 is the most extreme ectomorph. The somatotype 4-4-4 falls at the midpoint of the scale with respect to all three primary components. . . .

From William H. Sheldon, *Varieties of Delinquent Youth: An Introduction to Constitutional Psychiatry* (New York: Harper and Row Publishers, Inc., 1949). Reprinted with permission.

*Endomorphy,* or the first component: Relative predominance in the bodily economy of structure associated with digestion and assimilation. Relatively great development of the digestive viscera. In embryonic life the endoderm, or inner embryonic layer, grows into what becomes the functional element in a long tube, stretched or coiled from mouth to anus with a number of appendages. This is the digestive tube. Together with its appendages it is sometimes called the vegetative system. Its organs make up the bulk of the viscera. Endomorphy means relative predominance of the vegetative system, with a consequent tendency to put on fat easily. Endomorphs have low specific gravity. They float easily in the water. When well nourished they tend toward softness and roundness throughout the body, but it should be remembered that in learning to gauge one of the components it is necessary to learn to gauge the other two at the same time.

*Mesomorphy,* or the second component: Relative predominance of the mesodermally derived tissues, which are chiefly bone, muscle, and connective tissue. These are the somatic structures, or the motor organ-systems. Mesomorphs tend toward massive strength and muscular development. When their endomorphy is low, so that they remain lean, they retain a hard rectangularity of outline. If endomorphy is not low, mesomorphs tend to "fill out" heavily and to grow fat in middle life. However, because of the heavy underlying skeletal and muscular structure, they remain solid. When fat they are "hard-round", in contrast with the "soft-roundness" of endomorphy, and they continue in the general mold and the proportions of athletic shapeliness. Endomorphs get roly-poly, globular, and pendulous. Mesomorphs just swell up in their generally athletic mold. Mesomorphs are of higher specific gravity than endomorphs. They are less buoyant in water but because of superior muscular power are nevertheless often good swimmers. The mesomorphic heart and blood vessels are large, and the skin seems relatively thick because of heavy reinforcement with underlying connective tissue.

*Ectomorphy,* or the third component: Relative predominance of the skin and its appendages, which include the nervous system. All of these tissues are derived from the ectodermal embryonic layer. In the ectomorph there is relatively little bodily mass and relatively great surface area—therefore greater sensory exposure to the outside world. Endomorphs and mesomorphs appear to be biological conservatives, the former investing faith in superior assimilative power or digestive ability, the latter in superior resistive substance and striking power. Ectomorphs seem to have departed from *both* of these essential biological insurances and to have embarked on an exteroceptive adventure. They have given up mass for surface, in a sense suppressing the primacy of both the digestive organ-system and the motor organ-system in favor of the sensory organ-system. The Italian School of Clinical Anthropology . . . calls them hyperevolutes, suggesting that in departing from the secure advantages of the coarser and heavier bodies of the endomorphs and mesomorphs (in favor of extending the sensorium externally), they tend to move out toward the end of an evolutionary limb whence it may be difficult to return. Morphologically, ectomorphy means flatness and fragility throughout the body, with a comparatively high height/weight index.

*Mesomorphic endomorphs; endomorphic mesomorphs; ectomorphic mesomorphs; mesomorphic ectomorphs; endomorphic ectomorphs; ectomorphic endomorphs:* These terms refer to physiques in which all three of the primary morphological components are of different strength. Figure 16-1 is a schematic two dimensional presentation of the somatotypes in which these six various "families" are spatially delineated. An endomorphic mesomorph is an individual in whom mesomorphy predominates, with endomorphy second in order of strength, and ectomorphy third. Example: the somatotype 3-5-2.

*Balanced endomorphs; balanced mesomorphs; balanced ectomorphs:* These are individuals in whom one component is distinctly predominant, while the other two components are of equal strength. Example: 1-1-7. This is a balanced

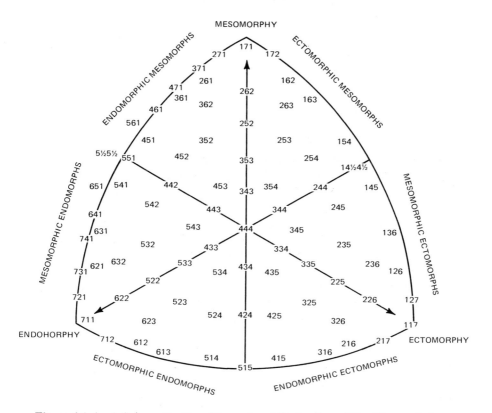

**Figure 16-1.** A Schematic Two-Dimensional Projection of the Theoretical Spatial Relationships among the Known Somatotypes

*extreme* ectomorph. The somatotype 2–2–6 is also considered a balanced extreme ectomorph, and the 2–6–2 a balanced extreme mesomorph. The 2–5–2 and 3–5–3 we call balanced *moderate* mesomorphs, and so on.

*Endomorph-mesomorphs; mesomorph-ectomorphs; ectomorph-endomorphs:* Individuals in whom the two primary components named are clearly predominant over the other component, *and are equal.* Examples: 5–5–1, 4–4–2, 2–4–4, 5–1–5, 4–2–4.

*The midrange somatotypes:* Those, other than the 4–4–4, in which no component has a strength greater than 4 or less than 3. These are: 3–3–4, 3–4–3, 3–4–4, 4–3–3, 4–3–4, 4–4–3.

*The overloaded somatotypes,* or 12-level somatotypes: Those in which the total strength of the three components adds up to 12. Eleven of these are known: 5–4–3, 4–5–3, 3–5–4, 3–4–5, 4–3–5, 5–3–4, and 4–4–4; and the 7–4–1, 6–5–1, 5–6–1, and 4–7–1. People whose somatotypes fall among the first seven of this group are often pulled strongly in several directions, but also are often unusually gifted. Such people abound in the mental hospitals and before academics became a branch of big business were probably common on college faculties.

* * *

## Behavioral Concepts

*TEMPERAMENT:* According to Webster: (1) A mixing in due proportion; (2) The internal constitution with respect to balance or mixture of qualities or components; (3) The peculiar physical and mental character of an individual; (4) Frame of mind or type of mental reactions characteristic of an individual.

The original meaning of the Greek verb is to mix. As I use the term, temperament is simply some quantification of the mixture of components that a person presents. In this literal sense temperament at the morphological level is the somatotype. At a slightly more dynamic or behavioral level it is the pattern of the mixture of the three primary components *viscerotonia, somatotonia,* and *cerebrotonia.* At more complex and more culturally conditioned levels, temperament may be defined more elaborately and may embrace any schema for quantification of the manifest components of a personality that a psychologist can devise. . . .

Temperament is the pattern at *all* levels. But as I use the term it is a little more specific than that. It is *the pattern quantitatively expressed, in terms of some schema of components which offers a frame of reference for an operational psychology.* . . .

*Viscerotonia:* The first component of temperament, measured at the least-conditioned level of dynamic expression. Endomorphy is the same component

measured at a purely structural or morphological level. Endomorphy is expressed
by the morphological consequences of a predominance of the first component.
Viscerotonia constitutes the primary or most general behavioral expression of
the same predominance; that is to say, predominance of the digestive-assimila-
tive function—the gut function. . . .

In briefest summary viscerotonia is manifested by relaxation, conviviality,
and gluttony for food, for company, and for affection or social support. When
this component is predominant the primary motive in life seems to be assimilation and conservation of energy.

*Somatotonia:* The second component of temperament, measured at the
least-conditioned level of dynamic expression. Mesomorphy is the same component measured at the morphological level. Somatotonia expresses the function
of movement and predation—the somatic function. . . .

In briefest summary somatotonia is manifested by bodily assertiveness
and by desire for muscular activity. When this component is predominant the
primary motive of life seems to be the vigorous utilization or expenditure of
energy. Somatotonics love action and power. Their motivational organization
seems dominated by the soma.

*Cerebrotonia:* The third component of temperament, measured at the least-
conditioned level of dynamic expression. Ectomorphy is the same component
at the morphological level. Cerebrotonia appears to express the function of
exteroception, which necessitates or involves cerebrally mediated inhibition
of both of the other two primary functions. It also involves or leads to conscious attentionality and thereby to substitution of symbolic ideation for
immediate overt response to stimulation. Attendant upon this latter phenomenon are the "cerebral tragedies" of hesitation, disorientation, and confusion.
These appear to be by-products of overstimulation, which is doubtless one
consequence of an overbalanced investment in exteroception. . . .

In briefest summary cerebrotonia is manifested by (1) inhibition of both
viscerotonic and somatotonic expression, (2) hyperattentionality or overcon-
sciousness. When this component is predominant one of the principal desires
of life seems to be avoidance of overstimulation—hence love of concealment
and avoidance of attracting attention. While cerebrotonia seems to result from
an evolutionary development in the direction of purchasing increased exteroception at the cost of *both* vegetative mass and motor strength, the *manifest traits*
of cerebrotonia (in a crowded society) are associated largely with escaping the
painful consequences of the increased exteroception thus attained. Yet cerebrotonia is probably in itself far from painful. There is a certain elemental
ecstasy in the heightened attentionality just as there is a somatotonic ecstasy
in vigorous muscular action and a viscerotonic ecstasy in first-rate digestive
action. . . .

# 17

## Twins and Crime

### Johannes Lange

In the first part of these investigations we applied the twin-method to criminals statistically. We ascertained in the case of the twins under investigation whether they themselves and their fellow-twins had come into conflict with the law. In every case we also endeavored to find out conclusively whether we were dealing with monozygotic twins, those with the same heredity, or dizygotic pairs, those with different heredity. In addition we confined ourselves exclusively to those of the same sex and also to such pairs of whom at least one partner had been sentenced.

Largely with the help of the Bavarian Ministry of Justice and the Institute of Criminal Biology at Straubing Prison, we found thirty pairs of twins, of whom thirteen were monozygotics and seventeen were dizygotics. Of the thirteen monozygotic pairs, both twins had been sentenced in ten cases. In three cases only one twin had come in conflict with the law. Of the seventeen dizygotic pairs, there were only two cases where both twins had been sentenced. In the other fifteen pairs only one twin had come before the courts. In addition, a comparison between the criminality of dizygotic twins with that of ordinary brothers and sisters showed that both of a pair of dizygotic twins escaped sentence more frequently than was to be expected.

Even allowing for all necessary reservations, which will be gone into later, these facts show quite definitely that under our present social conditions, heredity does play a role of paramount importance in making the criminal; certainly a far greater role than many are prepared to admit.

Our rough figures also permit the conclusion that heredity alone is not exclusively a cause of criminality, but that one must allow a certain amount for environmental influences. Even monozygotic pairs did not by any means show complete agreement in their attitudes to crime. The fact that in about one quarter of the cases, only one of the monozygotic twins was sentenced must be interpreted as showing that in these cases some environmental influence determined the criminal behavior.

This statistical result, clear as it is, is still somewhat unsatisfactory. We should have nothing more to say if we had counted out certain pathological

From Johannes Lange, *Crime and Destiny* (New York: Charles Boni Paper Books, 1930).

states. Crime, however, cannot be interpreted merely as the result of given biological factors; it is not a purely biological phenomenon which ceases with the criminal. It also presents a social picture and as such must always have a social background. . . .

Now, although no serious person really doubts that we must first look for the causes of crime in the criminal, in biological material, the circumstances nevertheless demand that the crudest statistical results should be amplified by detailed individual information which permits a closer investigation, particularly into the environmental influences.

Here, the dizygotic pairs, particularly the discordant ones, cannot help us very much. We saw that the criminal members of such pairs had committed the most various misdeeds. Several of them were habitual criminals, whereas their twins had fitted into the social scheme and had even gotten on well in life. It is worth calling attention to the fact that in a number of cases it was not the other twin, but a brother or sister who had been in trouble. This fact can be interpreted either to postulate an unusually bad environment, or particularly strong hereditary tendencies toward antisocial behavior in the families in question. Both points of view emphasize the relevance of the other twins' non-criminal conduct, and the importance of the innate tendencies with which each separate individual enters society.

We might have expected more conclusive information from the concordant dizygotic pairs. Unfortunately our investigations in these cases met with considerable obstacles; in them we were dealing with exceptional circumstances. The records clearly showed the pairs of twins differed in the manner and extent of of their crimes. We also know that there were great differences of personality between the twins examined. But apart from these facts we learned little that was certain. . . .

# 18 The Extra Y Chromosome

## W.M. Court-Brown

A recent development in human genetics has been the study of human chromosomes. In fact, this branch of biological science has been firmly established for only about ten years. The value of this study is that it is comparatively simple and is entirely objective. We are now in a position to examine moderately large and defined groups of males and females and compare the findings between different groups. At present, work in the Clinical Effects of Radiation Research Unit at Edinburgh and in the Department of Genetics at Sheffield is directed toward the study of males in the Special and State hospitals, in ordinary prisons and in Borstals (reform schools). The results of these studies may be compared with the findings in newborn babies and those from surveys of the mentally subnormal and mentally ill. Already there are clear indications that certain types of abnormality of the sex chromosomes complement are important in relation to criminal populations.

### The Normal Sex Chromosome Complement

In the normal man or woman there is one pair of sex chromosomes among the twenty-three pairs of chromosomes found in nearly every cell. In the woman the two sex chromosomes are alike and are the two X chromosomes, while in the man the sex chromosomes are dissimilar and consist of an X chromosome and a Y chromosome, the latter chromosome determining maleness at conception. The normal woman, therefore, has an XX and the normal male an XY sex chromosome complement. There is a simple screening test which enables individuals to be identified who have more than one X chromosome in their cells. This test involves the staining of smears of cell from the buccal aspect of the cheek and the examination of their nuclei for the presence of a sex chromatin body. In diploid or near diploid cells the number of sex chromatin bodies seen in a cell is one less than the number of X chromosomes present. Therefore a normal

From W.N. Court-Brown, *"Genetics and Crime," J. Roy. Coll. Phys. London* 1 (1967): 311. Published by Pitman Medical Publishing Co. Ltd. Reprinted with permission.

male shows no sex chromatin body whereas one body is seen in the cells of a normal female. A male with a sex chromatin body, therefore, would be presumed to have two X chromosomes in his cells. However, the technique does not give information on the Y chromosome, so a formal chromosome study is necessary on chromatin-positive males to determine their precise sex chromosome complement. To find males with an XYY complement in a group of males, it is clearly necessary to do a formal chromosome study of each member of the group, and this is a tedious process when substantial numbers are involved.

The abnormal sex chromosome complements of interest in relation to criminal behaviour are XXY, XY/XXY, XXYY and XYY.

## XXY Males

Males with this form of sex chromosome abnormality are born with a frequency of about 10 to 15 in every 10,000 live male births. The additional X chromosome increases their possibility of being mentally subnormal, and males with an XXY complement occur with a frequency of about 50 to 60 per 10,000 males in hospitals for the mentally subnormal. The data from the Special and State hospitals (Moss Side, Rampton, and Carstairs) show a striking increase in the frequency of XXY males, these being about 100 per 10,000 men, or about double the frequency in the ordinary hospitals for the mentally subnormal and some seven to ten times the frequency among newborn males. However, it is important not to conclude that the difference recorded between the frequencies of XXY males in hospitals for the mentally subnormal and in the Special and State hospitals is real, until comparisons are made after standardization for IQ. It seems quite possible that there will be a greater proportion of high-grade mental defectives in Special and State hospitals than in the ordinary hospitals for mental subnormality, and XXY males, if mentally subnormal, are likely to be high-grade defectives except in exceptional cricumstances. It is worth noting that the interest of the Clinical Effects of Radiation Research Unit in Edinburgh in the problem of criminal behaviour arose from a casual observation that there seemed to be an unusual proportion of chromatin-positive males in hospitals for the mentally subnormal who had been referred there by the courts.

The features of the XXY male are degenerative changes in the testes, eunuchoid proportions, anomalism of body and facial hair, and sometimes breast development. These males are found in all walks of life and clearly some are able to fill professional and business posts carrying considerable responsibility. However, it is generally felt that the presence of the additional X chromosome limits the IQ, so that it is reduced below what it would have been had the subject had a normal sex chromosome complement. It remains to be seen whether the presence of these individuals in an increased frequency in the State and Special hospitals reflects simply the effect of their sex chromosome complement on their IQ, or whether there is also some influence on behavioural characteristics. . . . It would not be surprising if these men were found in unusual numbers among ordinary adult prisoners.

## XY/XXY Males

The commonest form of sex chromosome mosaicism in males is the XY/XXY type. In chromosome mosaicism the relative proportions of the two cell lines may vary widely from tissue to tissue in any one person, and it is, of course, possible that in some instances the buccal mucosa may only contain XY cells. For this reason it cannot be concluded that all XY/XXY mosaics are detected by nuclear sexing. . . .

The frequencies of XY/XXY males do not materially change depending on whether they are ascertained in newborn males, the mentally subnormal, or the mentally ill, but . . . there is an increase among men in the Special and State hospitals. The interpretation is complex. In the first three categories the absence of any difference certainly supports the idea that in this type of mosaicism, where the cell line is normal, the individual is less prone to develop these features characteristic of individuals entirely composed of cells of the abnormal line. The increased frequency in patients from the Special and State hospitals is possibly due to the fact that, in studying such groups, we are selecting for individuals who, having an XY/XXY complement, will tend to be those showing the effects of the abnormal cell line.

XY/XXY males may show no physical abnormality or they may show some or all the abnormalities associated with an XXY sex chromosome complement. It is presumed that much depends on the representation of XXY cells in the gonads.

## XXYY Males

XXYY males are very rare in the newborn population, and so far only one has been found in over 13,000 randomly selected male babies in the Edinburgh area. Only one has been found in a study of over 2,400 males in hospitals for the mentally subnormal, and none in 6,000 mentally ill males. However, the combined data from Moss Side, Pampton and Carstairs indicate a frequency in these Special and State hospitals of 60 to 70 per 10,000 men.

The XXYY male has been the subject of various reports in the literature. Essentially he shows the physical features of the XXY male together with unusual height. In fact the evidence indicates the XXYY males are on average taller than XYY males. . . .

*XYY Males*

Casey and his colleagues at Sheffield (1966) were the first to focus attention on the high proportion of XYY males in a criminal population, in their study of men at Moss Side and Rampton. It was a comparison of their unpublished findings with those from the Scottish hospitals for the mentally subnormal that led Dr. Patricia Jacobs to suggest that the second Y chromosome was likely to be the important factor in their increased frequency, and that XYY males might be found in these particular hospitals. At this time, that is early 1965, very little was known about the XYY male. There had been less than a dozen reports in the literature, and many of these, it is now realized, were of quite atypical individuals.

Jacobs and her colleagues (1965) examined at the State Hospital, Carstairs, 315 our of a total 342 men. They found nine to have XYZ complement, or a frequency of about 300 per 10,000 men. It has to be remembered that in a number of these men there are quite adequate medical grounds for understanding their behaviour. For example, some have temporal-lobe epilepsy and others have residual damage following infections of the central nervous system. None of the XYY males at Carstairs were in this category, and if the Carstairs data are corrected to take account of these men, then the frequency of XYY males among men whose actions are inexplicable on any ordinary medical ground rises to between 450 and 500 per 10,000 men.

One other important feature was noted, namely that the XYY men are taller than average, and that their distribution of height differs significantly from that of men with an XY sex chromosome complement. Height, therefore, is a somatic marker, and so far it is the only obvious one, for the men at Carstairs have not been found to have any physical abnormality. Casey and his colleagues have studied men of 6 feet or more from Moss Side, Rampton and Broadmeer. Putting their findings together with those of Jacobs and her colleagues from men at Carstairs of 6 feet or more, we obtain a frequency of about 1,800 men per 10,000 males of 6 feet or more, a quite astonishing figure. Strictly speaking, it is scientifically incorrect to bulk the data like this, for some refer to findings among the mentally subnormal and some among psychotics. In fact the frequency appears to be higher among the mentally subnormal than among the psychotics by the order of a factor of 3. . . .

We know nothing about the frequency of the XYY male in the general population. A study of the chromosomes of 266 randomly selected male babies in Edinburgh did not reveal one XYY, and at any rate we would not expect such males to be as frequent as XXY males. In fact their frequency may well be substantially less, and it will be remembered that the frequency of XXY males at birth is between 10 and 15 per 10,000. Even supposing the XYY male turned out to be as common as the XXY male, we would still be dealing with the order of a twenty-fold increase in discussing their frequency in the Special and State hospitals. Finally, Casey and colleagues found no XYY males among thirty ordinary men of 6 feet or more or among thirty mentally ill men of 6 feet or more, while Jacobs and her colleagues (unpublished data) have found none so far in an incomplete study of a hospital for the mentally subnormal among 190 males of all ages and heights.

Recently Casey and his colleagues made a very significant advance. They examined twenty-four "intermediate stay" prisoners in Nottingham prison. None were mentally subnormal and all were 6 feet or more. Two XYY males were found, and assuming that further studies confirm this finding, then clearly there may well be many XYY males in our ordinary prisons.

## Conclusions

There is no doubt that men with XXY, XY/XXY, XXYY, and XYY sex chromosome complements are found in unusual numbers among males in the Special and State hospitals. There is preliminary evidence suggesting that XYY males may come to be found in unusual numbers among ordinary prisoners, while the data so far from a study of the new entrants to the Scottish Borstals indicate that they are uncommon in this group of young male offenders. It is more than likely that studies will show the presence of men with XXY or XY/XXY or possibly even XXYY complements among ordinary prisoners in increased frequencies by comparison with those in the newborn population or in the ordinary population of adult males.

The discovery of the XYY male in his setting in these criminal groups may be the most important discovery yet made in human cytogenetics, and it may provide a powerful lever to open up the study of human behavioral genetics. The four abnormal sex chromosome complements may in varying degrees influence intelligence and behavior. Being purely speculative, it is possible that the main influence of the XXY complement is on intelligence with perhaps some influence on behavior, while the situation is possibly reversed with the XYY complement. At all events, there are sufficient data to indicate that cytogenetic studies of criminal groups are likely to be rewarding in helping to further our understanding of the nature of criminal behavior.

# 19

## A Critique of the Anthropological View of Crime

*Robert K. Merton* and
*M.F. Ashley-Montagu*

Professor Hooton in two works recently published in the combined fields of physical anthropology and criminology has propounded some highly unorthodox theories and stated some startling conclusions. . . .

Since Hooton's work seems destined to exert an appreciable effect upon the thought of all those who make themselves acquainted with it, as well as upon the thought of many who do not, it is desirable that the significance of his results be critically examined from as many aspects as possible, for its implications are of the greatest importance. . . .

The study of the *Old American Criminal* reports on 4,212 native white prisoners of native white parentage from nine states and a civilian (noncriminal) check sample of 313 (146 Nashville firemen and 167 residents of Massachusetts). Observations included at least thirty-three anthropometric measurements and indices, ten sociological categories and thirty-three morphological categories for each person. It should be noted that almost one-half of the civilian check group are firemen. . . . Another part of the check group consists of Massachusetts militiamen. . . .

Hooton finds that "on the whole, the biological superiority of the civilian to the delinquent is quite as certain as his sociological superiority." "The evidence," he writes, "that the criminals are derived from the baser biological staff of their various ethnic stocks seems to me to be conclusive, although," he adds, "it might be argued that they came from families which are the anthropological victims of environmental depression."

Hooton finds that the "first generation criminals seem to adhere more closely than first generation civilians to the squat, broad-faced types which are often characteristic of the foreign born emigrant from Europe," and he goes on to make the astonishing suggestion that "it seems possible that such biological inadaptability, such phylogenetic conservatism, be responsible for the association of primitive features with retarded culture in modern savages."

It need hardly be said that for this suggestion there exists not the slightest

From Robert K. Merton and M.F. Ashley-Montagu, "Crime and the Anthropologist," *American Anthropologist* 42, number 3, 1940. Reprinted with permission of the American Anthropological Association.

113

factual support, but unexceptionally the evidence completely and unequivocally proves the contrary; that modern "savages" are biologically at least as perfectly adapted to the environments in which they live as the white man is to his. With respect to culture, it apparently requires to be pointed out that the culture of "savages" with rare exceptions, is anything but "retarded." It is a misunderstanding of the nature of culture, and of the history of our own, to speak of the culture of simpler peoples as retarded. Primitive cultures are no less complex and developed in their own ways than our own. . . .

Two distinct interpretative tendencies run throughout the work: one, a cautious and admirably restrained effort to assay the significance of biological factors in the determination of the incidence of criminal behavior; the other, a pugnacious and flamboyant insistence on the biological determination of crime. These two views do not rest comfortably in the same book but, conveniently enough, they are usually segregated.

In spite of all this laudable protestation that a statistical association is not to be confused with a causal relationship, Hooton insists that "the variation in physique and body build is *certain causally* related to the nature of offense." (p. 296; italics inserted.) And this, despite the absence of adequate evidence to demonstrate the causal connexion which he holds to be incontestable. . . .

Criminals are organically inferior. Crime is the resultant of the impact of environment upon low-grade human organisms. It follows that the elimination of crime can be effected only by the expiration of the physically, mentally and morally unfit, or by their complete segregation in a socially aseptic environment.

What are these *differences* which, we must infer, unquestionably signify *inferiority*? The first is age. The criminals are 3.80 years younger than the civilians. Youth, presumably, is to be included in this homespun category of biological inferiority. It hardly comes as an unheralded discovery that the age-group varies with the type of offense. The study of crime statistics had long ago led to this finding.

The second term involving statistically significant differences between the civilians and criminals is weight: the criminals are 11.70 pounds lighter, on the average. Presumably, deficiency of weight as compared with the "roly-poly" firemen, et al., is a mark of biological inferiority. In view of the frequently observed association between body weight and socio-economic status, might it not be advisable to equate the status of the criminal and check samples, before testing differences of weight as "biological" differences? Or are we to make the further assumption that socio-economic status is also biologically determined?

The five other indubitable differences involve the criminal's deficiencies in chest breadth, head circumference, upper face height, nose height, and ear length. One awaits with some impatience the demonstration that these deficiencies represent biological inferiority, as one awaits the proof that these "significant differences" mean anything more than a difference between two statistics computed from separate samples of such a magnitude that the probability that the samples were drawn from the same universe is inappreciable. We already know that Hooton's samples were drawn from different universes, and what we would be interested to know is why Hooton fastened upon a difference of a biological nature, rather than upon the many other characters of difference which are socio-economically known to exist between the civilians and criminals, as the causative factor in criminality. Statistically significant differences tell us no more than that the statistics involved are of different values; they do not tell us *why* or how they came to be so. The extrapolation of the "biological" factor, to the exclusion of all others, may satisfy Hooton's critical sense, but it does not satisfy ours. Furthermore, since some of Hooton's "significant differences" between the civilians and criminals are no more than 3 or 4 times the probable error, this renders those particular differences less clearly significant. It may be mentioned here that the employment of the critical ratio, i.e., difference/standard error of difference, rather than the difference/probable error of difference as used by Hooton, would have constituted a critically more exacting index of "statistical significance" of such differences as were found to exist between criminals and civilians. But in any event, the demonstration is altogether lacking that such differences as the criminals exhibit are marks of "inherited inferiority" which inevitably militates against the living of a legally acceptable life. . . .

As we have seen, Hooton speaks much of biological inferiority. To our knowledge, in only one passage does he specifically state what he means by this term. This statement is a truly remarkable example of *petitio principii.* Hooton is quite clear as to the characters which are biological inferiorities; namely, *any of the characters which are distinctive of the criminal aggregate when compared with the civilian sample.* In effect all differential characters of the criminal population are by fiat inferiorities. It is by virtue of a clearly circular definition that Hooton can arrive at the "indubitable" conclusion that "criminals are biologically inferior."

When we summate the findings for the anthropometric, indicial and morphological characters, we find that the percentage differences by which the criminals differ, in the characters which they exhibit, from the civilians are as follows: Advanced 49.5 per cent, and Indifferent 15.8 per cent. We conclude then that the aggregate of characters which the criminals exhibit more frequently than the civilians group comprise a very high percentage of advanced characters, and significantly lower proportions of primitive and indifferent characters as compared with the civilians.

Disregarding for the moment the existence of such large percentages of advanced and indifferent characters, it should be clear that if Hooton is to establish the correctness of his hypothesis that the criminal is on the whole biologically or organically inferior to the civilian, he must rest his case on this 34.7 per cent of so-called primitive characters. Now, let us inquire a little more closely into the nature of these characters, and let us examine first the anthropometric and indicial characters. Among the nineteen characters classed as primitive, we find that such characters as greater chest depth occur 4 times, shoulder breadth 1, nasal index 1, and sitting height 1. Since the criminals exceed the civilians in the measurements of all these characters, there can scarcely be any question of organic inferiority or degeneration here. Such characters amount to seven in number or 6.9 per cent of the total number of 101 combined anthropometric-indicial-morphological characters, and 20.0 per cent of the total of thirty-five combined primitive characters. The next group of characters we have to consider are narrow forehead 1, deficient head-height 1, deficient head-length 1, deficient length-height index of head 2, deficient head breadth-height index 2, deficient head circumference 1, deficient minimum frontal diameter 1, and deficient bigonial diameter 1. It is of importance to note here that all of these characters, amounting to 52.6 per cent of the anthropometric-indicial primitive characters, merely represent expression of a single factor, namely, relatively small-headedness. These ten measurements and indices must, therefore, properly be treated as multiple demonstration of the existence of a single character, namely, the relatively small size of the head; hence the number of primitive characters in this group must be reduced by nine, and the total of ten measurements and indices treated as one primitive character. The only "primitive" characters which remain are deficient ear length and greater nose breadth. Now, Hooton has himself rejected deficient ear length among the offense group of robbers as without significance. Out of a total of nineteen primitive characters in the anthropometric-indicial series we are left with only two primitive characters, namely small-headedness and greater nose breadth; a total of 4 per cent instead of our original 37.3 per cent of primitive characters. . . .

Primitive or inferior characters in the anthropometric-indicial series, that these are few in number and that they are far exceeded in number by characters of an agreed advanced and neutral or indifferent nature. When we turn to consider the sixteen "primitive" characters which characterize the morphological grouping, we must frankly confess that we fail to see in any one of them any sign which may be interpreted as a mark of physical or organic inferiority, although the arbitrary standard which we have adopted as a measure of the developmental status of such characters, these characters must remain in the "primitive" category. But there are only 32.0 per cent of these characters in this group as against 56.0 per cent of "advanced" characters. A more significant figure is obtained by taking these sixteen primitive characters together with the two characters of the same class from the anthropometric-indicial series and expressing them as a percentage of the total number of combined anthropometric-indicial-morphological characters, which amount to 101. In this way we find that only 17.8 per cent of characters fall into the primitive class as compared with 49.5 per cent in the advanced class. In the light of these findings then, is it a tenable hypothesis that the criminal is an organically inferior being? We think not. We believe it to be undemonstrated that such differences as we do find are marks of genetic or biological inferiority. We believe that Hooton's own findings, when subjected to a developmental analysis such as we have attempted, do not support his conclusion that "the evidence that the criminals are derived from the baser biological stuff of their various ethnic stocks seems . . . to be conclusive."

Hooton also imputes "sociological inferiority" to the criminal aggregate. It may be suggested, however, that his summary of significant sociological differences between the criminal and civilian samples attests above all to the glaring inadequacy, in some respects, of the check sample. This may be seen by examining the specific marks of sociological "inferiority." With respect to marital status, the excess of single men among criminals, and correlatively, the deficiency of married criminals, is acknowledged to be "partially attributed to the lower mean of age of the criminals." Some differences persist, however, apart from this factor of age. The criminals' excess of divorced men is allegedly due in part "to probable suppression of divorce on the part of civilians" (for not a single divorced person appears in the civilian check sample!). All of the differences in occupational distribution are exaggerated, Hooton acknowledges, by the disproportionate number of public service workers (those Nashville firemen again) in the check sample. To the naive reader it would seem that the occupational distribution (and perhaps other social and physical characteristics) of the criminal sample would have appeared even more "abnormal" and "inferior" if the entire civilian sample, instead of only some 50 per cent, were constituted by the "stout" firemen.

When it comes to the third set of clear cut social differences, namely, education, the criminals are found to be, as expected, clearly deficient in duration of formal schooling. However, here again the gross results must be interpreted cautiously in view of the fact that 60 per cent of the criminal sample come from Tennessee, Kentucky, and Texas. In fact, when comparison is made between the Tennessee criminal and the Tennessee firemen, some of the differences are sharply attenuated, if not reversed in direction (e.g., the criminals have a marked excess of those who have had from one to two years of high school training and a statistically insignificant excess of college men). All this is not to suggest that there are no social differences between the criminal and civilian population—on the contrary, other exacting studies have shown many such differences—but simply to indicate the inadequacy of the particular samples utilized in this study.

Moreover, there still remains the question as to what is meant by the oft-repeated phrase, "sociological inferiority" of the criminal sample. The possibility of selective commitment on the basis of social and economic status is not explored here for the ample reason that the relevant evidence is not available. Thus, granted the reliability of the observed differences, what is concretely meant by the unqualified imputation of sociological inferiority? Fortunately, Hooton is explicit on this point. "Excesses of single men and of divorced men indicate an inability or unwillingness to undertake successfully the normal family responsibilities of the adult male." The introduction of Hooton's personal attitude toward divorce and celibacy is illuminating, perhaps interesting, but hardly relevant. If those of us who have given hostages to Fortune are more kindly disposed toward benedicts than toward celibates, well and good; but is this considered judgement resting in part upon twelve years of anthropological research concerning the American criminal or is its source some arcanum into which we may not be admitted? In any event, if this evaluation is to be accepted at its face value, one must also conclude that the Massachusetts civilians are in this respect "sociologically inferior" to the Tennessee civilians inasmuch as 86 per cent of the latter are married whereas only 32 per cent of the Bay State representatives have attained this superior status. Moreover, on the same logic, the Massachusetts civilians are likewise inferior to the criminal aggregate since 45 per cent of the latter are confessed benedicts. The not wholly irrelevant point is that Hooton's conclusion of ingrained biological and sociological inferiority of the criminal will be and has been heralded as a finding derived by an unquestionably eminent scientist from a comprehensive analysis of objective data. In view of the painstaking and exact nature of a great part of the study, it is unfortunate that the interpretation is marred by such data.

Hooton set himself a task of unusual magnitude. His data appear to be inadequate for answering some of the questions with which he was fundamentally concerned. The substantial result of his research is an unparalleled array of metrical, indicial and morphological data, the significance of which still remains largely to be established. Should these researches be extended it is hoped that a sociological perspective will not be so conspicuously absent in the interpretation of the data and that a systematic effort will be made to equate some of the social, economic and cultural attributes of the civilian samples, before the facile conclusion is reached that one is dealing with exclusively "biological" data. Moreover, it would seem expedient to abandon the extreme biologistic preconception which is manifest in various sections of the present interpretation and to consider in more detail the interrelations of the biological and sociocultural factors in the determination of criminal behavior. The practice of setting up false dilemmas, the frequent implication that sociological and biological interpretations are mutually exclusive, serves to mislead not only the reader of this work but possibly the author as well. It may well be that many of these exaggerations arose from a polemical context; in that event, it would seem more sagacious to take the facts and let the polemics go. Above all, it would appear expedient for an impartial investigator to disentangle himself from the illusion that scientific toughmindedness requires the assumption of biological determinism or that sociocultural facts are born simply of the observer's sentiments and self-induced phantasies. This general biologism thwarts an adequate interpretation of an impressive mound of statistical data. . . .

**Part III**
**Psychological Factors in Crime**

# Introduction

A natural outgrowth of the concern with the body type, cranial characteristics, and other physiological features of the criminal was a concern for the relation of mental capacity to criminal conduct. An early belief that crime is caused by epilepsy or mental deficiency was apparently supported by discoveries by Richard L. Dugdale, Henry H. Goddard, and others who published their findings at the beginning of the century, that a large number of incarcerated individuals had one or both of these conditions. However, as methodology became more refined and the conceptualization of the problem more precise, many of the early presuppositions linking mental inadequacy to crime were questioned.

Freudian psychology assumes that the repressed personality is likely to substitute criminal conduct for normative role expectations. Conflict in the unconscious mind, the Freudians theorize, creates feelings of guilt and anxiety, and a wish to be rid of guilt feelings and their source, to restore the proper balance of good against evil through punishment. Consequently, the criminal completes his deviant act to be caught and punished. Such modern psychoanalytic theorists as August Alchorn, Kate Friedlander, and David Abrahamsen propose that all behavior is purposive in that environmental and social elements are only minor causative factors in human conduct. More recently, Fritz Redl and David Wineman have explained delinquency in terms of a malfunctioning ego. Many aggressive children, they believe, are unable to master the broad social demands which reality places upon them. Twentieth-century psychiatrists-psychoanalysts Franz Alexander and Hugo Staub, however, see delinquency and criminality in both chronic and accidental terms. Walter Bomberg, contemporary of Alexander and Staub, defines crime as a spontaneous expression of self-assertion that arises from the violator's inner needs and impulses.

Part III traces the growing emphasis on psychological influences in crime. The English physiologist Henry Maudsley (1835-1918), writing at the turn of the century and influenced by Benoit A. Morel's (1809-1873) concept of degeneracy, conceived of crime as a form of mental illness and of habitual criminals as deficient in moral sense. Anticipating the Freudian concept of the unconscious, many criminals are dominated, he held, by a pathology of will; others, however, enter the realm of criminality gradually or under the press of circumstances. Between these two extremes is a third group, which is oriented to criminality in some degree although not likely to become criminal if placed in a positive environment. While a criminal nature may be degenerate, all criminals are not automatically degenerate. Criminals will go mad if they are not criminals because crime is a substitute for mental illness.

Havelock Ellis, a contemporary analyst, passes beyond the level of Maudsley's analysis and examines the criminal's conduct from the offender's point of view. Socially, the criminal, Ellis the late nineteenth-century to middle twentieth-

century doctor and essayist contends, is likely to be viewed as hero by the uncultured despite the fact that closer analysis may reveal that he is a feebleminded or a distorted person who has violated societal norms. Whether the offender commits his act while sane or insane is unimportant because society must
still protect itself from his act. To accept insanity as a defense is to encourage
crime and vice. During a period of stress, antisocial attitudes and manifestations
become more common. Criminals may be categorized in terms of political criminals, criminals of passion, insane criminals, instinctive criminals, occasional
criminals, habitual criminals and professional criminals. Instinctive criminals are
usually "born criminals"; habitual criminals are usually unintelligent persons in
whom habit dominates; professional criminals are usually intelligent and guided
by rationality.

In the first of his two selections, Henry H. Goddard, an early 1900s analyst
of heredity who wrote about the Kallikak family, contends that the preadoles-
cent child is generally a creature of impulse and instinct. Not until he has
reached adolescence does he become responsible for his actions. Similarly, although those with imbecilic backgrounds may know the nature of their acts,
they commonly possess no understanding of their quality. Consequently, it is
unreasonable to hold either the normal child under the age of twelve years or the
imbecilic child responsible for his acts. If crime is ever to be fully controlled, the
mentally defective must be kept from producing his own kind.

In a study of the Juke family's 1,200 descendants, Richard Dugdale, an
investigator of the influence of the family tree upon crime and personality,
found 280 paupers, 60 habitual thieves, 140 other criminals, 300 premature
babies, 7 murderers, 50 prostitutes, 440 persons with venereal disease, and a
number of other deviants. He reached the tentative conclusion that crime is
typically found in the illegitimate lines of a family, that legitimate lines sometimes marry into crime, that streaks of crime in legitimate lines occur largely
where crosses have occurred in the X branch of the family, that the eldest child
of the family has the greatest tendency to criminality, that crime chiefly follows
the male line, and that the longest lines of crime are along the lines of the eldest
son. Unlike pauperism, which represents a degree of apathy, crime suggests
vigor. Therefore, a criminal career does not tend to include pauperism, except
occasionally in old age or in childhood, and criminal careers can be more easily
modified by environment than can pauperism. In general, "crime is a social
phenomenon," but it is "natural disposition and training" that make one man a
criminal and another an honest citizen.

In his second contribution, Goddard examines in a study slightly later than
Dugdale's, the heritage of the legitimate and illegitimate breaches of the Kallikak
family over six generations. Finding that the "good" branch (496 descendants)
of the family had a relative absence of criminality and feeblemindedness and the
"bad" branch (480 descendants) had a high incidence of crime, Goddard concluded that feeblemindedness is largely responsible for the existence of poverty,

crime, prostitution, alcoholism, and other social diseases. He recommended in 1913 that efforts be made to determine who the mentally defective are and to see to it that they do not reproduce either by placing them in a segregated environment or by sterilizing them. The continued transmission of defective heredity will result in degenerative mentality and continuing human problems.

German psychiatrist Gustave Aschaffenburg (1866–1944) argues that both criminality and mental disease are products of physical and mental degeneration, but disagrees with Lombroso's contention that atavism is a causative factor in the born criminal. Physical or mental inferiority is a reflection of the person's inability to resist social circumstances. Because they are weak, violators often succumb to the pressures placed upon them. Criminals may be categorized in terms of chance, affection, occasion, consideration, recidivism, habit or profession. Crimes involve multiple factors, especially psychological in the form of psychoses and other mental defects.

The English physician-psychologist William Healy focuses on the individual offender as the "dynamic center" of the problem of delinquency and crime. The nature of the offense is determined in part by the antecedent conditions and in part by the mental capacity and personality characteristics of the potential offender. Mental or emotional disturbances are more common in delinquents than in nondelinquents.

In commenting on the work of earlier psychological theorists, the deceased twentieth-century sociologist-criminologist Edwin H. Sutherland claims that they overstated the importance of feeblemindedness and emotional disturbance as causes of delinquency and crime. More recent studies, he pointed out, find fewer criminal offenders diagnosed as feebleminded. This decline is largely due to changes in the interpretation of intelligence measurement data which have resulted in lowering the standard of normality. Feeblemindedness, Sutherland believes, is not so important a cause of delinquency as has been assumed. In some situations, feebleminded persons become delinquent and others not. The significance of feeblemindedness for delinquency and crime can be ascertained only in relationship to a multitude of personal and situational factors.

# 20 Crime and Mental Illness

*Henry Maudsley*

## The Emotions

As we justly speak of the *tone* of the spinal cord by the variations of which its reactions are so much affected, so we may fairly also speak of a *psychical tone,* the tone of the supreme nervous centres, the variations of which so greatly affect the character of the mental states that supervene. And as it appeared when treating of the spinal cord that, apart from its original nature and accidental causes of disturbance, the tone of it was determined by the totality of impressions made upon it, and of motor reactions thereto, which had been organized in its constitution as faculties; so with regard to the supreme centres of our mental life, from the residua of past thoughts, feelings, and actions, which have been organized as mental faculties, there results a certain psychical tone in each individual. This is the basis of the individual's conception of the *ego*—the affections of which, therefore, best reveal his real nature—a conception which, so far from being, as is often said, fixed and unchanging, undergoes gradual change with the change of the individual's relations as life proceeds. Whosoever candidly reflects upon the striking modification, or rather revolution, of the *ego,* which happens at the time of puberty both in men and women, will surely not find it hard to conceive how the self may imperceptibly but surely change through life. The education and experience to which any one is subjected likewise modify, if less suddenly, not less certainly, the tone of his character. By constantly blaming certain actions and praising certain others in their children, parents are able so to form their character that, apart from any reflection, these shall ever in afterlife be attended with a certain pleasure; those, on the other hand, with certain pain. Experience proves that the customs and religions of different nations differ most widely; what one nation views as crime, another praises as virtue; what one nation glorifies in as a legitimate pleasure, another reprobates as a shameful vice: there is scarcely a single crime or vice that has not been exalted into a religious observance by one nation or another at one period or other

From Henry Maudsley, *The Physiology and Pathology of the Mind* (London: Macmillan & Company London, 1867). Reprinted with permission of Macmillan London and Basingstoke.

of the world's history. How much, then, is the moral feeling or conscience dependent upon the due educational development of the mind!

Between the inborn moral nature of the well-constituted civilized person and the brutal nature of the lowest savage, all question of education and cultivation put aside, the difference as a physical fact is not less than that which often exists between one species of animal and another. The exalted ideas of justice, virtue, mercy—which are acquired in the course of a true civilization, and which the lowest savage has not—do, without doubt, add something to the nervous endowment of succeeding generations; not only is there in their constitution the potentiality of such ideas, which there is not in the lowest savage, but there is generated an instinctive quality of mind, an excellent tone of feeling, which rebels against injustice of any kind: there is formed the potentiality of a so-called *moral sense.* Thus it is that the individual rightly developing in his generation is, by virtue of the laws of hereditary action, ordaining or determining what shall be preordained or predetermined in the original nature of the individual of a future age. But are we then to lose sight of the physical aspect of this development? Certainly not; the moral feeling betokens an improved quality, or higher kind of nervous element, which ensues in the course of a due development, and which may easily again be disturbed by a slight physical disturbance of the nervous element. In the exaltation of mankind through generations, in the progress of humanization, so to speak, this height of excellence is reached: in the deterioration or degeneration of mankind, as exhibited in the downward course of insanity proceeding through generations, one of the earliest evil symptoms is, as we shall hereafter see, the loss of this virtue—the destruction of the moral or altruistic feeling.

## Varieties of Insanity

There are certain mild forms of insanity, or rather certain eccentricities of thought, feeling, and conduct, that scarcely reach the degree of positive insanity, which not unfrequently cause great difficulty when the question of legal or moral responsibility is concerned. Many people who cannot be called insane notably have what may be called the insane temperament—in other words, a defective or unstable condition of nerve element, which is characterized by the disposition to sudden, singular, and impulsive caprices of thought, feeling, and conduct. This condition, in the causation of which hereditary taint is commonly detectable, may be described as the *Diathesis spasmodica,* or the *Neurosis spasmodica.*

*The Insane Temperament,* or Neurosis spasmodica. It is characterized by singularities or eccentricities of thought, feeling, and action. It cannot truly be said of anyone so constituted that he is mad, but he is certainly strange, or "queer," or, as it is said, "not quite right." What he does he must often do in a different way from all the rest of the world. If he thinks about anything, he is apt to think about it under strange and novel relations, which would not have occurred to an ordinary person; his feeling of an event is unlike that which other people have of it. He is sometimes impressionable to subtle and usually unrecognized influences; and now and then he does whimsical and apparently quite purposeless acts. There is in the constitution an innate tendency to act independently as an element in the social system, and there is a personal gratification in the indulgence of such disposition, which to lookers-on seems to mark great self-feeling and vanity. Such a one, therefore, is deemed, by the automatic beings who perform their duties in the social system with equable regularity, as odd, queer, strange, or not quite right.

The acts of the person who has the evil heritage of an insane temperament are, on the other hand, purposeless, irregular, and aim at the satisfaction of no beneficial desire; they tend to increase that discord between him and nature of which the purposeless acts are themselves evidences, and they must ultimately end in his destruction.

*Affective Insanity.* The feelings mirror the real nature of the individual; it is from their depths that the impulses of action spring; the function of the intellect being to guide and control. Consequently, when there is perversion of the affective life, there will be morbid feeling and morbid action; the patient's whole manner of feeling, the mode of his affection by events, is unnatural, and the springs of his action are disordered; and the intellect is unable to check or control the morbid manifestations, just as, when there is disease of the spinal cord, there may be convulsive movement, of which there is consciousness, but which the will cannot restrain. In dealing with this kind of derangement, it will be most convenient, as in the investigation of the insanity of early life, to distinguish two varieties—impulsive or instinctive insanity, and moral insanity proper.

*Impulsive Insanity.* Fixing their attention too much upon the impulsive act of violence, to the neglect of the fundamental perversion of the feelings which really exists, many writers appear to have helped to increase the confusion and uncertainty which unfortunately prevail with regard to these obscure varieties of mental disorder. [The] first symptom of an oncoming insanity commonly is an affection of the psychical tone—in other words, a perversion of the whole manner of feeling; and what we have here to fix in the mind is that *the mode of affection* of the individual by events is entirely changed: this is the fundamental fact, from which flow as secondary facts the insane impulses, whether erotic, homicidal, or suicidal. The result of the abnormal condition of nerve element is to alter the mode of feeling of impressions: in place of that which is for the individual good being agreeable, and exciting a correspondent desire, and that which is injurious being painful, and exciting an answering desire to eschew it, the evil impression may be felt and cherished as a good, and the good impression felt and eschewed as an evil. There are not only perverted appetites, therefore, but there are perverted feelings and desires, rendering the individual a complete discord in the social organization.

The morbid perversion of feeling may be general, so that all sorts and conditions of abnormal feelings and desires are exhibited, or it may be specially displayed in some particular mode, so that one persistent morbid feeling or desire predominates. In the latter case we have such instances of madness as those in which there is a persistent morbid desire to be hanged, and the victim of the diseased feeling is actually impelled to a homicidal act to satisfy his unnatural craving; or, again, such insanity as that of the father or mother who kills a child with the sincere purpose of sending it to heaven. The act of violence, whatever form it may take, is but the symptom of a deep morbid perversion of the nature of the individual, if a morbid state which may at any moment be excited into a convulsive activity, either by a powerful impression from without producing some great moral shock, or by some cause of bodily disturbance—intemperance, sexual exhaustion, masturbation, or menstrual disturbance. There are women, sober and temperate enough at other times, who are afflicted with an uncontrollable propensity for stimulants at the menstrual period; and every large asylum furnishes examples of exacerbation of insanity or epilepsy coincident with that function. In fact, where there is a condition of unstable equilibrium of nerve element, any cause, internal or external, exciting a certain commotion, will upset its stability, just as happens with the spinal cord under similar circumstances. . . .

[It] is quite evident in some cases of impulsive insanity . . . there is present in the mind of the sufferer the *idea* that he must kill someone: he is conscious of the horrible nature of the idea, struggles to escape from it, and is miserable with the fear that it may at any moment prove too strong for his will, and hurry him into a deed which he dreads, yet cannot help dwelling upon. . . .

*Moral Insanity.* Here the moral perversion is very evident and cannot be overlooked, while the outward reactions of the individual are less convulsive in their manifestations, and answer more exactly to the morbid feelings and desires, than is the case in impulsive insanity. Hence it is so difficult to induce the public to entertain the idea that moral insanity is anything more than a willful and witting vice. . . .

When compelled to give an opinion upon a particular case of suspected moral insanity, it is of some importance to bear in mind that the individual is a *social* element, and to have regard therefore to his social relations. That which would scarcely be offensive or unnatural in a person belonging to the lowest strata of society—and certainly nowise inconsistent with his relations there—would be most offensive and unnatural in one holding a good position in society, and entirely inconsistent with his relations in it.

* * *

*Ideational Insanity.* Under this general name may be included those different varieties of insanity usually described as *Mania* or *Melancholia*: the unsoundness affects *ideation,* and is exhibited in delusions and intellectual alienation. Cases of ideational insanity are easily recognized to be of two principal kinds, according to the character of the accompanying feeling: in one kind there is great oppression of the self-feeling with corresponding gloomy morbid idea; in the other there is excitement or exaltation of the self-feeling, with corresponding lively expression of it in the character of the thoughts or in the conduct of the patient. The former cases belong to *Melancholia*; the latter to *Mania,* acute or chronic.

\* \* \*

If a broad division were made of insanity into two classes, namely, insanity without positive delusion and insanity with delusion, in other words, into *affective* insanity and *ideational* insanity; and if the subdivisions of these two varieties were subsequently made—would not the classification, general as it may appear, and provisional as it should be deemed, be really more scientific than one which, by postulating an exactness that does not exist, is a positive hindrance to an advance in knowledge? One desirable result of great practical consequence could not fail to follow; that is, the adequate recognition of those serious forms of mental degeneration in which there are no delusions. I have ventured accordingly . . . to put forward the following classification:

| I. Affective or Pathetic Insanity | II. Ideational Insanity |
|---|---|
| 1. Maniacal Perversion of the Affective Life. Mania sine Delirio. | 1. General<br>  a. Mania<br>  b. Melancholia } Acute and Chronic |
| 2. Melancholic Depression without Delusion. Simple Melancholia. | 2. Partial<br>  a. Monomania<br>  b. Melancholia |
| 3. Moral Alienation Proper. Approaching this, but not reaching the degree of positive insanity, is the Insane Temperament. | 3. Dementia, primary and secondary.<br>4. General Paralysis.<br>5. Idiocy, including Imbecility. |

\* \* \*

*Partial Ideational Insanity.* This division will correspond with that originally described as monomania by Esquirol, and will include not only delusion accompanied by an exalted passion, but also delusion accompanied by a sad and oppressive passion—monomania proper and ordinary melancholia. In the former an exalted self-feeling gets embodied in a fixed delusion, or in a group of delusions, which fails not to testify an overweening self-esteem; it is clothed in a corresponding delusion of power or grandeur, and the personality of the patient, who may fancy himself king, prophet, or divine, is transformed accordingly: in the latter, the feeling of oppression of self becomes condensed into a painful delusion of being overpowered by some external agency, demonic or human, or of salvation lost through individual sins.

* * *

*General Ideational Insanity.* This division will include all those cases of intellectual alienation which are commonly described under *mania,* as well as many cases of general intellectual disorder in which, notwithstanding the excitement, the evidence of much mental suffering leads to their being placed under *melancholia.* In fact, it is not possible in practice to draw the line of distinction between acute mania and acute melancholia, which often blend, follow one another, or run into one another, in a way that defies exact division; for although we may properly say that there is in acute mania an excitement or exaltation of the self-feeling, the expression of which takes place chiefly in the actions of the patient, who sings, dances, declaims, runs about, pulls off his clothes, and in all ways acts most extravagantly, yet there may be equal excitement and restlessness of action in a patient who believes himself bewitched or lost, while another, exalted and furious one day, shall be frenzied with anguish next day. . . .

# 21

### Psychological and Psychiatric Factors in Crime

*Havelock Ellis*

One of the most interesting and instructive departments of criminal literature is that dealing with the criminal's mental attitude towards crime. In considering the problems of crime, and the way to deal with them, it is of no little importance to have a clear conception of the social justification for crime from the criminal's point of view. Not only is he free from remorse; he either denies his crime or justifies it as a duty, at all events as a trifle. He has a practical and empirical way of his own of regarding the matter, as Dostoevski remarks, and excuses these accidents by his destiny, by fate.

\* \* \*

The criminal is firmly convinced that his imprisonment is a sign that the country is going to the dogs. . . . Most people must have observed, in talking with persons of vicious instincts, the genuine disgust which these so often feel for the slightly different vices of others and their indifference to their own. So the man in prison feels indulgence for his own offense and contempt for his more cautious brother outside who continues to retain the respect of society, feelings which the latter heartily reciprocates. Every individual, whatever his position, feels the need of a certain amount of *amour propre.* "I may be a thief, but, thank God, I am a respectable man."

\* \* \*

The criminal has always been the hero, almost the saint, of the uncultured. . . . The same reverence or amazement that the educated feel for the man of genius, the uneducated feel for the criminal. . . . In a less crude form, and among persons who lay claim to a somewhat higher degree of culture, the same veneration has long existed and still exists.

\* \* \*

From Havelock Ellis, *The Criminal* (New York: Scribner and Welford, 1890).

It is not possible to regard the criminal as a hero or a saint after we have
once seriously begun to study his nature. He is simply a feeble or distorted
person to whom it has chanced—most often, perhaps, from lack of human
help—to fall out of the social ranks. It is as unreasonable and as inhuman for a
whole nation to become excited over him, and to crave for the minutest details
concerning him, as we now deem it to expose the miseries of any other abnormal person—man of genius or idiot, leper or lunatic—to the general and unmerci-
ful gaze. Not that any of these may not be studied; they must be studied, but
not delivered over to unrestrained curiosities, sentimentalities, cruelties. No
external force can change this attitude; no censorship of newspapers will avail.
Only the slow influences of education, and a rational knowledge of what criminality means, can effect a permanent change. But until this has been effected,
one of the most fertile sources of crime, will remain, as it is today, a danger in
all civilized countries, a danger which is suggesting heroic remedies. The minute
details of every horrible crime are today known at once by every child in re-
motest villages. The recital of it stirs up all the morbid sedimentary instincts
in weak and ill-balanced natures; and whenever a large community grows excited
over a crime, that community becomes directly responsible for a whole crop of
crimes, more especially among young persons and children.

We have, then, to reform our emotional attitude towards the criminal. On
the other hand, we have yet something to do in reforming our rational attitude
towards crime. . . .

A question which is constantly arising, and constantly leading to direct
divergence between the exponents of science and the exponents of law, is the
question of insanity. Under existing conditions it is frequently a matter of some
moment whether a criminal is insane or not. Now whether a man is insane or
not is largely a matter of definition. Even with the best definition we cannot
always be certain whether a given person comes within the definition, but it
is still possible to have a bad definition and a good definition. The definition
which lawyers in England are compelled to accept is of the former character.
The ruling still relied on is that of the judges in the McNaghten case, many
years ago: "That to establish a defense on the ground of insanity, it must be
clearly proved that at the time of committing the act the accused was laboring
under such a defect of reason from disease of the mind as not to know the
nature and quality of the act he was doing, or if he did know it, that he did
not know he was doing what was wrong." That this metaphysical and unprac-
tical test will not do has been clearly recognized by some of the most eminent
lawyers, who are quite in agreement with medical men. . . .

The point on which we must fix our attention, however, is that it should
make so much difference whether a criminal is insane or not. Our law is still
in so semi-barbaric a condition that the grave interests of society and of the
individual are made to hinge on a problem which must often be insoluble. Practically it cannot make the slightest difference whether the criminal is sane or

insane. Sane or insane, he is still noxious to society, and society must be protected from him. Sane or insane, it is still our duty and our interest to treat him
humanely, and to use all means in our power to render him capable of living a
social life. Under any system, at once fairly human and fairly rational, the
question of insanity, while still of interest, can make little practical difference,
either to society or to the criminal. It is unreasonable and antisocial to speak
of insanity as a "defense." It is an explanation, but, from the social point of
view, it is not a defense. Suppose we accept the definition of insanity which, as
we have seen, is now widely accepted by medical men and favored by many
eminent lawyers, that insanity is a loss of self-control, the giving way to an
irresistible impulse. It cannot be unknown to anyone that self-control may be
educated, that it may be weakened or strengthened by the circumstances of life.
If we define insanity as a loss of self-control and accept that as a "defense,"
we are directly encouraging every form of vice and crime, because we are removing the strongest influence in the formation of self-control.

* * *

Criminality, like insanity, waits upon civilization. Among primitive races
insanity is rare; criminality, in the true sense, is also rare. Conservatism and the
rigid cult of custom form as distinct a barrier against crime as they do against
progressive civilization. . . . In an epoch of stress, and of much change and
readjustment in the social surroundings and relations of individuals, ill-balanced
natures become more frequent, and the antisocial and unlawful instincts are
more often called out than in a stagnant society. . . . Like insanity, criminality
flourishes among migrants, and our civilization is bringing us all more or less
into the position of migrants.

But the problem of criminality is not thereby rendered hopeless. Rather
it is shown to be largely a social fact, and social facts are precisely the order of
facts most under our control. The problem of criminality is not an isolated one
that can be dealt with by fixing our attention on that and that alone. It is a
problem that on closer view is found to merge itself very largely into all those
problems of our social life that are now pressing for solution, and in settling
them we shall to a great extent settle it. The rising flood of criminality is not an
argument for pessimism or despair. It is merely an additional spur to that great
task of social organization to which during the coming century we are called.

It is useless, or worse than useless, to occupy ourselves with methods for
improving the treatment of criminals, so long as the conditions of life render the
prison a welcome and desired shelter. So long as we foster the growth of the
reckless classes we foster the growth of criminality. . . . Liberty is dear to every
man who is fed and clothed and housed, and he will not usually enter a career
of crime unless he has carefully calculated the risks of losing his liberty and
found them small; but food and shelter are even more precious than liberty,

and these may be secured in a prison. . . . Crime would be much commoner than it is if it were not for the communistic practice of mutual helpfulness which rules so largely among the poorest classes, and mitigates the stress of misery. . . .

It was at one time thought that the great panacea for the prevention of crime was education. Undoubtedly education has an important bearing on criminality, but we now know that the mere intellectual rudiments of education have very little influence indeed in preventing crime, though they may have a distinct influence in modifying its forms. Such education merely puts a weapon into the hands of the antisocial man. The only education that can avail to prevent crime in any substantial degree must be education in the true sense, an education that is as much physical and moral as intellectual, an education that enables him who has it to play a fair part in social life. . . . We seem to be approaching a point at which it will become obvious that every citizen must be educated to perform some useful social function. In the interests of society he must be enabled to earn his living by that function. If we close the social ranks against him he will enter the antisocial ranks, and the more educated he is the more dangerous he will then become.

All education must include provision for the detection and special treatment of abnormal children. We cannot catch our criminals too young. . . . It is our duty and our interest to detect such refractory and abnormal children at the earliest period, to examine them carefully, and to ensure that each shall have the treatment best adapted to him. It is much easier, and much cheaper, to do that, than to wait until he has brought ruin on himself and shame on his friends. . . . It is indispensable, if we are to deal effectually with the criminal, that we should be able to refer to the record of his physical, mental, and moral dispositions during childhood. . . .

While a wise modification of the educative influences is here of the greatest importance, we must not forget that to a very large extent the child is molded before birth. There is no invariable fatalism in the influences that work before birth, but it must always make a very great difference whether a man is well born and starts happily, or whether he is heavily handicapped at the very outset of the race of life; whether a man is born free from vices of nature, or buys freedom, if at all, at a great price. There is evidence to show how much of the welfare of the child depends on the general physical and emotional health of the parents, and that the child's fate may be determined by some physical weakness, some emotional trouble at conception or during pregnancy. No legislation can step in here, save at the most very indirectly. We can, however, quicken the social and individual conscience. The making of children is the highest of all human functions, and that which carries the most widespread and incalculable consequences. It is well to remember that every falling away from health, every new strain and stress, in man or woman, may lay an additional burden on a man or woman yet unborn, and perhaps wreck a life or a succession of lives. . . .

**Feeblemindedness and Crime**

*Henry H. Goddard*

## Responsibility

All students of the psychology of childhood agree that not until the dawn of adolescence does reasoning as such begin to show itself in the child mind; that judgment and foresight and self-control, such as enable a person to counteract his natural impulses and make himself fit into the conventions of society, are practically unknown previous to this age. It is true that many children are taught to say what the adult alone can feel in connection with such matters. But as for having the real feeling and the understanding of the situation, we seem to have no right to expect it before the beginning of this adolescent period, from twelve to fifteen years of age. Everything points to the correctness of the conclusion that during this early period of preadolescence the child is a creature of impulse and instinct and is controlled largely by counteracting one instinct by another. . . . Without going further into a discussion of the point, which would necessarily lead to many philosophical considerations, the writer may express his conviction, born of a study both of normal children and also of mental defectives of twelve years and under in mentality, that persons of this mentality do not know much about right and wrong. They act upon impulse and upon instinct, without very much thought. Even the child of the best opportunity and the most elaborate training in a good home may quite likely not know the wrongfulness of an act of homicide in the sense of having a real feeling of that wrong. He can doubtless, as already stated, *say* that the thing is wrong, because he has learned that this is the right thing to say.

Let us turn now to the other part of the legal phrase, "Does such a person know the nature and quality of his act?" If the writer understands these terms, the first may be translated into the expression, "Does he know what he is doing?" We take it that the expression originated in the attempt to cover those cases where persons, either momentarily or permanently deranged, literally do not know what they are doing. If this is correct, then one cannot, as a rule, say that a high-grade imbecile does not know what he is doing. He is not like

From Henry H. Goddard, *The Kallikak Family* (New York: Macmillan & Company, 1935).

the lunatic who acts blindly and is probably no more responsible for his acts than a person walking in his sleep. The imbecile[a] is not in this condition. He has, so to speak, full possession of all the mind that he has ever had and that, in the case of these high-grade imbeciles or morons, is certainly sufficient to enable him to know what he is doing. In the case of Jean Gianini, the writer testified that in his opinion he knew what he was doing. He knew the nature of his act. . . . Did he know the quality of his act?

By the quality of a thing is meant that which distinguishes it from all other things. This implies a complete  and extensive knowledge of the thing in question. To know the quality of an act—murder, for example—means to know all of the elements, forms, or modes of being or action which seem to make it distinct from all other acts. To know the quality of an act of murder is to know that it is unjustifiable; it is to know that it differs from the killing of a rat in that different consequences follow; that human suffering is involved, both that of the victim and of the victim's friends and associates. It is to know, at least in some vague way, that human society could not exist if murder were the rule. To know the quality of an act of murder is to know enough to be able to distinguish it from justifiable homicide, from killing in war, not to mention more obvious necessary distinctions.

Did Jean Gianini know the quality of his act? On the stand, under cross-examination, the writer was led to express the opinion that he did. Later study of the problem and consideration of the circumstances leads to the conclusion that this was erroneous. Such knowledge implies mental capacity which is not possessed by a boy under twelve years of age. It involves experience; it involves abstraction, which is notoriously lacking in such persons. If there is one characteristic more noticeable than another among the high-grade imbeciles or morons, it is their failure to deal with abstract ideas; to draw generalizations from specific instances.

Did Pennington know the quality of his act? There is not the slightest evidence that he did. Indeed, in his case we may go farther and hold very probably that he did not even know the nature of his act. It is easily conceivable that he struck the man with the blackjack without knowing that he was committing murder, without knowing that he might kill him. His stupidity was clearly of such a character that it is a perfectly tenable position that he thought he was to strike the man and stun him until they could rob him and escape.

Did Tronson know the nature and quality of his act? Using revolvers as he did, it seems undeniable that he knew the nature. He was familiar with revolvers; he knew what they would do. He, undoubtedly, knew that he was killing Emma Ulrich. That he did not know the quality of his act is equally certain. She would not marry him, he did not want her to marry anyone else, and

---

[a]"Imbeciles," as used by Goddard, include morons and idiots.—Eds.

he had no conception that he had no right to put her out of the way so that she could not marry another if she would not marry him.

Again, we might go further and deeper into the philosophy of the question, the logic and ethics of it. But these few considerations seem sufficient to make it of the highest probability that persons of a mental age under twelve years, like the normal boys and girls of the same age, do not know and cannot be expected to know the quality of their acts. And this is sufficient, because the law requires no more than a reasonable doubt, and there certainly is a very reasonable doubt as to whether such persons know the quality of an act of murder and know that it is wrong.

## The Punishment for Criminal Imbeciles

. . . We cannot have innocent people killed in accordance with the whim of the irresponsible. These imbeciles have killed innocent members of society. What shall the living do to prevent these particular persons from repeating the crime and to prevent other imbeciles from ever committing such a crime? This, of course, involves the whole problem of punishment or the treatment of the wrongdoer. Upon one thing everybody is agreed—we must make it impossible for these persons ever to do such a deed again. The surest way to accomplish this is to destroy them. Dead men commit no crimes. Society feels safe when a desperado is killed. If we can agree upon this solution, the problem is easily solved and further discussion is unnecessary. But society is not at one on this question . . .

It is somewhat difficult to draw a line of distinction between the persons involved in these crimes and the so-called responsible murderers. . . . Nevertheless, at the present time, we do draw the distinction, and many feel that the person who has full power over his action, who knows the nature and quality and wrongfulness of his act, should be executed, while those who do not know should not be executed.

If we take the latter view, the question still remains, What shall be done with these criminal imbeciles? The alternative to capital punishment is incarceration for life. Here at least we find a distinction between these persons and the normal intelligent wrongdoers. Of all persons in the world, the criminal imbecile should be placed in custody under conditions that will forever make it impossible for him to repeat his offense. The man who commits murder in a fit of insanity may recover from his insanity and be a useful citizen for the rest of his life. The man who commits murder under a strong impulse of anger or in calm meditation as the result of perverted reasoning may recover normal reasoning and be a useful citizen. This is not true of the imbecile. He will never recover; he will never have more mind than he has now; he will never be free from the danger of following the suggestion of some wicked person or of yielding to his own inborn and uncontrolled impulses. It will never be safe for him to be at large.

\* \* \*

An institution for feebleminded would seem at first glance to be the logical place to which such a person should be committed. But no one need seriously object to commitment to a penitentiary or a state prison. . . .

If we wish to save our teachers from the possibility of being murdered by their pupils or our daughters from being killed by their wooers or business men from being struck down by the blows of feebleminded boys, we must be on the watch for symptoms of feeblemindedness in our school children. When such symptoms are discovered, we must watch and guard such persons as carefully as we do cases of leprosy or any other malignant disease. . . .

One thing more. Careful studies have shown beyond the peradventure of doubt that at least two-thirds of these mental defectives have inherited their defect; in other words, that they belong to strains of the human family whose intelligence lies below that which is required for the performance of their duties as citizens. This points to a further precaution necessary in looking toward the ultimate prevention of feeblemindedness and the solution of a large part of our prison problem, and that is the prevention of the further propagation of this race of defectives. If it is true—and there is every evidence that it is—that children are daily being born of such a mentality that it requires the attention and thought of an army of normal people to prevent their growing up into criminal lives and that all of the best efforts can never make them able to take their place in society as useful citizens, then it certainly is our duty to see that such children are not born. How this is to be accomplished has not yet been worked out in detail. The colonization and segregation of all such people in institutions where they will not be allowed to propagate is one solution that is proposed. The other is by surgical interference, to render such people physically incapable of propagating. Probably both these methods and still others must be utilized to help solve this problem. . . .

# 23 The Juke Family

*Richard L. Dugdale*

To get a full record of the crimes of the "Juke" family the criminal records of three other counties need to be examined. As respects misdemeanors, these are to be found in the books of justices of the peace and the books of the sheriffs, both of which are either destroyed or laid away in private hands, packed in barrels or stowed in garrets, and are inaccessible. In addition we must note that in the latter part of the last century and the beginning of this, many acts which now subject a man to imprisonment then went unpunished, even cases of murder, arson and highway robbery, so that the absence of a man's name from the criminal calendar is no criterion of his honesty.

In the first place, the illegitimates who have become parent stocks are the oldest children of their respective mothers, Ada [and] Bell. . . . In the study of crime we take the males as the leading sex, skipping the women just as in studying harlotry we skipped the men, but at the same time it will be well to notice how harlotry prevails among these families where the boys are criminals.

## Case 23

We get an intermarriage of cousins, and the appearance of crime seems to be postponed for a generation. The word "seems" is used because no crime receiving punishment was committed; but there is no doubt that the two eldest sons of the next generation were both petty thieves, one of them an expert sheep stealer. Coming down to the next generation (fifth) we find the criminal children to be where there is a cross between the "Juke" and the X blood. We also find that the oldest male child of the fourth generation is the father of proportionately more criminals than the second male child, while the third male child, who is also the youngest and has intermarried into the "Juke" blood, is the father of honest children. The figures run thus: first son, 7 boys, 5 criminals; second son, 6 boys, 2 criminals; third son, 4 boys, no criminals.

Moreover, comparing the children of the fifth generation by families, we

From R.L. Dugdale, *The Jukes* (New York: G.P. Putnam, 1877).

find that it is the older brothers who are the criminals and not the younger ones while, if we trace down line 1 to the sixth generation, we find the heredity of crime seems to run in the line of the oldest child, and that the males preponderate in those lines.

## Case 24

Taking the illegitimate progeny of Bell, what do we find? That the preponderance is of males, and that the three eldest children are honest, industrious and self-supporting. . . .

But when we come to the fourth child we find, what? That he has married outside the "Juke" blood, that he is not a criminal himself, but that amongst his children are found criminals. The oldest of his boys, as in the previous generation, was industrious. He married, emigrated to Pennsylvania at least thirty years ago, and now owns a farm and is doing well.

The second child was a farmer and industrious, lived to seventy years of age, and neither committed crime nor went to the county-house, but received out-door relief at sixty-five for three years. The third child did tolerably well and had no criminal children, they being all girls. The fourth was a criminal and died of syphilitic consumption; the fifth was the father of a criminal; also the sixth, who had received outside relief at thirty-eight years of age; while the seventh, and last, was a harlot and an alms-house pauper who died of syphilitic disease.

Here we see crime immediately follows the cross of bloods, and that the criminal is born before the pauper of the family, as we also see that the honest is born before the criminal. It now remains to follow several lines, tracing the heredity of individual cases, and laying the environment alongside.

## Case 25

A boy seventeen years of age who has served six months in Albany penitentiary for petit larceny; his father (gen. five) has been twice in county jail for assault and battery, and is now serving a five-year sentence in State prison for a rape on his niece in her twelfth year. Going further back we find the father was a petty thief, though never convicted. This ends the information as to the hereditary. Now as to the environment.

The adults of generation four lived in a settlement mainly composed of their own relatives, situated in the woods around a chain of lakes. The greater proportion of these people having recourse to petty theft to help out their uncertain incomes, going on excursions of several miles during the night, and robbing hen-roosts, stripping clothes-lines, breaking into smoke-houses and stealing hams, corn, firewood and wood with which to make axe-handles, baskets or chair-bottoms. This general condition continued during the boyhood of generation five, only, the general wealth of the community having enormously increased, their field became broader and their offenses more grave than those of the previous generation. Going down to generation six, we find the boy of seventeen is suddenly deprived of support by his father being sent to prison. He is in want; his mother goes to the poor-house with the younger children, while he takes up the life of a vagrant, picking up his living as he best can. Want, bad company, neglect form the environment that predisposes to larceny. He will not go to the county-house with his mother; he feels it is more independent to steal and takes the risks. Now self-reliance, no matter how wrongly it asserts itself, is indicative of power, and this power should be availed of for better purposes. In these three generations is traced an environment which predisposes to crime and corresponds to the heredity.

## Case 26

Now turning to the sixth generation, a boy nineteen years of age throws another boy over a cliff forty feet high, out of malicious mischief. This boy is the second illegitimate child of his mother, but probably not of his father, which latter was the first illegitimate of his mother by X. This case then seems to follow the rule that the crime follows the lines of illegitimacy where the "Juke" blood marries into X. There is no evidence that the mother was a criminal, but her father was a petty thief. . . . Such is the heredity.

The environment, a home the scene of violence, debauch and drunkenness, father and mother both intemperate and idle; the mother becoming the procuress for her eldest son of a child twelve years of age, whom that illegitimate son seduces and is forced to marry to prevent criminal prosecution; the first born of this child forming the third bastard in a line of heredity. Here we have an environment corresponding to the heredity.

## Case 27

Case 27 seems to be an exception to the rule that the oldest is a criminal, but it is only a seeming exception. He, with his next brother aged twelve, engaged in a burglary, getting $100 in gold as booty. The boy was caught, but he, the leader in the crime, escaped. He being a sailor, it is impossible to get any reliable information about his career, but it is evident that at nineteen he was a leader in crime.

**Case 28**

[In] the fifth generation, brothers and sisters, we find the oldest son commits
a number of offenses, among them murder, but he escapes punishment as in the
case above. The second child, a girl, has become the contriver of the crimes
which the third child, a boy, has carried into effect, and for which he has
recently received twenty years' sentence of imprisonment. In this case the
boldest and most intelligent is the oldest child.

Of the crimes committed by the legitimate branch of the Juke family . . .
the same general rule holds good, that the eldest is the criminal of the family,
the youngest the pauper.

*Tentative inductions respecting crime:*

1.   The burden of crime is found in the illegitimate lines.
2.   The legitimate lines marry into crime.
3.   Those streaks of crime found in the legitimate lines are found chiefly where
     there have been crosses into X.
4.   The eldest child has a tendency to be the criminal of the family.
5.   Crime chiefly follows the male lines.
6.   The longest lines of crime are along the line of the eldest son.

**Crime and Pauperism Compared**

The ideal pauper is the idiotic adult unable to help himself, who may be justly
called a living embodiment of death. The ideal criminal is a courageous man in
the prime of life who so skillfully contrives crime on a large scale that he
escapes detection and succeeds in making the community believe him to be
honest as he is generous. Between these two extremes there are endless gradations which approximate each other, till at last you reach a class who are too
weak to be contrivers of crime, and too strong to be alms-house paupers; they
are the tools who execute what others plan and constitute the majority of those
who are found in prison during their youth and prime, and in the poor-house
in their old age. These men prefer the risks and excitements of criminality and
the occasional confinement of a prison where they meet congenial company,
to the security against want and the stagnant life of the alms-house.

\* \* \*

*Tentative inductions on the relations of crime and pauperism:*

1.   Crime as compared to pauperism indicates vigor.
2.   With true criminals pauperism occurs either in old age or in childhood,
     and is not synchronous with the term of the crime career.

3.  Imprisonment of the parent may produce induced pauperism in the children, especially if they be girls who are thrown into the alms-house and remain inmates long enough to become mothers.
4.  Criminal careers are more easily modified by environment, because crime, more especially contrived crime, is an index of capacity, and wherever capacity is found, there environment is most effective in producing modifications of career.
5.  The misfortune of one generation which throws the children into an alms-house may lay the foundation for a criminal career for that generation if the children are of an enterprising temperament, for pauperism if of low vitality and early licentious habits.

\* \* \*

## The Formation of Character

Where there is heredity of any characteristic, it would seem there is a tendency and, it might almost be said, a certainty to produce an environment for the next generation corresponding to that heredity, with the effect of perpetuating it. Where the environment changes in youth the characteristics of heredity may be measurably altered. Hence the importance of education. In treating the subject it must be clearly understood and practically accepted, that the whole question of the educational management of crime, vice, and pauperism rests strictly and fundamentally upon a physiological basis, and not upon a sentimental or a metaphysical one. These phenomena take place not because there is any aberration in the laws of nature, but in consequence of the operation of these laws; because disease, because unsanitary conditions, because educational neglects, produce arrest of cerebral development at some point, so that the individual fails to meet the exigencies of the civilization of his time and country, and that the cure for unbalanced lives is a training which will affect the cerebral tissue, producing a corresponding change of career. This process of atrophy, physical and social, is to be met by methods that will remove the disabilities which check the required cerebral growth, or where the modification to be induced is profound, by the cumulative effect of training through successive generations under conditions favorable to such strengthening.

We have seen that disease in the parent will produce idiocy in the child; this is arrest of cerebral development: that it will cause early death; this is arrest of development. Besides these, arrest of development takes place in various other forms, at different stages and under widely differing circumstances. Excess of the passions prevents mental organization; and neglected childhood even, produces the equivalent of arrest of development; for, as in the case of the idiot, the arrest of cerebral development is caused by want of alimentary nu-

trition to the brain, so in the untaught child we get arrest of cerebral development caused by neglecting to furnish properly organized experience of the right
relations of human beings to each other, which gives us a corresponding moral
idiot.

Men do not become moral by intuition, but by patient organization and
training. Indeed, the whole process of education consists of the building up of
cerebral cells. For the purpose of a concise explanation, it may be said that
there are four great subdivisions of the nervous system, each one of which
presides over, coordinates and controls a separate set of functions: (1) the
ganglionic nervous centers which connect the heart, lungs and internal viscera
with each other and with the brain, bringing them into sympathetic action;
(2) the spinal cord, which chiefly presides over the movements of the limbs
and body; (3) the sensational centers, which register the impressions gathered
by the senses; (4) the ideational centers, that enable us to reason, to think, to
will, and, with this last, the moral nature. The ganglionic centers are, in a
certain sense, subordinate to the spinal nerve centers; these, in their turn, are
subordinate to the sensory centers; and these last are subordinate to the controlling action of the hemispheres of the brain. . . . While the mind is the last
in order of development, it is the first in importance. . . . This all-important will
does not usually reach its full growth till between the thirtieth to the thirty-
third years. . . . We must therefore distinctly accept as an established educational
axiom, that the moral nature—which really means the holding of the emotions
and passions under the dominion of the judgment by the exercise of will—is the
last developed of the elements of character, and, for this reason, is most modifi-
able by the nature of the environment.

* * *

The analysis of what we have ascertained concerning the body and mind
of the criminal leads to the same conclusions. Intellectually and physically they
fall below the average. This does not apply to the individual, but to criminals
as a class, just as we may say of a race that it stands on a low plane without
intending to intimate that it lacks physically strong and intellectually eminent
men. . . .

Inferiority is the result of descent and training. Thus, the roots of the evil
are transferred to the social sphere. The great advantage of this is that we can
confront the whole phenomenon with more courage, because we then realize
how it must be combated. . . .

The social evils, wretchedness and poverty, drunkenness and disease,
produce a generation of men who are not equal to the storms of life; they are
socially useless, in the same sense that those who are rejected, when recruits
are examined for the army, are physically unfit. . . .

So, too, for us the establishment of a low intelligence, of physical and mental inferiority, is merely a sign of the lack of the power to resist social circumstances, a signal that warns us to be cautious and not to ask too much of these socially unfit. If we could tear up all these people out of the foul soil in which they are rooted, if we could strengthen them physically and steel them by education, if, above all, we could protect them from the dangers of life, we should be able to save most of them from social ruin.

But that would be Utopia. Life takes its course and grinds him who cannot keep up. As the struggle for existence is going on at present, as national customs force everyone into the yoke of "doing likewise," we are obliged thus to judge the dangers to which we are all exposed. They are greater than the power of resistance of all these inferior persons; where the strong swimmer breasts and surmounts the surf, the weak one perishes. And those that perish are many. . . .

We must reckon with an army of criminals who, under existing conditions, cannot be fitted into a regulated life. If we look closer at these men, we shall find that outward causes play a very different part in their lives; one gives way at the slightest touch, another only after resisting temptation for a long time, but, as far as human power can judge, they one and all eventually succumb.

Now, are all these socially "incorrigibles" morally insane persons, incorrigible because they lack the ability to perceive and follow the laws of morality? "Moral insanity" is a much disputed conception, and the controversy as to whether a disease can appear exclusively in ethical defects is not yet at an end. Hence, I can only give my own personal point of view here: I do not believe in the existence of this disease. All the cases diagnosed as such with which I have come in contact either were accompanied by pronounced intellectual defects or were merely symptoms of serious neuroses and psychoses which had failed to be recognized. . . .

The establishment of the outward circumstances under which a crime is committed made it possible clearly to perceive a number of causes of crimes, of which I would mention again the influence of the seasons, the economic situation, and popular or national customs. From this it follows that crime is, in the first place, a social phenomenon; every age has the crimes that it produces. But not everyone becomes a criminal. Every crime is the product of natural disposition and training, of the individual factor on the one side, and of the social conditions on the other.

# 24 The Kallikak Family

*Henry H. Goddard*

## What It Means

. . . We have here a family of good English blood of the middle class, settling upon the original land purchased from the proprietors of the state in Colonial times, and throughout four generations maintaining a reputation for honor and respectability of which they are justly proud. Then a scion of this family, in an unguarded moment, steps aside from the paths of rectitude and, with the help of a feebleminded girl, starts a line of mental defectives that is truly appalling. After this mistake, he returns to the traditions of his family, marries a woman of his own quality, and through her carries on a line of respectability equal to that of his ancestors.

We thus have series from two different mothers but the same father. These extend for six generations. Both lines live out their lives in practically the same region and in the same environment, except in so far as they themselves, because of their different characters, changed that environment. . . . That we are dealing with a problem of true heredity, no one can doubt, for, although of the descendants of Martin Kallikak, Jr., many married into feebleminded families and thus brought in more bad blood, yet Martin, Jr., himself married a normal woman, thus demonstrating that the defect is transmitted through the father, at least in this generation. Moreover, the Kallikak family traits appear continually even down to the present generation, and there are many qualities that are alike in both the good and the bad families, thus showing the strength and persistence of the ancestral stock.

\* \* \*

[The] Kallikak family, in the persons of Martin Kallikak, Jr., and his descendants . . . were feebleminded, and no amount of education or good environment can change a feebleminded individual into a normal one, any more than it

From Henry H. Goddard, *The Criminal Imbecile* (New York: Macmillan and Company, 1915).

can change a red-haired stock into a black-haired stock. The striking fact of the enormous proportion of feebleminded individuals in the descendants of Martin Kallikak, Jr., and the total absence of such in the descendants of his half brothers and sisters is conclusive on this point. Clearly it was not environment that has made that good family. They made their environment; and their own good blood, with the good blood in the families into which they married, told.

\* \* \*

In the good branch of the Kallikak family there were no criminals. There were not many in the other side, but there were some, and, had their environment been different, no one who is familiar with feebleminded persons, their characteristics and tendencies, would doubt that a large percentage of them might have become criminal. . . .

Such facts as those revealed by the Kallikak family drive us almost irresistibly to the conclusion that before we can settle our problems of criminality and pauperism and all the rest of the social problems that are taxing our time and money, the first and fundamental step should be to decide upon the mental capacity of the persons who make up these groups. We must separate, as sharply as possible, those persons who are weak-minded, and therefore irresponsible, from intelligent criminals. Both our method of treatment and our attitude towards crime will be changed when we discover what part of this delinquency is due to irresponsibility.

\* \* \*

We have claimed that criminality resulting from feeblemindedness is mainly a matter of environment, yet it must be acknowledged that there are wide differences in temperament and that, while this one branch of the Kallikak family was mentally defective, there was no strong tendency in it towards that which our laws recognize as criminality. In other families there is, without doubt, a much greater tendency to crime, so that the lack of criminals in this particular case, far from detracting from our argument, really strengthens it. It must be recognized that there is much more liability of criminals resulting from mental defectiveness in certain families than in others, probably because of difference in the strength of some instincts.

\* \* \*

We learn from a responsible member of the good branch of the family that the appetite for alcoholic stimulants has been strong in the past in this family and that several members in recent generations have been more or less addicted to its use. Only two have actually allowed it to get the better of them to the extent that they became incapacitated. Both were physicians. In the other branch, however, with the weakened mentality, we find twenty-four victims of this habit so pronounced that they were public nuisances. . . .

It is such facts as these . . . that lead us to the conclusion that drunkenness is, to a certain extent at least, the result of feeblemindedness and that one way to reduce drunkenness is first to determine the mentally defective people, and save them from the environment which would lead them into this abuse.

Again, eight of the descendants of the degenerate Kallikak branch were keepers of houses of ill fame, and that in spite of the fact that they mostly lived in a rural community where such places do not flourish as they do in large cities. . . .

From this comparison the conclusion is inevitable that all this degeneracy has come as the result of the defective mentality and bad blood having been brought into the normal family of good blood, first from the nameless feeble-minded girl and later by additional contaminations from other sources. . . .

[In] view of such conditions as are shown in the defective side of the Kalli-kak family, we begin to realize that the idiot is not our greatest problem. He is indeed loathsome; he is somewhat difficult to take care of; nevertheless, he lives his life and is done. He does not continue the race with a line of children like himself. Because of his very low-grade condition, he never becomes a parent.

It is the moron type that makes for us our great problem. . . . The real sin of peopling the world with a race of defective degenerates who would probably commit [Martin Kallikak's] sin a thousand times over, was doubtless not per-ceived or realized. It is only after the lapse of six generations that we are able to look back, count up and see the havoc that was wrought by that one thoughtless act. . . .

**Conclusion and Resume**

The Kallikak family presents a natural experiment in heredity. A young man of good family becomes through two different women the ancestor of two lines of descendants—the one characterized by thoroughly good, respectable, normal citizenship, with almost no exceptions; the other being equally characterized by mental defect in every generation. This defect was transmitted through the father in the first generation. In later generations, more defect was brought in from other families through marriage. In the last generation it was transmitted through the mother, so that we have here all combinations of transmission, which again proves the truly hereditary character of the defect.

We find on the good side of the family prominent people in all walks of life and nearly all of the 496 descendants owners of land or proprietors. On the bad side we find paupers, criminals, prostitutes, drunkards, and examples of all forms of social pest with which modern society is burdened.

From this we conclude that feeblemindedness is largely responsible for these social sores.

Feeblemindedness is hereditary and transmitted as surely as any other character. We cannot successfully cope with these conditions until we recognize feeblemindedness and its hereditary nature, recognize it early, and take care of it.

In considering the question of care, segregation through colonization seems in the present state of our knowledge to be the ideal and perfectly satisfactory method. Sterilization may be accepted as a makeshift, as a help to solve this problem because the conditions have become so intolerable. But this must at present be regarded only as a makeshift and temporary, for before it can be extensively practiced, a good deal must be learned about the effects of the operation and about the laws of human inheritance.

# 25 On Psychological Factors
*Gustave Aschaffenburg*

Both criminality and mental disease are plants that draw their nourishment from the same soil, physical and mental degeneration. The fact that this soil is not able to produce better fruit must be attributed to intemperance and wretchedness, to the marriage of mentally deficient persons, in short, to unfortunate social conditions. Why it is that one child of a drunkard will be epileptic, idiotic, or insane, and another, with no discernible psychic defect, but irritable and unstable, will become a criminal; why one of a depraved family's badly brought up children will turn drunkard and end in the insane asylum, while another finds his way to prison, we do not and never shall know.

In spite of some alterations in his classification of criminals, Lombroso continued to maintain that perhaps one-third of all criminals represented a special type distinguished by common physical and mental qualities. He considered the proof of these physical and psychic anomalies of particularly great value, because to him they were signs that the *delinquente nato* was an atavistic step in the development of mankind. This assertion is, at present certainly, entirely unfounded. The dividing line between the really atavistic formations and the anomalies that arise in earliest youth, or during foetal development in consequence of pathological processes, is just as difficult to draw as that between the anomalies themselves and the variations that still lie within the margin of normality. . . .

Similarity in anatomy and mental qualities to savages and the peoples of former ages has been used to support the theory that the criminal signifies a relapse which may lead "beyond the savage, to the animal itself." This hypothesis stands on very uncertain feet; the life and doings of primitive peoples are often very different from the rough and unchecked brutality, cruelty, and other characteristics which are advanced as the basis of the likeness between savages and criminals.

Entirely mistaken is the comparison between crime and epilepsy. . . . This view is based on an entire misunderstanding of epilepsy. A criminal never shows epileptic characteristics unless he is suffering from this disease. This is common

From Gustave Aschaffenburg, *Crime and Repression* (Little, Brown and Company, 1915). Reprinted with permission of Patterson-Smith Publishing Corporation.

enough and is easily explicable, if we know the frequency of epilepsy among drunkards and the children of drunkards. But the only thing that crime has in common with epilepsy is the common soil of degeneration.

All of Lombroso's attempts to separate the born criminal from the normal man by bringing him into connection, partly with atavistic, partly with pathological, states, have come to grief; and so has the endeavor to characterize the criminal "clinically and anatomically." . . .

# 26

## The Intricacy of Causation

### William Healy

The dynamic center of the whole problem of delinquency and crime will ever be the individual offender. . . . [No] general theories of crime, sociological, psychological or biological, however well founded, are of much service when the concrete issue, namely the particular offense and the individual delinquent, is before those who have practically to deal with it. The understanding needed is just that craved by Solomon—the understanding of the one who has actually to deal with people, the one who formally is the therapeutist. . . .

Nothing is shown by our data more convincingly than the predictable inadequacy of social measures built upon statistics and theories which neglect the fundamental fact of the complexity of causation, determinable through study of the individual case. Many of the works on social misconduct deal with what is often denominated "general causation," and attempt to establish geographical, climatological, economic and many other correlations. Much of this is interesting and even seductive intellectually, and it is true that there are some relationships, such as that between alcoholism and crime, well enough verified to justify social alteration. But that many of these suggested correlations contain only half-truths one is constrained to believe after prolonged attempt to gather in all available facts in many individual cases. . . .

Thorough study of individual cases does not imply that we shall always find the main cause of the offender's tendency in his own make-up—it merely implies the logical balancing of causative factors. One has seen an extensive family chart exhibited as proof that criminalism is inherited, because of its springing up in several side lines. But in addition to the chart the investigator possessed information that the various persons showing delinquent tendencies all lived in an atrocious environment. The facts not plotted on the chart could be used to show, if we took them also by themselves, that in this family criminalism was uniformly the result of bad social circumstances. On the other hand, it may be conditions in the home, or other environmental agents, which at first sight loom large. But then one finds other individuals in the same family turning out well, others on the same street or with the same associates who do not become crim-

From William Healy, *The Individual Delinquent* (Boston: Little, Brown and Company, 1915). Reprinted with permission of Patterson-Smith Publishing Corporation.

inals. Complicating the argument again, we may discover grave delinquent tendencies appearing in some one member of the most upright families, while, contrariwise, we have occasionally found all the numerous immediate descendants of a terrible drunkard successfully arising in full strength of character from the squalor in which he placed them. So it goes; to single out and blame this or that specific condition, without proceeding by the scientific process of elimination and attempting to rule out other possible causes, will not lead far towards real solutions. Indeed, without well-rounded studies of the pivotal facts in the particular case it ensues that "experience is fallacious and judgment difficult."

The idea that the individual must be carefully studied in order that crime may be ameliorated has been steadily growing since the day of Lombroso. The . . . view of Lombroso was that of the scientific man who sees in this field the inexorable laws which govern man's nature and environment. It makes little difference which theoretical view of penology is held; the problem of society ever is to handle a given offender satisfactorily. . . .

A person is not fairly to be regarded merely as the soul and body of the moment. It is only our own temporal limitations which prevent us from seeing people as they really are—as products of the loom of time. Every individual is partly his ancestors, and partly the result of his developmental conditions, and partly the effects of many reactions to environment, and to bodily experiences, and even of reactions to his own mental activities. An ideal description of a human person would refer each trait or condition to its proper source. Most serviceable to us is the conception of the individual as the product of conditions and forces which have been actively forming him from the earliest moment of unicellular life. To know him completely would be to know accurately these conditions and forces; to know him as well as is possible, all of his genetic background that is ascertainable should be known. The interpretations that may be derived from acquaintance with the facts of ancestry, ante-natal life, childhood development, illnesses and injuries, social experiences, and the vast field of mental life, lead to invaluable understandings of the individual and to some ideas of that wonderful complex of results which we term personality.

Out of the chaos, which some of our previous statements might seem to imply exists in the study of delinquents, we rejoice to see strongly marked causal types or classes emerging. These evidently are not to be factitiously categorized, but nevertheless represent the centering of clear-cut practical issues. Now we see mental, now social, now physical factors uppermost as each type appears, and one observes greatly mixed causes which insistently have to be interpreted for the individual case itself. Our card schedule of causative factors shows sufficient illustration of this. The main factor gives a clue to the most logical grouping. The minor and antecedent issues may, however, have their bearing on direct treatment or on public measures of prevention. Any grouping of similar factors may be fairly denominated causal groups, standing by themselves simply because they represent answers to our formal inquiry concerning the causes of delinquency. These represent pragmatic and not theoretical groups.

We find there is much overlapping of the types and groups, and that there is occasional difficulty in differentiation. There are borderline cases of feeble-mindedness; the influence of bad companions, of mental conflicts, of physical defect, may not be separable from other influences. Different ways of looking at cases may lead to some little confusion. . . .

As we have gone on with the grouping according to ascertained factors in individual cases, we have seen that many subtypes can be discriminated and related to various prognoses. This comes out distinctly in our case studies, and turns out to be the logical center for the making of case summaries. As an example, we might take the instance of an epileptic offender. Now, apart from the question of the disease itself, we must take up as a subhead his environment. Let him there be tempted to alcoholism, and we have a combination that at once determines a bad prognosis in the matter of his delinquent tendencies. But if his home control is good, we can pass to another point, the form of his disease. If he has epileptic lapses with wandering, the prognosis is bad, and so on. This brings us to the conclusion that even though his epilepsy be justifiably regarded as the main antecedent, still that factor unconsidered in the light of subconditions is not enough to base the prognosis on, nor enough to form the unit of statistics which shall give accurate data concerning ultimate causes and remedies.

Finding direct mental determination of delinquency demonstrates prime consideration of the mental life of the individual as being the straightforward way of discriminating most causal factors. Not only is this shown by the undue proportion of feeblemindedness, epilepsy and insanity among delinquents, but also by the mental disappointments, irritations and conflicts which very frequently are at the roots of offending careers. Our groupings, by weight of the facts, show much more necessary allegiance to psychological than to any other classification of both offenders and causes. Not that even here we achieve consistency, since we deal now with static abilities, now with functionings, now with mechanisms, and now with content. We are forced first to the use of a differential individual psychology, and then, as best we can, later, to the formulations of group psychology, as well as to analysis of mental mechanisms and mental content. . . .

The discovery of great intricacy in causations appears so momentous for the treatment of the individual, for those who are concerned in any way with general causes, and for the projection of interpretation of any statistics, that we have diagramed group connections of some simple findings to bring out sharply their vital interrelationships. We show in this at three levels the delinquency, the offender as a member of some general class, and the causal antecedents back of his tendency to delinquency. The combinations are made from only a few of the ascertained facts and types and could, of course, by the addition of facts, be made infinitely more complex. The combining lines represent either sequence of conjunction of the portrayed elements.

We observe from the diagram in figure 26–1 that classification on any level tells very little of what is of practical importance on other levels. For example, petty thieving may be committed by any one of the types of offenders on our diagram, who may in turn have been influenced by any of a number of different remotely antecedent or immediately inciting factors. As an instance, the feeble-minded individual, the least difficult of all to group, may be with his deficiency the result of several possible causes, may be directly incited towards crime by inward or outward influences apart from his defect, and may commit any of the diagramed offenses.

The criminal is not in himself to be grouped according to any logical system, and mere classification of either the antecedent or the consequent of his tendency leads only a short distance along the path of scientific and practical aims. The second is that each nucleus of fact cannot, in any fair-minded way, be interpreted as being or having a sole antecedent or a sole consequent. . . .

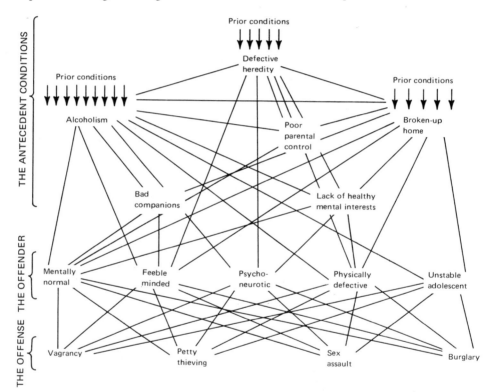

**Figure 26-1.** Diagram of Sequence or Conjunction of Some Simple Antecedents and Consequents

# 27 Mental Deficiency and Crime

*Edwin H. Sutherland*

Approximately 350 American studies of the intelligence of delinquents are accessible; these studies contain the results of psychometric tests of about 175,000 offenders. The present survey is an attempt to appraise this method of studying delinquents and to summarize the results which have accrued from its use.

The first conclusion derived from this survey is that the proportion of delinquents diagnosed feebleminded has been steadily decreasing. . . . This downward trend . . . may be interpreted in two ways: one is that intelligent people are relatively more likely to commit crime now than they were a generation ago, the other is that the methods of measurement of intelligence have changed. The invalidity of the first interpretation cannot be demonstrated, but the second seems much more plausible in view of the well-known changes in the methods of measurement of intelligence. About 1915 much criticism of mental testing methods developed. Many of the testers pointed out the lack of standardization in these tests. . . . In those early days of mental testing the influence of Goddard was very great; he had asserted that the more expert the mental tester the larger the proportion of delinquents he would find to be feebleminded. Many of the testers attempted to demonstrate their superiority in that manner. . . . The criticisms, discussion, and comparison of results did result in lowering the standards of normal intelligence so that many who had previously been classified as feebleminded came to be included among the normal. These changes appear to be the principal factor in the decrease of the proportion of delinquents diagnosed feebleminded.

A second conclusion from this survey of psychometric studies of delinquents is that the proportions of delinquents feebleminded have varied widely even in the studies made since 1919. In this group of more recent studies at one extreme stand two studies in which only 1 per cent of the delinquents were found to be feebleminded, at the other extreme one study in which 69 per cent were found to be feebleminded. One-fourth of these studies report

From Edwin H. Sutherland, "Mental Defficiency and Crime" in Kimball Young, *Social Attitudes* (New York: Holt, Rinehart & Winston, 1931). Reprinted with permission.

less than 10 per cent of the delinquents feebleminded, one fourth report from 10 to 21 per cent feebleminded, one fourth 22 to 36, and one fourth more than 36 per cent.

This scattering may be interpreted as the result of difference either in the intelligence of the groups tested or in the methods of diagnosing intelligence. Both interpretations are evidently partially correct. . . .

Methods of testing and methods of grading the tests vary widely. Some testers use an IQ of 75 as the upper limit of feeblemindedness, some use 70, and Dearborn and Burt maintain that the dividing line, so far as it can be located by tests, should be closer to 50 than to 70. Some take into account nothing except the tests, while others include a wide variety of other facts regarded as pertinent, especially race, nationality, formal education, economic status, and previous behavior. Some diagnose as feebleminded only those with low intelligence scores who are not found, in a complete physical and psychopathic examination, to be psychotic, epileptic, neurotic, psychopathic personalities, deteriorated by drugs or alcohol, or in other ways mentally or nervously abnormal, while others distribute the entire sample on a unilinear curve of intelligence. Some include only vocabulary ability in their tests, others include a wide variety of other abilities. Some administer tests when the delinquents first enter the institution, others after the delinquents have had considerable time in which to adjust to the institutional life. Some have a much better technique than others of putting the delinquent at ease and inducing him to perform to the maximum of his efficiency.

Mental tests of delinquents are certainly not standardized to the extent of eliminating important personal variations. . . .

A third conclusion from this survey of psychometric tests of delinquents is that feeblemindedness has not been demonstrated to be a generally important cause of delinquency. The studies from which this conclusion is derived are of two types; first, comparison of the mental scores of delinquent and of the general population; second, comparison of behavior of the feebleminded and normal minded.

The early mental testers were very certain that they had discovered the most important cause of crime. Goddard and others called the feebleminded "potential criminals" as though other people were not potential criminals. Moreover, Goddard stated that a diagnosis of feeblemindedness "fully explains any delinquency of which the child has been guilty." In accordance with that proposition many of the early testers, after finding 50 per cent of the delinquents tested feebleminded, concluded that feeblemindedness was the cause of 50 per cent of all delinquency and crime. The first difficulty about that conclusion was the lack of a satisfactory measure of the intelligence of the general population with which the delinquents were compared. . . .

A second reason for discounting the early conclusion regarding the importance of feeblemindedness as a cause of delinquency is that delinquents who

have been tested are always a selected portion of the entire delinquent population and are probably selected partly because of their feeblemindedness.
Delinquents who are smarter than policemen are less likely to be caught than
those who are less intelligent. . . .

A third objection to the conclusion regarding the importance of feeblemindedness as a cause of delinquency is the report by several investigators
that the group with the highest rate of delinquency is not the definitely deficient
group but the dull group. Wallim, especially, has stressed this. Some others
have reported that the superior group ranks next to the feebleminded group,
so that the delinquency rate drops from the deficient group to the normal and
then rises from the normal to the very superior. . . .

In view of the upward trend in the proportion of the general population
reported feebleminded, the downward trend in the proportion of delinquents
reported feebleminded, the striking similarity in some studies in the distribution
of intelligence of the delinquents who are tested and the portion of the general
population tested, especially by Army Tests, and the fact that delinquents who
are tested are likely to include an undue proportion of feebleminded because
of the greater probability of arrest, conviction, and commitment to institutions,
and the smaller probability of early parole, the claim of the early testers regarding the general importance of feeblemindedness as a cause of crime does not
seem to be substantiated.

The second type of studies from which a conclusion regarding the importance of feeblemindedness as a cause of delinquency has been derived, consists
of attempts to determine delinquency records of groups of feebleminded persons. . . . In general, though these studies . . . show some very large percentages
of delinquency among the feebleminded, they all need to be discounted because
of the selected nature of the group studied and because of the lack of a suitable
group for purposes of comparison. These studies, therefore, tend to substantiate
the conclusion that the great importance of feeblemindedness as a cause of
delinquency has not been demonstrated. . . .

A fifth conclusion is that these studies do not in general indicate that the
amount of intelligence exercises a decisive influence in determining goodness
of behavior on parole. . . .

A sixth conclusion is that no generally significant relationship between
intelligence and recidivism has been demonstrated. . . .

A final conclusion is that the type of crime is affected somewhat by
intelligence. Those convicted of fraud are generally a more intelligent group,
those convicted of sex offenses generally a less intelligent group. The evidence
is not conclusive, however, regarding many other particular offenses. . . .

The most significant conclusion from this evidence is that the relation
of feeblemindedness to delinquency cannot be determined by dealing with it
in isolation from other factors. We find feebleminded persons well behaved in
some situations, delinquent in others; even in one objective situation some

feebleminded persons become delinquent, other feebleminded persons do not become delinquent. The significance of feeblemindedness apparently can be determined only when studied in relation to a great many other personal and situational factors. . . .

Part IV:
Sociocultural Causes of Crime

# Introduction

The search for the causes of crime widened in scope as many theorists rejected both biological and psychological explanations. Human ecologists Clifford R. Shaw and Henry D. McKay conclude as a result of their studies of Chicago, Birmingham, Cleveland, Denver, Philadelphia, Richmond, and Seattle in 1929 and the years following that delinquency and crime are transmitted through a cultural and ecological system that supports such deviant attitudes and practices. Delinquency rates tend to be constant in delinquency areas despite the ethnic group composing the community at a particular time in history. Delinquency rates systematically decline as one moves away from the center of the city. To a large extent, slum delinquency and crime result from the intimate relationships of youth with older, more experienced criminals. These conclusions have been challenged by other criminologists such as sociologist Andrew Lind and delinquency specialist Sophia Robison who find that all cities do not follow these patterns. Sociologist William F. Whyte, in addition, finds that the urban slum, although unintegrated into the society surrounding it, is characterized by some degree of internal integration. Success in rackets and politics provides the deviant with prompt recognition and meaningful rewards. Studies by British analysts Terrence Morris and David M. Downes speak to the same issue. To some, delinquency is a response that children learn as they become members of delinquent groups within a delinquent subculture. To others, however, their activity reflects the values of a counterculture, which opposes conventional society. Some analysts relate delinquency and crime to subcultures of violence, processes of social deviance, exaggeration of particular social concerns, structural change, criminogenic culture, family relationships, poverty and economic factors, social-class relationships, and other sociocultural factors.

Psychiatrist Gustave Aschaffenburg of Germany (1866-1944) places great emphasis upon the role of society in crime causation, arguing that society is basically responsible both for criminal conduct, which emerges within society, and for the eradication of crime, which undermines social coherence. Consequently, penal judgments should be based on social (for example, habits, professions, chance elements), and to some extent biological criteria and not merely theological or metaphysical concepts of free will.

The further development of sociocultural thinking regarding crime is recorded in the selections that follow. Italian criminal lawyer, professor, and legislator Enrico Ferri (1856-1929) probes the character of criminal sociology, which is founded on a science of positive observation. Crime, Ferri idealistically contends, is a complex phenomenon involving not only biological, physical, and social elements, but such other influences as persons, things, times, and places.

163

To comprehend crime, one must understand the composite elements which make up the criminal act. Because so many elements enter into the criminal's actual violation, the idea that his act is one of free will is only an illusion. Criminal acts are not solely caused by social factors; biological and physiosocial elements must also be considered. Penal substitutes must be created to offer alternative means of social protection. Because traditional punishments' forms are ineffective, greater emphasis must be placed upon prevention. Ferri calls for complete renovation of the scientific method in its application to criminal social pathology. Because criminal man is not a normal man, society must have a wide range of alternatives available to deal with the man's problems.

Cyril Burt, writing in 1925, argues that it is not possible to differentiate sharply the delinquent from the nondelinquent. Delinquency is a matter of degree and is a form of behavior just as normal conduct is a form of behavior, a theme originally articulated by Émile Durkheim. Burt agrees with Ferri that crime is a product of multiple causes. Although heredity, environment and physical and psychological conditions are positively correlated with delinquency, no single factor is correlated to a very high degree. Some 170 factors relevant to delinquency may be classified into nine major categories.

The late-nineteenth-century French writer Henry Joly, however, sees the criminal as the voluntary architect of his own downfall, who alone bears responsibility and guilt for his actions. Crime is, he argues, a moral disorder, the point at which all egotistical or coarse human inclinations converge.

French philosopher-lawyer-behavioral scientist Gabriel Tarde (1843–1904), for example, concluded that the social environment is of ultimate significance in the development of a criminal pattern of conduct. Although chance influences a potential criminal career, at the bottom of every criminal career commitment, he held, are individual choices, which are in part imitation and, therefore, a product of the dominant judgment of the social group. The concept of crime depends upon the degree of public alarm and indignation which is evident in the definition of the criminal act. Crime is a form of learned behavior, a theme amplified in the middle 1900s by Edwin H. Sutherland. Men imitate one another to varying degrees depending upon the closeness of their contact and also upon whether the other's actions are regarded as inferior or superior. Men imitate the customs and fashions of others so that the more contact they have the more imitation takes place. The superior is often imitated by his inferior. If two mutually exclusive fashions or customs conflict, the newer one will be the more imitative.

Edwin H. Sutherland, drawing heavily from Tarde, proposes what has become known as the differential-association theory, arguing that criminal behavior is a product of the character of one's association with others and of the process one encounters in learning. First offering his theory in seven and later in nine propositions, Sutherland relates crime to human processes. Behavior is the same for all people. What differs is the type of act completed and the valuation placed upon that act. Criminal conduct is determined through a process of association with criminals even as legitimate conduct is learned through association with law-abiding persons. The frequency, consistency, intensity and duration of association determine in large degree the likelihood of criminal conduct. Although cultural conflict is the underlying cause of differential association, social organization is the basic cause of actual criminal conduct.

Seminal French sociologist Émile Durkheim (1858-1917), who focused primarily on social integration and social disorganization and contributed little to the philosophy of law, nevertheless defines a concept which has since been applied to criminal processes by Robert K. Merton and Richard A. Cloward and Lloyd E. Ohlin. Durkheim, who uses suicide as an example of deviant behavior, attributes the criminogenic process to more than learning and the association of relationships. The absence of norms and rules may create a condition of anomie, of nonbelonging. This may lead to deviant behavior. Egoistic suicide, he says, is a product of man's inability to find a life purpose; altruistic suicide is a result of concern for something beyond life itself and involves giving oneself for another or a cause; anomic suicide is a product of inadequate social regulation. Repressive law, Durkheim believed, has its origin in common beliefs and sentiments and is an index of the strength of the collective conscience of the group (society). Criminal conduct in society is both normal and necessary. It is useful to society because it permits the normal evolution of morality necessary to bring about change in law and in society. Individuality, even if expressed in criminal acts, needs to be acted out. If the balance between cultural aspirations and social opportunity is negated, deviant or criminal conduct results.

Contemporary American sociologist Robert K. Merton, extending Durkheim's concepts, maintains that anomie is a result of lack of coordination between the means and goal phases of the social structure. Deviance and crime are related to the uneven achievement of men in society. Although deviant conduct may be generated by lack of opportunity to succeed in normative terms or by an exaggerated emphasis on monetary goals, it is generally when the approved modes of acquiring common success symbols are restricted or eliminated for part of the population that antisocial behavior emerges on a large scale. When a person finds his aspirations thwarted, he searches for ways to escape from the unacceptable situation through illegitimate as well as legitimate means. Some social structures exert pressures upon certain people to commit deviating acts. When man's cultural aspirations and the institutional norms or acceptable procedures for achieving these goals do not mesh, deviance is a normal result.

Nineteenth-century Italian sociologist Napoleone Colajanni, anticipating the socialist explanation of crime, tends to disregard the emphasis upon cultural conflict and theorizes that delinquency and crime are products of historical phenomena and social need. Human behavior is related to ideas of morality and economic conditions. Criminal conduct is characterized by antisocial and antiindividual motives. War, industry, family, and marriage patterns, education, politics and revolutions, prostitution and vagrancy among others are products of the capitalist economic system and are directly related to the development of delinquency. When the economic system is unable to satisfy wants adequately, men naturally turn to crime for relief. The least possible delinquency in a society, Colajanni contends, results when the means of subsistence are secure, economic conditions are stable and the distribution of wealth is relatively equal.

Dutch criminologist-sociologist Willem Adriaan Bonger, who committed suicide on the eve of the Nazi invasion of the Netherlands in 1940, finds that crime involves more than the economic system. It is a serious immoral act which is harmful to the interests of the group. Egoistic tendencies alone do not make a criminal, but egotism brought about by the demands of the capitalistic system in the long run undermine social integration and make crime inevitable. In this situation, social reciprocity is lessened and the moral force that normally would help the man to combat an inclination toward criminal acts is weakened. A person with diminished social instincts, Bonger contends, has a greater likelihood of becoming a criminal; whether he does or not depends largely upon the environment. Because large differences exist between criminal offenders and offender types, crime should be divided into economic crimes against property, crimes for economic or noneconomic reasons, crimes with heterogeneous motives, and political crimes.

Frenchman A. Lacassagne, a member of the "French school" of criminal theory, concludes in a short selection translated from the original published in the late 1800s that, despite the orientation and direction of law, societies tend to have the criminals they deserve. They must be blamed for their emergence. Criminal offenders are characteristic products of their societies. Instinctive criminals commit crimes due to inherited or acquired penchants; insane criminals, because they are mentally ill; but action criminals are naturally inclined in this direction.

Belgian Adolphe Prins (1851–1919), a colleague of Lacassagne, defines what must be done to defend society against the abuses of the offenders which it produces. The mere repression of delinquency and crime is an inadequate solution to the problem. Society must assume responsibility for the protection of its members and for assisting those in need. This cannot be accomplished through a single approach but must be achieved through utilization of diverse programs and institutions designed to meet the varying needs of those who attack society.

Marc Ancel, writing in 1962, extends this basic conception, calling for a new social defense that rejects both traditionalism and positivism and presupposes a new penal policy. This social defense presupposes that criminal justice is relative; that its purpose is not to punish some fault according to an absolute, but rather to examine the social offense of a particular individual, considering his unconscious motivation. The efforts of scientists and lawyers must be coordinated both nationally and internationally if the long-range goal of social defense is to prevent crime in order to protect both society and the delinquent from himself. Rather than exclude the delinquent from the community, the new social defense calls for his reintegration within it so that the offender can "recover his place as a free man in that society in which he will no longer feel himself the enemy."

# 28

## Criminal Sociology and the Multiplicity of Causes

*Enrico Ferri*

### Criminal Sociology: The Program

The positive criminal school does not consist, as it seems convenient for many of its critics to feign to believe, only in the anthropological study of the criminal; it constitutes a complete renovation, a radical change of scientific method in the study of criminal social pathology and in the study of what is most effectual among the social and juridical remedies that social pathology presents. The science of crimes and punishments was formerly a doctrinal exposition of the syllogisms brought forth by the sole force of logical fantasy. Our school has made of it a science of positive observation, which, based on anthropology, psychology, and criminal statistics, as well as on criminal law and studies relevant to imprisonment, becomes the synthetic science to which I myself gave the name "Criminal Sociology." . . .

The juridical valuation of criminal acts strictly concerns the criminologist. There are two main reasons why he can no longer put off considering it. The first is to prevent laymen drawing extravagant and erroneous conclusions from the facts which belie the old theories; the second, that while the other juridical sciences are concerned with social relations (abstracting individual particularities which do not directly change their value) the doctrine of crimes and punishments, unlike them, has man, as he really lives and acts in the social medium, as its immediate object. It is clear that the classical criminologists would oppose this new scientific movement, were it only through the force of inertia. Accustomed as they are to build abstract theories with the aid of pure logic and without other tools than paper, pen, ink, and the volumes of their predecessors, it is natural that they should regret finding themselves forced, if not to make personal researches, at least to procure some positive knowledge of anthropology, psychology, and statistics. But the historical reasons for modern scientific thought, as we have indicated them above, render an increasing complexity in the science of crimes and punishments inevitably arising from the law that things must develop in becoming more and more complex, which is so in the

From Enrico Ferri, *Criminal Sociology* (New York: Appleton and Company, 1897). Reprinted with permission of Prentice-Hall, Inc.

169

physical as well as in the intellectual and moral order. Now, in recapitulating the most serious and most flagrant divergences between the new results of the positive sciences (which study man as a physio-psychic organism, born and living in the midst of a fixed physical and social medium) and the metaphysical doctrines on crime punishment and penal justice of the past, I think I can reduce them to the following points.

Among the fundamental bases of criminal and penal law as heretofore understood are these three postulates:

1.  The criminal has the same ideas, the same sentiments as any other man.
2.  The principal effect of punishment is to arrest the excess and the increase of crime.
3.  Man is endowed with free will or moral liberty and, for that reason, is morally guilty and legally responsible for his crimes.

On the other hand, one has only to go out of the scholastic circle of juridical studies and a priori affirmations to find in opposition to the preceding assertions these conclusions of the experimental sciences:

1.  Anthropology shows by facts that the delinquent is not a normal man; that on the contrary he represents a special class, a variation of the human race through organic and psychical abnormalities, either hereditary or acquired.
2.  Statistics prove that the appearance, increase, decrease, or disappearance of crime depends upon other reasons than the punishments prescribed by the codes and applied by the courts.
3.  Positive psychology has demonstrated that the pretended free will is a purely subjective illusion. . . .

The very purpose of this work is to prove that penal law, whether as a function exercised by society in self-defense, or as a collection of scientific principles intended to regulate this function, always has its reason for existence. But it will at the same time point out the thorough renovation which is being produced in the spirit and in the practical applications of penal law. And this renovation finds its synthetic expression in the following declaration: We should henceforth devote ourselves not to doctrinal criminal law but to positive criminal sociology. . . .

The inseparable concurrence of the anthropological, physical, and social factors in every form of human activity and on the variable importance of each of them in every particular case not only assist us to develop and give precision to our idea on the origin and nature of criminality but are useful as well in showing the insufficiency of the other group of hypotheses which are still to be examined. According to many of our critics, and especially those who have rarely or never studied criminals with a truly scientific method and by direct observation, criminality is a phenomenon of exclusively social origin, while showing one or another of the particular aspects which this kind of cause may take. There are some who maintain that the whole social medium is determined by economic conditions, and that consequently crime, in whatever form it presents itself, is but the effect of economic disease. . . . Yet I think that this theory should be supplemented by admitting in the first place that the economic conditions of each people are in turn the natural resultant of its racial energies which unfold in a given telluric medium; and by admitting in the second place that the moral sentiments, ideas, and political and legal institutions also have their own relatively autonomous existence, i.e., within the limits of the variations of a given economic constitution on which they also have their more or less superficial reaction but which are nevertheless worthy of being noticed. . . .

I consider the opinion inaccurate and prejudiced which holds that crime is exclusively or even principally the product of the social environment. . . . In the indissolubility and infinite complexity of natural causes, it is certain that every cause is also an effect and every effect in turn becomes a cause. Moreover, bearing in mind that I have said above, namely, that economic and social conditions are, in their turn, a resultant of racial energies in a given telluric medium, and that there is a relatively autonomous development of each order of social facts in the field of economic conditions—one sees that it is more positivistic to admit and define by scientific observations the respective and concomitant influences of the different factors of crime. . . .

Hence, in conclusion, we return to our fundamental assertion which should control not only criminal anthropology but all the inductions of criminal sociology: that crime, like all other human acts, is a phenomenon of complex origin, both biological and physio-social, with different modalities and degrees according to the different circumstances of persons and things, of times and places.

**29** The Multiplicity of Causes

*Cyril Burt*

What . . . are the commonest causes that tend to issue in crime? How can their nature and likelihood be learned? . . .

All the causes observed have been counted and classified. They fall into half a dozen main divisions. The frequency of a given factor among the delinquents, as compared with its frequency among the remainder, may be taken as indicating its relative importance, and the likelihood of its operation in any future set of cases. . . .

**Definition of Delinquent**

The offenses committed comprise, for the most part, such breaches of the law as would be punishable in an adult by penal servitude or imprisonment—stealing, burglary, damage, common assault, indecent assault, and soliciting; to this list must also be added certain other misdeeds which none but a child can commit, as truancy and being beyond parental control; and one or two, which, while offending against no explicit legal enactment, may become the ground for official intervention, for example, inordinate lying and sexual impropriety. . . .

There is, however, no sharp line of cleavage by which the delinquent may be marked off from the nondelinquent. Between them no deep gulf exists to separate the sinner from the saint, the white sheep from the black. It is all a problem of degree, of a brighter or a darker gray. This graded continuity, the normal melting into the abnormal by almost imperceptible shades, is entirely in accord with what we now know of most other forms of mental deviation. The insane, the neurotic, the mentally deficient are, none of them, to be thought of as types apart, anomalous specimens separated from the ordinary man by a profound and a definite gap; the extreme cases merge into the borderline, as the borderline merges into the average, with no sudden break or transition. It is the same with the moral faults of children; they run in an uninterrupted series, from the most

From Cyril Burt, *The Young Delinquent* (New York: Appleton Century Company, 1938). Reprinted with permission of Prentice-Hall, Inc.

heartless and persistent crimes that could possibly be pictured, up to the mere occasional naughtiness to which the most virtuous will at times give way. The line of demarcation is thus an arbitrary line, not a natural line; and delinquency is, at bottom, a social rather than a psychological concept. A child is to be regarded as technically a delinquent when his antisocial tendencies appear so grave that he becomes, or ought to become, the subject of official action. . . .

I have now worked through the whole list of characteristics discovered or discoverable in delinquents such as those we have been studying. . . .

Is there, we may ask in conclusion, any all-pervading principle, whether of causation or of treatment, deducible from our detailed discussions? When we glance back through page after page and turn in succession to table after table, one striking fact leaps out in bold relief—the fact of multiple determination. Crime is assignable to no single universal source, nor yet to two or three: it springs from a wide variety, and usually from a multiplicity, of alternative and converging influences. So violent a reaction, as may easily be conceived, is almost everywhere the outcome of a concurrence of subversive factors: it needs many coats of pitch to paint a thing thoroughly black. The nature of these factors and of their varying combinations differs greatly from one individual to another, and juvenile offenders, as is amply clear, are far from constituting a homogeneous class. . . .

Crime . . . is the outcome of many confluents.


**Variety of Major Factors**

Yet, in any given case, amid all the tangle of accessory factors, some single circumstance not infrequently stands out as the most prominent or the most influential. Often, as we have seen, it can be definitely established that the child in question showed no delinquent tendencies until the year of some unfortunate event. An illness, a new demoralizing friendship, the death or the remarriage of a parent, the emergence within the growing child himself of some fresh interest or instinct—some dated crisis of this kind has often ascertainably preceded, and perhaps has plainly precipitated, his first violation of the law. At times, and with the same abruptness, so soon as the untoward condition has been removed, his perversity has diminished and his outbreaks have ceased. In other instances, some salient quality of the child's own mind, existing from birth or inherited from his parents, goes far to explain his misconduct—a strong sex instinct, a weak and suggestible temper, or a general deficiency of common sense. In many cases, however, to look for one paramount influence is a more doubtful and precarious business; and to sift causative conditions into major and minor may be little more than an arbitrary assortment, based, it is true, on long inquiries and on many consultations, but of value only for a rough and summary review. If we restrict our reckoning to the main, predominating factors, thus singled out wherever possible, we are still confronted with a long catalogue of causes, each making straight for lawless conduct: and we may still count up as many as seventy different conditions, each forming, in one instance or another, the principal reason for some child's offense. . . .

All the conditions enumerated—hereditary, environmental, physical, and psychological—are positively correlated with delinquency; but no one of them singly to a very high degree. To attribute crime in general either to a predominantly hereditary or to a predominantly environmental origin appears accordingly impossible; in one individual the one type of factor may be preeminent; in another, the second; while, with a large assortment of cases, both seem, on an average and in the long run, to be of almost equal weight.

Judged by the coefficients, the following proves to be the order of importance of the various conditions we have reviewed: (1) defective discipline; (2) specific instincts; (3) general emotional instability; (4) morbid emotional conditions, mild rather than grave, generating or generated by so-called complexes; (5) a family history of vice or crime; (6) intellectual disabilities, such as backwardness or dullness; (7) detrimental interests, such as a passion for adventure, for the cinema, or for some particular person, together with a lack of any uplifting pursuits; (8) developmental conditions, such as adolescence or precocity in growth; (9) a family history of intellectual weakness; (10) defective family relationships—the absence of a father, the presence of a stepmother; (11) influences operating outside the home—as bad street companions and lack or excess of facilities for amusement; (12) a family history of temperamental disorder—of insanity or the like; (13) a family history of physical weakness; (14) poverty and its concomitants; and, last of all, (15) physical infirmity or weakness in the child himself.

Heredity appears to operate, not directly through the transmission of a criminal disposition as such, but rather indirectly, through such constitutional conditions as a dull or defective intelligence, an excitable and unbalanced temperament, or an overdevelopment of some single primitive instinct. Of environmental conditions, those obtaining outside the home are far less important than those obtaining within it; and within it, material conditions, such as poverty, are far less important than moral conditions, such as ill discipline, vice, and, most of all, the child's relations with his parents. Physical defects have barely half the weight of psychological and environmental. Psychological factors, whether due to heredity or to environment, are supreme both in number and strength over all the rest. Intellectual conditions are more serious than bodily, and emotional than intellectual; while psycho-analytic complexes everywhere provide a ready mechanism for the direction of overpowering instincts and of compressed emotional energy into open acts of crime. . . .

# 30 Crime: A Social Study
*Henri Joly*

## A. The Idea of Crime

Awareness of guilt and of the right to punish is one thing, but quite another is the formulation of a clear and logical criminal law, which we pretend to have successfully attained. Without doubt a good number of distinctions must be clarified in order to unravel the fundamental concepts of our codes. Certain writers view crime as an assault against the society, yet this idea of crime can only become precise when one has succeeded in distinguishing between the idea of a wrong done to an individual person and the idea of a sin, that is to say, the infraction of a law emanated from God Himself. Repression of a wrong done to an individual, one can say, is a matter of civil law; punishment of sin is a problem for religious authority. Properly stated, criminal law is an intermediate conception; it can break away and establish itself only by grace of the progress accomplished by the intelligence of the state's own laws. Such distinctions are assuredly plausible, they correspond to a division of social work by which one could acknowledge necessity. But the synthesis, which sees crime as a wrong and a sin at the same time, does not merit scorn. It is one view, perhaps confusing, but very interesting, and strives to embrace all of the truth. In summary, conscience preceded statute; those who wrote the law had to overcome the scruples of extremes of the conscience much more often than to impose or extend minor obligations.

## B. Criminal Association

The first form of association is parasitism. A parasite is a being that lives at the expense of another. In order to succeed better at this, it habitually installs itself either beside its victim or within him; animal or physiological parasites even introduce themselves into the person of the host and stay there for good.

The parasitism of which we would like to speak and in which we see a

From Henri C. Joly, *Le Crime: Étude Sociale* (Paris: Librairie Léopold Cerf, 1894).

complimentary criminal association has two characteristics: First, the individuals at whose expense the parasites live are responsible to a degree for the evil committed on them; second, the destruction inflicted by the parasites only serves to incite their voluntary dupes of hosts to proceed in their turn to more and more serious misdeeds. It is this twofold characteristic that makes parasitism deserving of emphasis in our study.

A healthy, active organism, developing regularly according to its species, rarely knows parasites. At least, it promptly succeeds in eliminating them without having been seriously attacked by them. However, all organisms that slacken or become exhausted as a result of deviation, decay, or excess fatally become the prey of the parasites. It is the same in social life.

At times one may either through naivete or stupidity allow himself to be penetrated and overrun by parasitism; even then the individual is partially responsible. Moreover, with what is commonly called corruption, that is to say, vice, begins a sort of association in which the parasite is not the only one guilty of the wrongdoings, small or large, that are committed. . . .

## C. Conclusion

In giving a clear idea of the nature of evil doers the criminal and his victim share a relationship of necessity and dependence. In this approach more than one reader will find undoubtedly that we have been too intent on distinguishing them from the insane and the sick and that we have exaggerated the responsibility that rests on them. Others will decide that we are too inclined to differentiate criminals from the rest of men, to explain the deterioration of their consciences in terms of influences from which very few know how to escape and by which few are completely unaffected.

But between these two ways of understanding the criminal there is no contradiction. In our eyes, the criminal is the voluntary artisan of his own downfall; he is guilty and responsible for it. Criminals do not form groups so isolated that there exists no other group of men, more or less guilty themselves, who provide a link to those whom the law respects. Crime is that culminating point at which all the egotistical or base inclinations of our nature converge. To study this form of evil is to study the common miseries of humanity; it is to contemplate the germs of immorality and injustice that tend to develop in each of us, that more or less always develop there, that always contribute to the perils of contagion for some people. Only seeing them under a magnifying glass or in these projections enables the hidden mysteries of nature to stand out to all eyes.

If crime is fundamentally a moral disorder done voluntarily, society is not obliged to wait until secular selection has eliminated the defective organism; it has the duty to take immediate and continuous measures to retard its actions and reduce the seriousness of the offense. . . . But if crime is also a social disorder, how can we close our eyes to the collective influences that encourage evil inclinations by offering a thousand temptations, a thousand facilities, that increase the audacity of the evil doers and diminish the capacity for resistance of honest people.

\* \* \*

The environment in which ordinary illnesses develop, subside, or sometimes even disappear is made up of elements whose study belongs to physics and chemistry. The environment of crime is society, it is the confluence not only of affection, sympathy, encouragement and cooperation, but also of rivalry, agreement, jealousy, hostility, and hate, which constitute the common life of humanity. All reflection, moral inspiration, and effort lead inevitably to personal conscience. But society is like an environment in which each sound emitted redoubles, reverberates, and finally produces a thousand echoes. It is in society that individual thought develops; becomes transformed, and organizes itself, and it does this for evil as well as for good.

\* \* \*

The moral illness that one calls crime is known to us, therefore, by its essence. It is necessary for us to examine more closely those factors that provoke it, unleash it, and spread it in the diverse parts of the great environment in which we live.

# 31

## The Laws of Imitation

*Gabriel Tarde*

Before anything else, we ought summarily to define and analyze the powerful, generally unconscious, always partly mysterious, action by means of which we account for all the phenomena of society, namely imitation. In order to judge of its inherent power, we must first of all observe its manifestations among idiots. In them the imitative inclination is no stronger than in ourselves, but it acts without encountering the obstacle which is met with in our ideas, our moral habits, and our wishes. . . .

All the important acts of social life are carried out under the domination of example. One procreates or one does not procreate, because of imitation; the statistics of the birth rate have shown us this. One kills or one does not kill, because of imitation; would we today conceive of the idea of fighting a duel or of declaring war, if we did not know that these things had always been done in the country which we inhabit? One kills oneself or one does not kill oneself, because of imitation. . . .

After this how can we doubt that one steals or does not steal, one assassinates or does not assassinate, because of imitation? But it is especially in the great tumultuous assemblages of our cities that this characteristic force of the social world ought to be studied. The great scenes of our revolutions cause it to break out, just as great storms are a manifestation of the presence of the electricity in the atmosphere, while it remains unperceived though none the less a reality in the intervals between them. . . .

Reciprocal imitation, when it is exercised over *similar* beliefs, and generally speaking, over *similar* psychological states, is a true multiplication of the intensity proper to these beliefs, to these various states, in each one of those who feel them simultaneously.

When, on the contrary, in imitating one another, several persons exchange *different* states, which is what ordinarily takes place in social life, when, for example, one communicates to the other a taste for Wagnerian music and in return the other communicates to him a love for realistic fiction; these persons

From Gabriel Tarde, *Penal Philosophy* (Boston: Little, Brown and Company, 1912). Reprinted with permission of Patterson-Smith Publishing Corporation.

no doubt establish between themselves a bond of mutual assimilation, just as when they express to each other two similar ideas or needs which take root in this manner. But in the first case, the assimilation is, for each of them, a *complication* of their internal state—this is essentially an effect of civilization—and in the second case the assimilation is, for each of them, a mere *reinforcement* of their inner life. Between these two cases there is the musical interval between unison and a chord. . . .

It is not immaterial to know whether the inclination to crime is the fruit of a bad family education or of a dangerous companionship. It is always either a family, or a sect, or a cafe full of comrades, which drives to crime the individual who is wavering; and, in this last case, the enthusiasm which carries him away recalls, to almost the very highest degree, the popular current which drives a rioter to commit murder.

#####

After these few words as to the force and the forms of imitation, we must set forth its general laws, which must be applied to crime as well as to every other aspect of societies. But the limits of this work will only allow us a brief indication of the subject. We already know that the example of any man, almost like the attraction of a body, radiates around himself, but with an intensity which becomes weaker as the distance of the men touched by his ray increases. "Distance" should not here be understood merely in the geometrical sense, but especially in the psychological sense of the word; the increase in the relations established by correspondence or by printing, of the intellectual communication of all kinds between fellow-citizens scattered over a vast territory, has the effect of diminishing in this sense the distance between them. Thus it may happen, let us repeat, that the honest example of an entire surrounding but distant society may be neutralized in the heart of a young vagabond by the influence of a few companions. From the economic, philological, religious, and political point of view, it is the same. . . .

Now instead of taking each example by itself, let us examine the connection between several examples and let us seek to find the result of the exchange. First of all, however mean and however despised an individual may be, repeated contact with him does not fail to stamp the highest and the proudest persons with a certain vague tendency to copy him. We have the proof of this in the contagion of *accents*; the proudest master, if he lives alone in the country with his servants, eventually borrows some of their intonations and even of their phrases. . . . [In] our societies, the impressive action exercised by the example of slaves upon their masters, of children upon adults, of the laity upon the clergy (in the prosperous days of the theocracy), of the ignorant upon the literate, the ingenuous upon the clever, the poor upon the rich, the plebians upon the patricians (in the prosperous period of the aristocracy), of the inhabitants of the country upon the inhabitants of the cities, of the provincials upon the Parisians,

in a word, of the inferior upon the superior, and only take into account the opposite action, which is the true explanation of history. There is during every
period a recognized superiority, sometimes wrongly recognized as such. It is the
privilege of the man who, richer in needs and ideas, has more examples to give
than he has to receive. The unequal exchange of examples, such as it is governed
by this law, has the effect of causing the social world to progress towards a
leveling state, which may be compared to that universal uniformity of temperature which the law of the radiation of the heat of bodies has a tendency to
establish.

* * *

It is especially in fostering the spread of example that a social hierarchy is
useful; an aristocracy is a fountain reservoir necessary for the fall of imitation in
successive cascades, successively enlarged. If industry on a large scale has become
a possibility in our day, if the diffusion of needs, of tastes, of identical ideas in
the hearts of immense masses of people has opened up the vast outlets which it
needs, is it not to the old inequalities that we are indebted for this existing
equality? . . .

# # # # #

Let us see how all this applies to our subject. Strange as it may seem, there
are serious reasons for maintaining that the vices and the crimes of today, which
are to be found in the lowest orders of the people, descended to them from
above. In every nascent or renascent society when the producing of wine becomes
difficult or limited, drunkenness is a royal luxury and a privilege of the aristocracy. It is quite certain that the kings of Homer's time got drunk far more often
than did their subjects, the Merovingian chiefs than their vassals, and the lords of
the Middle Ages than their serfs. . . .

The smoking habit, at present so widespread in every sort of surroundings,
perhaps already more widespread among the people than among the socially
elect, where they have begun to combat this passion, was propagated in the same
manner. James I of England, Roscher tells us, put a very heavy tax upon tobacco
in 1604, "because," says the law, "the lowest classes, incited by the example of
the upper classes, impair their health, taint the air, and corrupt the soil." The
irreligiousness of the masses, which today here and there contrasts with the
relative religiousness of the last survivors of the old aristocracy, is just as much
due to this same cause. Vagabondage, under its thousand and one existing forms,
is an essentially plebian offense. but by going back into the past, it would not be
very difficult to connect our vagabonds, our street singers, with the noble pilgrims and the noble minstrels of the Middle Ages.

Poaching, another hotbed of crime, which in the past, together with smuggling, has played a part which may be compared with that played by vagabond-

age at the present time, is still more directly connected with the life of the lords. . . .

Poisoning is now a crime of the illiterate; as late as the seventeenth century it was the crime of the upper classes, as is proven by the epidemic of poisonings which flourished at the court of Louis XIV, from 1670 to 1680, following the importation of certain poisons by the Italian Exili. . . .

Must not murder by bravos, by "bravi," so much used in Germany and Italy in the Middle Ages, have been the transition phase which homicide passed through in descending from the highest stratum of society to the lowest? The fact remains that the power to kill, from which was derived the right to kill, has been, in every primitive society, the distinguishing indication of the upper classes. . . .

Arson, the crime of the lower classes today, was one of the prerogatives of the feudal lords. . . . Counterfeiting today takes refuge in a few caverns in the mountains, in a few underground places in towns; we know that for a long time it was a royal monopoly. . . . Finally theft, so degrading in our day, has had a brilliant past. Montaigne tells us, without being very indignant about it, that many young gentlemen of his acquaintance, to whom their fathers did not give enough money, got funds by stealing. . . .

[The] last descendants of these pickpockets of feudal times are now the most unblemished representatives of French honor and honesty! If heredity were the principal "factor" as far as morality is concerned, could this be as it is? . . . This propagation from those above to those below applies to urban crime and rural crime equally well. When, in a country such as Sicily, we see country brigandage flourish by reason of a continual recruiting among the lower agri- cultural classes, we may be sure that at an earlier period the upper rural classes, which at the present time limit themselves to protecting this bold plundering, themselves used formerly to practice it. . . .

\* \* \* \* \*

While crime formerly spread, like every industrial product, like every good or bad idea, from the nobility to the people, and while the nobility, in those remote times, drew to itself the audacious and criminal elements of the people, today we can see crime spreading from the great cities to the country, from the capitals to the provinces, and these capitals and great cities having an irresistible attraction for the outcasts and scoundrels of the country, or the provinces, who hasten to them to become civilized after their own manner, a new kind of en- nobling. For the time being this latter fact is a fortunate one for the provinces, which are being purified by means of this emigration and passing through an era of comparative security. Never, perhaps, in rural regions has there been less fear of assassination and even of robbery with violence than at the present time. But unfortunately the attraction of the great cities for criminals is closely connected with the influence exercised by them over the remainder of the nation, with the fascinating power their example has in all matters. As a consequence it is to be feared that the benefits derived from this betterment of conditions in the provinces is but temporary. The capitals send to the provinces not only their political and literary likes and dislikes, their style of wit or folly, the cut of their clothes, the shape of their hats and their accent, but they also send their crimes and their misdemeanors.

Indecent assault upon children is an essentially urban crime, as is demonstrated by its chart; in its spread it is seen to form a dark spot around the great cities. Each variety of murder or theft invented by evil genius is born or takes root in Paris, Marseilles, Lyons, etc., before becoming widespread throughout France. . . .

With regard to thefts the same thing applies. There is not a single means of swindling employed at village fairs which did not first see the light of day upon a sidewalk of Paris. . . .

# The Differential Association Theory

## Edwin H. Sutherland

The following statement refers to the process by which a particular person comes
to engage in criminal behavior:

1. *Criminal behavior is learned.* Negatively, this means that criminal behavior is not inherited, as such; also, the person who is not already trained in
crime does not invent criminal behavior, just as a person does not make mechanical inventions unless he has had training in mechanics.

2. *Criminal behavior is learned in interaction with other persons in a process
of communication.* This communication is verbal in many respects but includes
also "the communication of gestures."

3. *The principal part of the learning of criminal behavior occurs within
intimate personal groups.* Negatively, this means that the impersonal agencies
of communication, such as movies and newspapers, play a relatively unimportant
part in the genesis of criminal behavior.

4. *When criminal behavior is learned, the learning includes (a) techniques of
committing the crime, which are sometimes very complicated, sometimes very
simple; (b) the specific direction of motives, drives, rationalizations, and attitudes.*

5. *The specific direction of motives and drives is learned from definitions
of the legal codes as favorable or unfavorable.* In some societies an individual
is surrounded by persons who invariably define the legal codes as rules to be
observed, while in others he is surrounded by persons whose definitions are
favorable to the violation of the legal codes. In our American society these
definitions are almost always mixed, with the consequence that we have culture
conflict in relation to the legal codes.

6. *A person becomes delinquent because of an excess of definitions favorable to violation of law over definitions unfavorable to violation of law.* This is
the principle of differential association. It refers to both criminal and anticriminal associations and has to do with counteracting forces. When persons

From Edwin H. Sutherland and Donald R. Cressey, *Criminology* (New York: J.B. Lippincott Company). Reprinted with permission of the publisher, J.B. Lippincott Company.
© 1966.

become criminal, they do so because of contacts with criminal patterns and also because of isolation from anticriminal patterns. Any person inevitably assimilates the surrounding culture unless other patterns are in conflict; a Southerner does not pronounce "r" because other Southerners do not pronounce "r." Negatively, this proposition of differential association means that associations which are neutral so far as crime is concerned have little or no effect on the genesis of criminal behavior. Much of the experience of a person is neutral in this sense, e.g., learning to brush one's teeth. This behavior has no negative or positive effect on criminal behavior except as it may be related to associations which are concerned with the legal codes. This neutral behavior is important especially as an occupier of the time of a child so that he is not in contact with criminal behavior during the time he is so engaged in the neutral behavior.

7. *Differential associations may vary in frequency, duration, priority, and intensity.* This means that associations with criminal behavior and also associations with anticriminal behavior vary in those respects. "Frequency" and "duration" as modalities of associations are obvious and need no explanation. "Priority" is assumed to be important in the sense that lawful behavior developed in early childhood may persist throughout life, and also that delinquent behavior developed in early childhood may persist throughout life. This tendency, however, has not been adequately demonstrated, and priority seems to be important principally through its selective influence. "Intensity" is not precisely defined but it has to do with such things as the prestige of the source of a criminal or anticriminal pattern and with emotional reactions related to the associations. In a precise description of the criminal behavior of a person these modalities would be stated in quantitative form and a mathematical ratio be reached. A formula in this sense has not been developed, and the development of such a formula would be extremely difficult.

8. *The process of learning criminal behavior by association with criminal and anticriminal patterns involves all of the mechanisms that are involved in any other learning.* Negatively, this means that the learning of criminal behavior is not restricted to the process of imitation. A person who is seduced, for instance, learns criminal behavior by association, but this process would not ordinarily be described as imitation.

9. *While criminal behavior is an expression of general needs and values, it is not explained by those general needs and values since noncriminal behavior is an expression of the same needs and values.* Thieves generally steal in order to secure money, but likewise honest laborers work in order to secure money. The attempts by many scholars to explain criminal behavior by general drives and values, such as the happiness principle, striving for social status, the money motive, or frustration, have been and must continue to be futile since they explain lawful behavior as completely as they explain criminal behavior. They are similar to respiration, which is necessary for any behavior but which does not differentiate criminal from noncriminal behavior.

It is not necessary, at this level of explanation, to explain why a person has the associations which he has; this certainly involves a complex of many things. In an area where the delinquency rate is high, a boy who is sociable, gregarious, active, and athletic is very likely to come in contact with the other boys in the neighborhood, learn delinquent behavior from them, and become a gangster; in the same neighborhood the psychopathic boy who is isolated, introverted, and inert may remain at home, not become acquainted with the other boys in the neighborhood, and not become delinquent. In another situation, the sociable, athletic, aggressive boy may become a member of a scout troop and not become involved in delinquent behavior. The person's associations are determined in a general context of social organization. A child is ordinarily reared in a family; the place of residence of the family is determined largely by family income; and the delinquency rate is in many respects related to the rental value of the houses. Many other aspects of social organization affect the kinds of associations a person has.

The preceding explanation of criminal behavior purports to explain the criminal and noncriminal behavior of individual persons. As indicated earlier, it is possible to state sociological theories of criminal behavior which explain the criminality of a community, nation, or other group. The problem, when thus stated, is to account for variations in crime rates and involves a comparison of the crime rates of various groups or the crime rates of a particular group at different times. The explanation of a crime rate must be consistent with the explanation of the criminal behavior of the person, since the crime rate is a summary statement of the number of persons in the group who commit crimes and the frequency with which they commit crimes. One of the best explanations of crime rates from this point of view is that a high crime rate is due to social disorganization. The term "social disorganization" is not entirely satisfactory and it seems preferable to substitute for it the term "differential social organization." The postulate on which this theory is based, regardless of the name, is that crime is rooted in the social organization and is an expression of that social organization. A group may be organized for criminal behavior or organized against criminal behavior. Most communities are organized for both criminal and anticriminal behavior and in that sense the crime rate is an expression of the differential group organization. Differential group organization as an explanation of variations in crime rates is consistent with the differential association theory of the process by which persons become criminals.

# 33 On Anomie

## Emile Durkheim

[Society] is not only something attracting the sentiments and activities of individuals with unequal force. It is also a power controlling them. There is a relation between the way this regulative action is performed and the social suicide rate.

It is a well-known fact that economic crises have an aggravating effect on the suicidal tendency.

In Vienna, in 1873 a financial crisis occurred which reached its height in 1874; the number of suicides immediately rose. From 141 in 1872, they rose to 153 in 1873 and 216 in 1874. The increase in 1874 is 53 per cent above 1872 and 41 percent above 1873. What proves this catastrophe to have been the sole cause of the increase is the special prominence of the increase when the crisis was acute, or during the first four months of 1874. From January 1 to April 30 there had been 48 suicides in 1871, 44 in 1872, 43 in 1873; there were 73 in 1874. The increase is 70 per cent. The same crisis occurring at the same time in Frankfurt-on-Main produced the same effects there. In the years before 1874, 22 suicides were committed annually on the average; in 1874 there were 32, or 45 per cent more.

The famous crash is unforgotten which took place on the Paris Bourse during the winter of 1882. Its consequences were felt not only in Paris but throughout France. From 1874 to 1886 the average annual increase was only 2 per cent; in 1882 it was 7 per cent. Moreover, it was unequally distributed among the different times of the year, occurring principally during the first three months or at the very time of the crash. Within these three months alone 59 per cent of the total rise occurred.

\* \* \*

If . . . industrial or financial crises increase suicides, this is not because they cause poverty, since crises of prosperity have the same result; it is because they are crises, that is, disturbances of the collective order. Every disturbance of equilibrium, even though it achieves greater comfort and a heightening of general vitality, is an impulse to voluntary death. Whenever serious readjustments take place in the social order, whether or not due to a sudden growth or to an unexpected catastrophe, men are more inclined to self-destruction. How is this possible? How can something considered generally to improve existence serve to detach men from it? . . .

No living being can be happy or even exist unless his needs are sufficiently proportioned to his means. In other words, if his needs require more than can be granted, or even merely something of a different sort, they will be under continual friction and can only function painfully. Movements incapable of production without pain tend not to be reproduced. Unsatisfied tendencies atrophy, and as the impulse to live is merely the result of all the rest, it is bound to weaken as the others relax.

* * *

Man's characteristic privilege is that the bond he accepts is not physical but moral; that is, social. He is governed not by a material environment brutally imposed on him, but by a conscience superior to his own, the superiority of which he feels. Because the greater, better part of his existence transcends the body, he escapes the body's yoke, but is subject to that of society.

But when society is disturbed by some painful crisis or by beneficent but abrupt transitions, it is momentarily incapable of exercising this influence; thence come the sudden rises in the curve of suicides. . . .

In the case of economic disasters, indeed, something like a declassification occurs which suddenly casts certain individuals into a lower state than their previous one. Then they must reduce their requirements, restrain their needs, learn greater self-control. All the advantages of social influence are lost so far as they are concerned; their moral education has to be recommenced. But society cannot adjust them instantaneously to this new life and teach them to practice the increased self-repression to which they are unaccustomed. So they are not adjusted to the condition forced on them, and its very prospect is intolerable; hence the suffering which detaches them from a reduced existence even before they have made trial of it.

It is the same if the source of the crisis is an abrupt growth of power and wealth. Then, truly, as the conditions of life are changed, the standard according to which needs were regulated can no longer remain the same; for it varies with social resources, since it largely determines the share of each class of producers. The scale is upset; but a new scale cannot be immediately improvised. Time is required for the public conscience to reclassify men and things. So long as the social forces thus freed have not regained equilibrium, their respective values are unknown and so all regulation is lacking for a time. The limits are unknown between the possible and the impossible, what is just and what is unjust, legitimate claims and hopes and those which are immoderate. Consequently, there is no restraint upon aspirations. If the disturbance is profound, it affects even the principles controlling the distribution of men among various occupations. Since the relations between various parts of society are necessarily modified, the ideas expressing these relations must change. Some particular class especially favored by the crisis is no longer resigned to its former lot, and, on the other hand, the example of its greater good fortune arouses all sorts of jealousy below and about it. Appetites, not being controlled by public opinion become disoriented, no longer recognize the limits proper to them. Besides, they are at the same time seized by a sort of natural erethism simply by the greater intensity of public life. With increased prosperity desires increase. At the very moment when traditional rules have lost their authority, the richer prize offered these appetites stimulates them and makes them more exigent and impatient of control. The state of de-regulation or anomie is thus further heightened by passions being less disciplined, precisely when they need more disciplining.

* * *

Anomie, therefore, is a regular and specific factor in suicide in our modern societies; one of the springs from which the annual contingent feeds. So we have here a new type to distinguish from the others. It differs from them in its dependence, not on the way in which individuals are attached to society, but on how it regulates them. Egoistic suicide results from man's no longer finding a basis for existence in life; altruistic suicide, because this basis for existence appears to man situated beyond life itself. The third sort of suicide . . . results from man's activity's lacking regulation and his consequent sufferings. By virtue of its origin we shall assign this last variety the name of *anomic suicide.*

Certainly, this and egoistic suicide have kindred ties. Both spring from society's insufficient presence in individuals. But the sphere of its absence is not the same in both cases. In egoistic suicide it is deficient in truly collective activity, thus depriving the latter of object and meaning. In anomie suicide, society's influence is lacking in the basically individual passions, thus leaving them without a checkrein. In spite of their relationship, therefore, the two types are independent of each other. We may offer society everything social in us, and still be unable to control our desires; one may live in an anomic state without being egoistic, and vice versa. These two sorts of suicide therefore do not draw their chief recruits from the same social environments; one has its principal field among intellectual careers, the world of thought—the other, the industrial or commercial world.

# 34 Anomie and Crime

*Robert K. Merton*

Among the elements of social and cultural structure, two are important for our purposes. These are analytically separable although they merge imperceptibly in concrete situations. The first consists of culturally defined goals, purposes, and interests. It comprises a frame of aspirational reference. These goals are more or less integrated and involve varying degrees of prestige and sentiment. They constitute a basic, but not exclusive, component of what Linton aptly has called "designs for group living." Some of these cultural aspirations are related to the original drives of man, but they are not determined by them. The second phase of the social structure defines, regulates, and controls the acceptable modes of achieving these goals. Every social group invariably couples its scale of desired ends with moral or institutional regulation of permissible and required procedures for attaining these ends. These regulatory norms and moral imperatives do not necessarily coincide with technical or efficiency norms. Many procedures which from the standpoint of *particular individuals* would be most efficient in securing desired values, e.g., illicit oil-stock schemes, theft, fraud, are ruled out of the institutional area of permitted conduct. The choice of expedients is limited by the institutional norms.

To say that these two elements, culture goals and institutional norms, operate jointly is not to say that the ranges of alternative behaviors and aims bear some constant relation to one another. The emphasis upon certain goals may vary independently of the degree of emphasis upon institutional means. There may develop a disproportionate, at times, a virtually exclusive, stress upon the value of specific goals, involving relatively slight concern with the institutionally appropriate modes of attaining these goals. The limiting case in this direction is reached when the range of alternative procedures is limited only by the technical rather than institutional considerations. Any and all devices which promise attainment of the all important goal would be permitted in this hypothetical polar case. This constitutes one type of cultural malintegration. A second polar type is found in groups where activities originally conceived as

From Robert K. Merton, "Social Structure and Anomie," *American Sociological Review* 3 (October 1938). Reprinted by permission of the author.

instrumental are transmuted into ends in themselves. The original purposes are forgotten and ritualistic adherence to institutionally prescribed conduct becomes virtually obsessive. Stability is largely ensured while change is flouted. The range of alternative behaviors is severely limited. There develops a tradition-bound, sacred society characterized by neophobia. The occupational psychosis of the bureaucrat may be cited as a case in point. . . . Finally, there are the intermediate types of groups where a balance between culture goals and institutional means is maintained. These are the significantly integrated and relatively stable, though changing groups.

An effective equilibrium between the two phases of the social structure is maintained as long as satisfactions accrue to individuals who conform to both constraints, viz., satisfactions from the achievement of the goals and satisfactions emerging directly from the institutionally canalized modes of striving to attain these ends. Success, in such equilibrated cases, is twofold. Success is reckoned in terms of the product and in terms of the process, in terms of the outcome and in terms of activities. Continuing satisfactions must derive from sheer *participation* in a competitive order as well as from eclipsing one's competitors if the order itself is to be sustained. The occasional sacrifices involved in institutionalized conduct must be compensated by socialized rewards. The distribution of statuses and roles through competition must be so organized that positive incentives for conformity to roles and adherence to status obligations are provided *for every position* within the distributive order. Aberrant conduct, therefore, may be viewed as a symptom of dissociation between culturally defined aspirations and socially structured means.

Of the types of groups which result from the independent variation of the two phases of the social structure, we shall be primarily concerned with the first, namely, that involving a disproportionate accent on goals. This statement must be recast in a proper perspective. In no group is there an absence of regulatory codes governing conduct, yet groups do vary in the degree to which these folkways, mores, and institutional controls are effectively integrated with the more diffuse goals which are part of the culture matrix. Emotional convictions may cluster about the complex of socially acclaimed ends, meanwhile shifting their support from the culturally defined implementation of these ends. As we shall see, certain aspects of the social structure may generate countermores and antisocial behavior precisely because of differential emphases on goals and regulations. In the extreme case, the latter may be so vitiated by the goal-emphasis that the range of behavior is limited only by considerations of technical expediency. The sole significant question then becomes, which available means is most efficient in netting the socially approved value? The technically most feasible procedure, whether legitimate or not, is preferred to the institutionally prescribed conduct. As this process continues, the integration of the society becomes tenuous and anomie ensues.

Thus, in competitive athletics, when the aim of victory is shorn of its institutional trappings and success in contests becomes construed as "winning the game" rather than "winning through circumscribed modes of activity," a premium is implicitly set upon the use of illegitimate but technically efficient means. . . .

Of course, this process is not restricted to the realm of sport. The process whereby exaltation of the end generates a *literal demoralization,* i.e., a deinstitutionalization of the means is one which characterizes many groups in which the two phases of the social structure are not highly integrated. The extreme emphasis upon the accumulation of wealth as a symbol of success in our own society militates against the completely effective control of institutionally regulated modes of acquiring a fortune. Fraud, corruption, vice, crime, in short, the entire catalog of proscribed behavior, becomes increasingly common when the emphasis on the *culturally induced* success-goal becomes divorced from a coordinated institutional emphasis. . . .

The competitive order is maintained, but the frustrated and handicapped individual who cannot cope with this order drops out. Defeatism, quietism and resignation are manifested in escape mechanisms which ultimately lead the individual to "escape" from the requirements of the society. It is an expedient which arises from continued failure to attain the goal by legitimate measures and from an inability to adopt the illegitimate route because of internalized prohibitions and institutionalized compulsives, *during which process the supreme value of the success-goal has as yet not been renounced.* The conflict is resolved by eliminating *both* precipitating elements, the goals and means. The escape is complete, the conflict is eliminated and the individual is socialized.

Be it noted that where frustration derives from the inaccessibility of effective institutional means for attaining economic or any other type of highly valued "success," that Adaptations II, III, and V (innovation, ritualism and rebellion) are also possible. The result will be determined by the particular personality, and thus, the *particular* cultural background, involved. Inadequate socialization will result in the innovation response whereby the conflict and frustration are eliminated by relinquishing the institutional means and retaining the success-aspiration; an extreme assimilation of institutional demands will lead to ritualism wherein the goal is dropped as beyond one's reach but conformity to the mores persists; and rebellion occurs when emancipation from the reigning standards, due to frustration or to marginalist perspectives, leads to the attempt to introduce a "new social order."

Our major concern is with the illegitimacy adjustment. This involves the use of conventionally proscribed but frequently effective means of attaining at least the simulacrum of culturally defined success—wealth, power, and the like. As we have seen, this adjustment occurs when the individual has assimilated the cultural emphasis on success without equally internalizing the morally prescribed norms governing means for its attainment. The question arises, Which phases of our social structure predispose toward this mode of adjustment;

We may examine a concrete instance, effectively analyzed by Lohman,[1] which provides a clue to the answer. Lohman has shown that specialized areas of vice in the near North Side of Chicago constitute a "normal" response to a situation where the cultural emphasis upon pecuniary success has been absorbed, but where there is little access to conventional and legitimate means for attaining such success. The conventional occupational opportunities of persons in this area are almost completely limited to manual labor. Given our cultural stigmatization of manual labor, and its correlate, the prestige of white collar work, it is clear that the result is a strain toward innovational practices. The limitation of opportunity to unskilled labor and the resultant low income cannot compete *in terms of conventional standards of achievement* with the high income from organized vice.

For our purposes, this situation involves two important features. First, such antisocial behavior is in a sense "called forth" by certain conventional values of the culture *and* by the class structure involving differential access to the approved opportunities for legitimate, prestige-bearing pursuit of the culture goals. The lack of high integration between the means-and-end elements of the cultural pattern and the particular class structure combine to favor a heightened frequency of antisocial conduct in such groups. The second consideration is of equal significance. Recourse to the first of the alternative responses, legitimate effort, is limited by the fact that the actual advance toward desired success-symbols through conventional channels is, despite our persisting open-class ideology, relatively rare and difficult for those handicapped by little formal education and few economic resources. The dominant pressure of group standards of success is, therefore, on the gradual attenuation of legitimate, but by and large ineffective, strivings and the increasing use of illegitimate, but more or less effective, expedients of vice and crime. The cultural demands made on persons in this situation are incompatible. On the one hand, they are asked to orient their conduct toward the prospect of accumulating wealth and on the other, they are largely denied effective opportunities to do so institutionally. The consequences of such structural inconsistency are psychopathological personality, and/or antisocial conduct, and/or revolutionary activities. The equilibrium between culturally designated means and ends becomes highly unstable with the progressive emphasis on attaining the prestige-laden ends by any means whatsoever. Within this context, Capone represents the triumph of amoral intelligence over morally prescribed "failure," when the channels of vertical mobility are closed or narrowed *in a society which places a high premium on economic affluence and social ascent for* all *its members.*

This last qualification is of primary importance. It suggests that other phases of the social structure, besides the extreme emphasis on pecuniary success, must be considered if we are to understand the social sources of antisocial behavior. A high frequency of deviate behavior is not generated simply by "lack of opportunity" or by this exaggerated pecuniary emphasis. A comparatively rigidified class structure, a feudalistic or caste order, may limit such opportunities far beyond the point which obtains in our society today. It is only when a system of cultural values extols, virtually above all else, certain *common* symbols of success *for the population at large* while its social structure rigorously restricts or completely eliminates access to approved modes of acquiring these symbols *for a considerable part of the same population,* that antisocial behavior ensues on a considerable scale. In other words, our egalitarian ideology denies by implication the existence of noncompeting groups and individuals in the pursuit of pecuniary success. The same body of success-symbols is held to be desirable for all. These goals are held to *transcend class lines,* not to be bounded by them, yet the actual social organization is such that there exit class differentials in the accessibility of these *common* success-symbols. Frustration and thwarted aspiration lead to the search for avenues of escape from a culturally induced intolerable situation; or unrelieved ambition may eventuate in illicit attempts to acquire the dominant values. The American stress of pecuniary success and ambitiousness for all thus invites exaggerated anxieties, hostilities, neuroses and antisocial behavior.

This theoretical analysis may go far toward explaining the varying correlations between crime and poverty. Poverty is not an isolated variable. It is one in a complex of interdependent social and cultural variables. When viewed in such a context, it represents quite different states of affairs. Poverty as such, and consequent limitation of opportunity, are not sufficient to induce a conspicuously high rate of criminal behavior. Even the often mentioned "poverty in the midst of plenty" will not necessarily lead to this result. Only insofar as poverty and associated disadvantages in competition for the culture values approved for *all* members of the society is linked with the assimilation of a cultural emphasis on monetary accumulation as a symbol of success is antisocial conduct a "normal" outcome. Thus, poverty is less highly correlated with crime in southeastern Europe than in the United States. The possibilities of vertical mobility in these European areas would seem to be fewer than in this country, so that neither poverty per se nor its association with limited opportunity is sufficient to account for the varying correlations. It is only when the full configuration is considered, poverty, limited opportunity and a commonly shared system of success symbols, that we can explain the higher association between poverty and crime in our society than in others where rigidified class structure is coupled with *differential class symbols of achievement.*

In societies such as our own, the pressure of prestige-bearing success tends to eliminate the effective social constraint over means employed to this end. "The-end-justified-the-means" doctrine becomes a guiding tenet for action when the cultural structure unduly exalts the end and the social organization unduly limits possible recourse to approved means. Otherwise put, this notion and associated behavior reflect a lack of cultural coordination. In international relations, the effects of this lack of integration are notoriously apparent. An emphasis upon national power is not readily coordinated with an inept organization of legitimate, i.e., internationally defined and accepted, means for attaining this goal. The result is a tendency toward the abrogation of international law, treaties become scraps of paper, "undeclared warfare" serves as a technical evasion, the bombing of civilian populations is rationalized, just as the same societal situation induces the same sway of illegitimacy among individuals.

The social order we have described necessarily produces this "strain toward dissolution." The pressure of such an order is upon outdoing one's competitors. The choice of means within the ambit of institutional control will persist as long as the sentiments supporting a competitive system, i.e., deriving from the possibility of outranking competitors and hence enjoying the favorable response of others, are distributed throughout the entire system of activities and are not confined merely to the final result. A stable social structure demands a balanced distribution of affect among its various segments. When there occurs a shift of emphasis from the satisfactions deriving from competition itself to almost exclusive concern with successful competition, the resultant stress leads to the breakdown of the regulatory structure. With the resulting attenuation of the institutional imperatives, there occurs an approximation of the situation erroneously held by utilitarians to be typical of society generally wherein calculations of advantage and fear of punishment are the sole regulating agencies. In such situations, as Hobbes observed, force and fraud come to constitute the sole virtues in view of their relative efficiency in attaining goals—which were for him, of course, not culturally derived.

It should be apparent that the foregoing discussion is not pitched on a moralistic plane. Whatever the sentiments of the writer or reader concerning the ethical desirability of coordinating the means-and-goals phases of the social structure, one must agree that lack of such coordination leads to anomie. Insofar as one of the most general functions of social organization is to provide a basis for calculability and regularity of behavior, it is increasingly limited in effectiveness as these elements of the structure become dissociated. At the extreme, predictability virtually disappears and what may be properly termed cultural chaos or anomie intervenes.

This statement, being brief, is also incomplete. It has not included an exhaustive treatment of the various structural elements which predispose toward one rather than another of the alternative responses open to individuals; it has neglected, but not denied the relevance of, the factors determining the specific incidence of these responses; it has not enumerated the various concrete responses which are constituted by combinations of specific values of the analytical variables; it has omitted, or included only by implication, any consideration of the social functions performed by illicit responses; it has not tested the full explanatory power of the analytical scheme by examining a large number of group variations in the frequency of deviate and conformist behavior; it has not adequately dealt with rebellious conduct which seeks to refashion the social framework radically; it has not examined the relevance of cultural conflict for an analysis of culture-goal and institutional-means mal-integration. It is suggested that these and related problems may be profitably analyzed by this scheme.

**Note**

1. Joseph D. Lohman, "The Participant Observer in Community Studies," *American Sociological Review* 2 (1937): 890–898.

# 35

## The Socialist Approach to Crime

*Napoleone Colajanni*

There has always been persistent opposition to the analogy of organisms and human collectivities. Some critics find this analogy erroneous, and ridicule it as an aberration because they wish to find in human societies a *quid proprium* that would distinguish them sharply from other societies.

Certainly there must be a difference between sociology and other sciences; otherwise there would be no need to concern oneself with it as a separate item. Neither can the abyss be crossed and a bridge built between the two kinds of science, nor is the recourse to analogy equivalent to establishing an identity. The most illustrious sociologists have always protested drawing explicative examples of social phenomena and laws from the biological field.

We are not justified in denying the existence of sociology just because some one or other of its great exponents, I mean particularly Spencer, considers all humanity to be a single organism. There are many objection to this hypothesis, but there is no need to adhere to it. Furthermore, it has been duly rejected by Gumplowicz, who saw in the great variety of grades of evolution among contemporary societies a valid argument in favor of the plurality of organisms.

In human societies things do not always happen normally; these collective organisms, so complex and so special, suffer from illnesses and present anomalies, precisely as does the individual organism. Hence, the necessity of studying their pathological and abnormal state alone with their healthy one; hence, the need for a pathological sociology as complementary to the normal, just as we have pathology and *Clinica* in addition to physiology.

The study of pathology is subdivided into that of diverse illnesses and anomalies which impair single tissues, organs, and functions. There is one among these that can be said to summarize all special social illnesses and anomalies because it draws from each and from each derives its component elements. It includes the study of anomalies of opposite character and demonstrates their co-existence in the social organism and the derivation of the one from the others, of atrophy and hypertrophy, of anemia and hyperemia. It is that which concerns the *sociology of crime,* which concerns itself with criminal manifestations.

From Napoleone Colajanni, *La Sociologia Criminale* (Catania, Italy: Felippo Tropea, 1889).

We must remember here how before others had found the name, a great Italian had already precisely described the thing, by recourse to those same analogies between social and biological sciences that some claim to be modern inventions and others reject as childish fantasies. "Crimes," wrote Romagnos, "are diseases of the social body, which always betray some general or local disturbance, permanent or transitory, growing or fading away." Crime is a signal of an individual voicing his resentment at his state of mental unbalance.

In the sociology of crime we meet, at first, a not inconsiderable objection. Looking at the social organism from the perspective of its entire evolution, we see that crime originates in a norm, and the physiological phenomenon, largely in its ulterior social development, becomes a censurable deviation, a pathological phenomenon. In carrying out these analogies in social organisms, according to their different stages, we not only observe special diseases, those that men and women, children and adults, present, but we meet non-diseased states that are normal at first and constitute a crime later. . . .

From this continuous evolution in the characterization of social phenomena, it follows that in the normal order the passage from the normal state of physiology to pathological abnormality is infinitely graduated among different classes in a given society, among several contemporary societies, and within successive periods in the same society in that same way as the passage in the biological and physical order from health to disease and madness is imperceptible.

The sociology of crime, then, serves to strengthen the analogies between biology and sociology in general, which, however, are never such as to confuse the two, but suffice only to show the derivation of the one from the other. . . . The usefulness of the sociology of crime is twofold; indirect and direct.

The first is manifest with reference to biology if we consider that the careful study of pathological changes has often proved valuable for the advancement of our knowledge concerning normal functions, permitting us to determine the organs involved and certain circulatory modalities, which are important for the maintenance of life and health.

Who does not see how fruitful, not to say indispensable, pathological sociology is for the determination of the relative importance and efficiency of every social institution and for establishing the relation between cause and effect among the various social phenomena?

Knowledge of the anomalies and deviations is especially useful in the social sciences in which one cannot resort to the direct experimentation and vivisection so serviceable to the biological sciences . . . Studying the anomalies and sick conditions of a people is a method followed not by choice but out of necessity.

The *direct* utility of the study of social ills, and specifically of the sociology of crime, is intuitive. It prescribes the cure and the prevention of crime; yet from the moral aspect it tends to save a great amount of pain, assuring individuals the tranquil enjoyment of their blessings, the complete development of their faculties, the free exercise of their rights—the impediments and violations of which become more odious as life becomes more peaceful, less uncertain, and better appreciated. The diminution and attenuation of criminality, if not its total disappearance, are not possible without opportune prevention and fitting repression.

The place of sociology in general and of the sociology of crime in particular in the hierarchy of the sciences is a matter of special importance in Italy, where, more than any other place, unexpected rebellious and unjustified protests have been raised against the place assigned to sociology in the classification of the sciences. We have seen sociology treated as a pretentious parvenu, invading the field of others. Scientists cannot tolerate the prospective subordination of the other venerable sciences which preceded sociology in the intellectual arena to this most recent arrival. Generally, it is easier to deny the existence of sociology, having once accorded it the right of citizenship among the sciences, than to deny that the branches concerned with the other social phenomena are subordinate to it. And yet that is precisely what many have done who acknowledge its existence and utility, with or without reservations, while holding the science of law hierarchically superior or at least wholly independent. We dwell on this controversy because it gives us occasion to discuss and establish with more precision the place and significance of sociology.

This leads to the logical and correct differentiation of the contents of the sociology of crime into anthropology and criminal psychology. The study of anthropology is indispensable for sociology. . . .

The tripartation to which I shall hold in this work is this: (1) genesis and etiology of crime; (2) treatment of crime, which in turn is subdivided into prevention or social hygiene; and into repression or penal law. We need not take the time to discuss the distinction that some have drawn between penology, which would be concerned with the technical, hygienic, economic and moral side of the application of punishment, and penal law, to which is left the purely legal part. (3) History and development of delinquency, by means of which one might ascertain the degree of effectiveness, or noneffectiveness, of the preventive and repressive means adopted to combat it; and in this way, with knowledge of the effects obtained, in a position to set out the negative part of moral progress. . . . The etiology of delinquency must be sought with the most decided preference in social contingencies: crime is above all a social and historical phenomenon. . . .

In beginning our examination of the social factors, we find ourselves disposed to accord them the greatest, if not exclusive, influence. But this general judgment is of little use to the sociologist because it supplies no acceptable indication of the precise causes of criminal phenomena, without which prevention is impossible. It seems impossible that there still are thinkers who doubt the pre-eminence and precedence of the economic factor in social evolution, allowing themselves to be misled by the complexity of present-day life in which, not infrequently, superior men subordinate and sacrifice material needs (that is to say, economic needs) to the needs of another order, namely moral and intellectual. The illusion comes from looking at the individual and not the species. Philogeny in this case illustrates and explains ontogeny and tells us that these noble and admirable men are the final product of all evolution before them, in which the economic factor was patent and even brutal.

Still, it is an exaggeration to affirm that every social event—political, religious, esthetic, moral— is the direct and exclusive product of an economic phenomenon, since at certain moments the sentiments and passions of superior men, devoid of all material preoccupations which become the motors of social transformations, are communicated as by irresistible contagion to the masses. But it is correct to affirm that the consequences of these events are almost always economic, because in the complexity of interests that all have you cannot touch one without striking the others, and because material needs, put for a moment in second place or completely put aside, will again take up their natural hegemony.

The intimate rapport between economic conditions and morality has inspired the most illustrious thinkers of all times and all races: philosophers and historians, moralists and statisticians, poets and economists. All saw in economic conditions the first and true cause of the moral condition, and thus of delinquency; and they expressed their own thought in different ways but with the same content.

In 1516 Thomas More said that the English economic and civil legislation of his time was a conspiracy of the rich few against the disinherited masses. Monsignor Savarese is of the same opinion of the legislation of today. But if the judgment of the utopist and the ascetic is suspect, here is that of a penologist and magistrate, whose experience derives from the study of books and from the contingencies of real life. From private property, says Pietro Ellero, come all, or almost all, crimes. Property inspires greed, dominance, and pride, on the one hand, and debasement, on the other, even when it does not produce perfect tyranny of some and complete degradation of others. It is the author of most of the evil passions, of the faults and crimes that are committed, of the straits and anxieties, etc., etc., that both haves and have-nots suffer on earth. The immoral influence of property is felt, too, in the present phenomenon of the planned family. . . . Otherwise it is held that misery is the *causa causorum* of crimes, and that property is the great moralizer.

Economic conditions have a direct and incontestable effect on the genesis of delinquency insofar as the scarcity of means to satisfy the numerous needs of man (different for different societies and more numerous among those who have reached a higher stage of civilization and have a higher standard of living) is sufficient stimulus to provide them for oneself by any means, honest and dishonest. And certain peculiarities in the present social order are a greater spur to dishonest activity, particularly in certain environments. In fact, sometimes there is greater reward and less risk in this than in honest activity. . . .

This form of direct influence of economic conditions on the making of criminals, especially those who perpetrate crimes against property, is enormous; but no less evident and powerful is the indirect influence. . . .

Where do well-being, comfort and wealth end and poverty begin? This is a question to which neither historians, economists, nor moralists have given sufficient and adequate answer. Nor can they answer it because wealth and poverty are essentially relative and mobile categories, in continuous transformation. But if we can give no answer to that question, we do possess innumerable facts that tell us that distribution is more important than the absolute quantity of goods, that stability and security in the means of subsistence are more important than desultory increments. Poverty is essentially relative to created needs and becomes habitual if they cannot be satisfied. It can be established that in a given society we obtain the least possible delinquency with the greatest security of the possession of the means of subsistence, stability of the economic conditions, and equality in the distribution of wealth.

The truth is that present-day socialism represents conscious and collective protest against the present order of things, for which one would like to substitute an order more useful for all and consistent with justice, while crime is nothing but the product of bad social organization—the unconscious and individual rebellion. Both may proceed concomitantly under the influence of poverty, but that is not desirable. Fortunately, history and statistics show that between the two movements there is at least a partial inverse proportion.

Doubts regarding the relationship between crime and the wealth of a people and an individual cease when we look at the dynamics of this relationship. The facts are so numerous and are so consistently unrelated to suppose any influence of climate and race that students of social science phenomena have acknowledged as a general principle that changes in economic conditions cause alterations in the conditions of delinquency.

# 36

## The Economic System, Egoistic Tendencies, and Class Differentiation

*Willem Adriaan Bonger*

The period of civilization during which [a] social modification . . . has taken place is generally lauded to the skies, as compared with preceding epochs. In certain relations this is justifiable. Technique has made immense progress and especially during the last phase of civilization, capitalism; the power of man over nature has advanced greatly; the productivity of labor has been so increased that one class of men, exempted by this from permanent care for their daily bread, are able to devote themselves to the arts and sciences. All this is indisputable. But the development of the arts and sciences and of technique has only an indirect importance for the etiology of crime. The question first of all to be asked is this: What influence has this modification in the economic and social structure had upon the character of man? And the answer to this question can only be the following: This modification has engendered cupidity and ambition, has made man less sensitive to the happiness and misery of his fellows, and has decreased the influence exercised upon men's acts by the opinions of others. In short, it has developed egoism at the expense of altruism.

### Egoistic Tendencies Resulting from the Present Economic System and from Its Consequences

The etiology of crime includes the three following problems:

First: Whence does the criminal thought in man arise?

Second: What forces are there in man which can prevent the execution of this criminal thought, and what is their origin?

Third: What is the occasion for the commission of criminal acts? . . .

For the moment we are still occupied with general considerations with regard to crime; it is clear then that the first and third questions will be examined

From Willem Adriaan Bonger, *Criminality and Economic Conditions* (Boston: Little, Brown and Company, 1916). Reprinted with permission of Agathon Press, Inc.

only when we are treating of crimes according to the groups into which they must be divided because of the great differences which their nature presents.

It is otherwise with the second question. . . . [It] is certain that man is born with social instincts, which, when influenced by a favorable environment, can exert a force great enough to prevent egoistic thoughts from leading to egoistic acts. And since crime constitutes a part of the egoistic acts, it is of importance, for the etiology of *crime in general,* to inquire whether the present method of production and its social consequences are an obstacle to the development of the social instincts, and in what measure. . . .

[The] egoistic tendency does not *by itself* make a man criminal. For this something else is necessary. It is possible for the environment to create a great egoist, but this does not imply that the egoist will necessarily become criminal. . . . [As] a consequence of the present environment, man has become very egoistic, and hence more *capable of crime,* than if the environment had developed the germs of altruism.

The present economic system is based upon exchange. . . . A society based upon exchange isolates the individuals by weakening the bond that unites them. When it is a question of exchange the two parties interested think only of their own advantage even to the detriment of the other party. In the second place the possibility of exchange arouses in a man the thought of the possibility of converting the surplus of his labor into things which increase his well-being in place of giving the benefit of it to those who are deprived of the necessaries of life. Hence the possibility of exchange gives birth to cupidity.

The exchange called simple circulation of commodities is practiced by all men as consumers, and by the workers besides as vendors of their labor power. . . .

Capitalistic exchange, on the other hand, has another aim—that of making a profit. A merchant, for example, does not buy goods for his own use, but to sell them to advantage. He will, then, always try, on the one hand, to buy the best commodities as cheaply as possible, by depreciating them as much as he can; on the other hand, to make the purchaser pay as high a price as possible, by exaggerating the value of his wares. *By the nature of the mode of production itself* the merchant is therefore forced to make war upon two sides, must maintain his own interests against the interests of those with whom he does business. If he does not injure too greatly the interests of those from whom he buys, and those to whom he sells, it is for the simple reason that these would otherwise do business with those of his competitors who do not find their interest in fleecing their customers. . . . [The] merchant and the thief are alike in taking account *exclusively* of their own interest to the detriment of those with whom they have to do.

The fact that in our present society production does not take place generally to provide for the needs of men, but for many other reasons, has important effects upon the character of those who possess the means of production. Production is carried on for profit exclusively; if greater profits can be made by stopping production it will be stopped—this is the point of view of the capitalists. The consumers, on the other hand, see in production the means of creating what man has need of. The world likes to be deceived, and does not care to recognize the fact that the producer has only his own profit in view. The latter encourages this notion and poses as a disinterested person. If he reduced the price of his wares, he claims to do it in the interest of the public, and takes care not to admit that it is for the purpose of increasing his own profits. This is the falsity that belongs inevitably to capitalism.

In general this characteristic of capitalism has no importance for the morality of the consumer, who is merely duped, but it is far otherwise with the press, which is almost entirely in the power of the capitalists. . . .

As we have seen above the merchant capitalist makes war in two directions; his interests are against those of the man who sells to him, and of the man who buys from him. This is also true of the industrial capitalist. He buys raw materials and sells what he produces. But to arrive at his product he must buy labor, and this purchase is "sui generis."

Deprived as he is of the means of production, the workingman sells his labor only in order not to die of hunger. The capitalist takes advantage of this necessitous condition of the worker and exploits him. We have already indicated that capitalism has this trait in common with the earlier methods of production. Little by little one class of men has become accustomed to think that the others are destined to amass wealth for them and to be subservient to them in every way. Slavery, like the wage system, demoralizes the servant as well as the master. With the master it develops cupidity and the imperious character which sees in a fellow man only a being fit to satisfy his desires. It is true that the capitalist has not the power over the proletarian that the master has over his slave; he has neither the right of service nor the power of life and death, yet it is none the less true that he has another weapon against the proletarian, a weapon whose effect is no less terrible, namely enforced idleness. The fact that the supply of manual labor always greatly exceeds the demand puts this weapon into the hands of every capitalist. It is not only the capitalists who carry on any business that are subjected to this influence, but also all who are salaried in their service.

Capitalism exercises in still a third manner an egoistic influence upon the capitalistic "entrepreneur." Each branch has more producers than are necessary. The interests of the capitalists are, then, opposed not only to those of the men from whom they buy or to whom they sell, but also of those of their fellow producers. It is indeed claimed that competition has the effect simply of making the product better and cheaper, but this is looking at the question from only one point of view. The fact which alone affects criminality is that competition forces the participants, under penalty of succumbing, to be as egoistic as possible. Even the producers who have the means of applying all the technical improvements to perfect their product and make it cheaper, are obliged to have recourse to gross deceits in advertising, etc., in order to injure their competitors. Rejoicing at the evil which befalls another, envy at his good fortune, these forms of egoism are the inevitable consequence of competition. . . .

[The] bourgeoisie . . . without having any occupation, consumes what has been made by others. Not to feel obliged to contribute to the material well-being of humanity in proportion to one's ability must necessarily have a demoralizing influence. A parasite, one who lives without working, does not feel bound by any moral tie to his fellows, but regards them simply as things, instruments meant to serve and amuse him. Their example is a source of demoralization for those about them, and excites the envy of those who see this easy life without the power of enjoying it themselves, and awakes in them the desire to exchange their painful existence for this "dolce far niente."

The egoistic tendencies work less strongly in the third group of the bourgeoisie, those who practice the liberal professions. However, the products of the arts and sciences having become commodities, the egoistic influence of exchange here too is not to be neglected. . . .

[The] state owes its origin to the formation of opposition of interests in society; the first task of the state being, therefore, the maintenance of a certain amount of order. This requires above all the holding of the great mass in subjection. As long as this mass is weak the dominant class has no need to resort to trickery; but as soon as the oppressed class can oppose the domination of the others, as soon as brutal power no longer gives the desired result, the dominant class changes its tactics. It attempts to create the impression that the concessions it has been forced to make are acts of charity; and presuming upon the ignorance of the oppressed, it pretends that their condition is not so bad, etc. Many of those engaged in politics play this part without being conscious of their duplicity. However, the contest between the classes exercises its baleful influence upon them also, for they involuntarily distort the facts, whereas the evolution of society has reached such a point that a new social order is necessary.

The power in the state sometimes passes from one party of the ruling class to another. All profit by the temporary opportunity not only for the realization of their political program, but also to procure advantages for their partisans. This struggle for power is carried on partly by means prejudicial to the character of those interested, while the end aimed at by some parties can be frankly avowed. It is for the same reason that international politics is such a source of lying and hypocrisy, the states not being able to avow their real intention—the weakening of their neighbors. . . .

The oppressed resort to means which they would otherwise scorn. As we have seen above, the basis of the social feelings is reciprocity. As soon as this is trodden under foot by the ruling class the social sentiments of the oppressed become weak towards them.

* * *

The lack of steady work, the horrors of the penury into which he and his fall, and the long train of evils which result from both, kill the social feelings in a man, for, as we have seen above, these feelings depend upon reciprocity.

* * *

Because of [egoistic] tendencies the social instinct of man is not greatly
developed; they have weakened the moral force in man which combats the
inclination towards egoistic acts, and hence towards the crimes which are one
form of these acts. To mention only the most important things, in a society in
which, as in ours, the economic interests of all are in eternal conflict among
themselves, compassion for the misfortunes of others inevitably becomes
blunted, and a great part of morality consequently disappears. The slight value
that is attached to the opinion of others is also a consequence of the strife of
economic interests, for we can be responsive to that opinion only when we do
not see adversaries in our fellows.

The fluctuations of the mind of the person in whom the criminal idea is
born may be compared with the oscillations of a balance; and it is upon sociology
that must devolve the task of examining the forces which throw a weight on one
side or the other. When the organization of society influences men in an altruistic way there is then a considerable force which can prevent the balance from
inclining towards the egoistic side. In our present society, the organization of
which does not exert an altruistic influence, this force is very weak, or does not
exist at all. Since, however, in every society, man must abstain from a number
of egoistic acts, substitutes have been devised to take the place of the weak or
wanting social sentiments. The hope of reward (whether terrestrial or celestial)
and the fear of being punished (whether by man or God) are charged with the
duty of keeping men in order. As believers themselves know very well, most
men are not very responsive to divine rewards and punishments—heaven and hell
are too far off. Is it not believers who are the strongest partisans of rewards and
punishments here below for human acts? However, this expedient is only a
very insufficient one. We know too well that the rewards are very often lacking,
and the punishments as well. This is why many persons take the risk of committing the crime they have planned.

The present environment exercises an egoistic influence upon all men. We
all participate, for example, in exchange, which, as we have seen, is a great
egoistic factor; and other similar factors could be named that act upon all. On
the other hand there are other egoistic factors which exercise their influence
only upon some of us.

* * *

He who is born with weak social instincts runs more *danger* of becoming
a criminal. But the *certainty* that he will become such does not exist—that
depends upon the environment. . . .

# 37 The Criminals Society Deserves

*Alexander Lacassagne*

This is a study of homicidal suicide, one of the most serious disorders of our social state, which seems to demonstrate, in our time, a crisis of nervous irritations. But all things considered, there are compensations—suicide is a process of selection involving the elimination of egotistical, unbalanced natures. Like emigration, it is a modifier of criminality. . . .

Behavior, moreover, is governed by laws in addition to those inscribed in statute books. And so criminality increases despite a terrifying arsenal of laws. Hence, we witness the impotence or failure of legislation.

In positing the existence of the cerebral unbalances, class distinction, more desire and less desire, laziness, imitation and alcohol, there arises the need to establish social therapy which would include: protection of childhood, right to work, assistance for liberated, discharged prisoners, modifications to be brought to the record of punishments, and necessity for work, I conclude:

Societies have the criminals they merit.

From Alexandre Lacassagne, "Les Suicides a Lyon," *Archives D'Anthropologie Criminelle de Medicine Legale,* vol. II (Paris: 1896).

# 38 On Social Defense

*Adolphe Prins*

The rhythm of crime accompanies the rhythm of honest activity, it accelerates with civilization according to the principle by which the number of accidents increases with an increase in the number of drives; criminality is only, after all, one of the forms of social life. It too, is in the current where useful and detrimental forces collide and merge, a current with uncertain limits, whose waters from time to time meet those of other currents. This leads to the development of a diversified group whose composition intersects misery, sickness, degeneration, vice, ignorance, unwholesome passion, symptoms of an overflowing and uncurbed life or an improverished and anemic life as well as all the manifestations of health, beauty, fecundity and work.

Yet nothing in this domain is absolutely clear-cut and the observer who pays attention only to facts sees so many intermediate degrees appear in every direction that he has difficulty discerning where one type of being ends, where another begins.

Just as we are guided from hot to cold, through a series of stages, sensitive to the atmosphere which the thermometer registers, so from the fullness of intellectual or physical equilibrium to insanity and incurable sickness there is a ladder of imperceptible gradations; so from the honest man doing good for the love of good to the criminal doing evil for the love of evil, there is a broad zone of multiple shades, from virtue to perversity.

## The Principle

Whether we turn the determinist or the non-determinist, we come to no clear, precise, satisfactory conclusion. Each of these theories has the same fault; each claims to explain by a simplified formula a complex, obscure, and contradictory human nature.

We have in ourselves atavistic attitudes which influence the course of our lives, and thus we have to admit a certain internal necessity for our acts.

From Adolphe Prins, *Social Defense and the Transformation of The Penal Law* (Paris: Marcil Riviere, 1886).

We have in ourselves a faculty of reaction against the surroundings, an activity directed toward a goal, and thus we have to admit a certain internal liberty of conduct.

At the core of our being these two tendencies meet. Liberty and necessity work together to mold our personality, making us energetic and determined or weak and indecisive; causing me to be myself and not another, to act in a certain way and not in another. . . .

How, then, can I wish that the things I ignore the judge would be able to know or to adopt as a principle for his decisions? What one says to him does not facilitate his task.

Here is, before repressive justice, an assassin who, in a peaceful village had waited for his adversary at the bend of a footpath and then stabbed him. The agent of the law will be satisfied to show the result and its immediate cause; that is to say, the murdered victim and the weapon aimed by the arm of the guilty, driven himself by a free and reflective will. The agent of the defense will go further back in the sequence of motives and causes and will search to bring out all the circumstances that led astray and subjugated the will. . . .

The reality here is the social aspect of the drama: the population terrified by the horror of the crime, the attack on the tranquility of rural life and the necessity to re-establish it in the regular and normal course. . . .

Penal law has a relative goal. It causes a relative order to prevail in the relationships between men. It guarantees, in the greatest possible measure, the person, life, patrimony, and honor of the citizens. . . .

This system, however, comes up against three categories of objections. The first consists in pretending that one makes the discussions on the degrees of responsibility disappear from the horizon of judiciary sessions; we make the conception of moral liberty disappear on the horizon of the world. The second consists of affirming that which is practiced; it is impossible to dispense with the criterion of the responsibility. The third consists of maintaining that our system no longer takes into account the individuality of the guilty. We have met with all three.

## Social Defense and Liberty

Assuredly moral liberty is indispensible to the moral development of humanity. But the question is to know if the destiny of moral liberty is bound to the text of repressive judgment which condemns or acquits the author of the illegal deed. It is very evident that there are two orders of ideas. The idea of moral liberty does not depend on the way in which the state exerts its high mission of policing and security; it depends on the sense that one gives to the ensemble of the world; it varies according to whether one considers the cosmos as the expression of a private mechanism of the senses or as intelligent finality, and it is related to the theory of evolution.

* * *

It is in the same conditions in penal law that the theory of social defense arises responding, in turn, to the transformations of the contemporary judicial conscience, and conceives a right of the state in certain cases, independent of the idea of fault and responsibility.

## Social Defense and Individual Disposition of the Delinquent

The difference between the classical law and the new law is not that the first affirms the moral individuality of the guilty and the second denies it; it is that the angle from which one considers it is no longer the same and that consequently new points of view have arisen . . . Let us bring to attention the mentality of certain specialists in immorality (exhibitionists, thieves, authors of [criminal] attempts and outrages of the morals and acts of debauchery), which appear to be produced by irresistible deviations and inclinations. Let us also bring to attention the mentality of beggars and vagabonds, who without having the energy to engage in criminality, never have the energy to work when they are free and only quit begging to return again after they have spent the little savings gathered during reclusion. And if one examines the psychic state of the most dangerous criminals, one will discern again in them the persistence of perverse or brutal instincts which only old age will succeed in dulling.

The theoretically justifiable conditions for punishing do not always fit the true psychic predispositions of the individual to whom the punishment is directed; and when all the conditions for punishing are present, I see only one that exists independent of the moral dispositions of the guilty. It is the exemplary: that is to say, the effect of chastisement not on the guilty but on the masses.

It is, then, also comprehensible that the penitentiary school, with its dream of guidance and reform of the will, or moralization and final reclassification of the majority of the prisoners, has not been able to realize its hopes, and such is, above all, the motive which causes the penal science to incline more to social defense than to expiration. . . . The method of differentiation of the modern school is otherwise; as it is occupied more with the nature of the agent than with the transient proportion of volition which enters into the act, it is also occupied more with the nature than the quota of punishment. It correlates severity and benevolence with the concrete measure of the social necessity. This specific measure is in agreement, in its turn, with the permanent psychic state of the delinquent.

And the differentiation is more precise at two points of view: In the first place, society has more to fear from the professional delinquent than the first offender; from associated delinquents than the isolated delinquent; from cunning persistence or cold maliciousness, or brutality than sudden anger, flippancy, or passion. Thus, justice finds a basis for the determination of punishment in the [threat a] guilty person poses against society.

Society has another thing to fear. It should take other measures of defense and preservation according to whether it is dealing with criminals acting out of passion or desperation, whose liberty should be abolished, above all, for the example that it sets, or with anti-social people rebelling against society, who must be prevented from doing harm, or with defective or degenerate criminals, who must be submitted to an appropriate regimentation of custody and preservation.

And it is here that the frame of classical penology becomes too narrow and that our uniform penal system no longer responds to our modern needs. We can no longer limit ourselves to mathematical calculations of the duration of the detention and to the study of the details of the organization of the cell. We no longer have to diversify only the restrictions of a single punishment; we have to diversify the programs themselves and create new institutions and establishments. I will specifically cite four groups: incompetents by degeneration; epileptics; alcoholics; and immoral sexual deviates. For these criminalists and penologists henceforth have to organize differentiated and specialized programs according to the nature of the delinquents. One sees, and it is not futile to note, that to occupy oneself less with the degree of the penal responsibility of the guilty person is not to occupy oneself less with the degree of the penal responsibility of the guilty person is not to occupy oneself less with the psychology of the delinquents. Quite to the contrary.

A last point to bring to attention: the principle of social defense extends beyond the horizon of penal law and penalty. In general, social danger results from criminality. Nevertheless, one can conceive it before the crime and independent of the crime . . . The state, then, cannot remain indifferent to crime and ignore private actions. Even here, it has the responsibility to guarantee social order.

Social defense manifests itself then in its highest and most productive form. It is no longer repression; it is protection and assistance.

# Social Defense Extended

## Mark Ancel

The term "social defense" is almost unknown in English and American legal literature. The term is found, however, in a number of recent works on criminology, especially in the United States. The United Nations has also made the term known by the creation in 1948 of a "Social defense section" charged with the task of studying the organization of *the prevention of crime and the treatment of offenders.* This last formula is itself to some extent a definition of social defense because it shows that the repression of crime, in the traditionally accepted sense of the word "repression," is not the purpose of social defense.

On the Continent of Europe and in the countries of Latin America, the expression "social defense" has long been in current use. The Italian positivist school at the end of the nineteenth century extended the use of the term by according it a greater significance. *Lombroso, Garofalo* and *Enrico Ferri* postulated, in principle, that repression of crime, as traditionally understood, had failed. As determinists, they considered that except for occasional offenders, criminals were always inevitably led to crime by biological, psychological or social causes. In any case, it became impossible to speak of moral responsibility and of repressive punishment. Therefore, the aim of criminal law should no longer be the punishment of fault, nor deterrence, but simply the protection of society.

This positive doctrine led to the suppression of punishment, replaced by *"mesures de sûreté,"* which could very roughly be translated as "preventive measures." The doctrine as a whole has not been accepted, but two of its important notions were taken up by the International Criminal Law Union, established by *von Liszt, van Hamel* and *Adolphe Prins* in 1889: these were the ideas of "perilousness" (*pericolosita*) and of *mesures de sûreté*, that is to say, of a criminal sanction aimed not at the delinquent's fault, but at his dangerous condition. . . .

However, this original social defense movement envisaged only the passive protection of society. It was mainly interested in two classes of criminals, habitual offenders and mental defectives, but it was to some extent a severe

From Marc Ancel, "Social Defense," *Law Quarterly Review* 78 (London, 1962), pp. 497–603. Reprinted with permission.

221

system as regards these two kinds of offenders. After the Second World War, there were various attempts to react against the excesses of totalitarianism and the assaults on the dignity of the individual. . . .

This doctrine broadly adopted the extreme positivist arguments in advocating the abolition of the traditional system of repressive criminal law and its replacement by a system which would be exclusively preventive in character and would no longer recognize the terms *crime* or *criminal.* The notion of criminal responsibility would be replaced by that of "antisociality" (*antisocialita*). This doctrine aroused criticism and opposition. Even within the International Society of Social Defense, founded in 1949, there arose another tendency which received the name of *new social defense.* . . . This new doctrine does not purport to abolish criminal law nor to suppress the notions of crime, criminal, criminal responsibility, or even punishment. But the doctrine nevertheless proposes to inspire an entirely new concept of penal policy. I will now deal only with this new social defense.

The first purpose of this conception of social defense is to constitute a new approach to the problem of crime. From this point of view it is equally opposed to traditional criminal law (the "neoclassical school") and to the system derived from positivist theory.

In the traditional system, the struggle against crime is considered as a legal problem. The principal weapon used in this struggle is punishment inflicted on the offender in accordance with the gravity of his offense. The offense is thus considered as a moral or social *fault* for which the offender must be punished in the name of society. The neoclassical or traditional law rests upon the culpability of the offender, author of the criminal act. Unless insane, he is presumed wholly responsible. . . .

Positivism, on the other hand, ever since *Lombroso's* "born criminal," explains the offense, as we have already observed, in terms of the inner condition or outward environment of the offender. The criminal offender is therefore either abnormal from a biological or psychological standpoint, or else a social misfit, who is always irresponsible, at least to a very large extent. . . .

The new doctrine of social defense is opposed to both these points of view. It blames the traditional, neoclassical law for being based on fictions and on legal metaphysics in contradiction with the facts. According to the theory of social defense, criminal justice can only be relative; its business is not to punish a fault according to some absolute standard, but to cause one man to be judged by other men. This is not a metaphysical question concerned with good or evil, but the problem of dealing with the particular criminal offense of a distinct individual. It is for this reason that traditional criminal law has shown itself inadequate to fight crime and in particular habitual crime. Such neoclassical law even purports to leave out of account the offender's real motives in order to classify the offense according to some abstract intention. This school of thought always looks on crime as a "legal entity," whereas it is above all an act perpe-

trated in society by an individual human being. Even the modern development
of this traditional law merely produces artificial and oversimplified concepts
such as diminished responsibility, and the distinctions of first offenders and
recidivists, mental defectives and habitual offenders, or "normal" offenders
and psychopaths. Beyond these legal ideas and fictions, the offender as an individual must be rediscovered. To accomplish this, it must be understood that the
scientific revolution of the nineteenth century has stripped the criminal law
of its former autonomy and exclusiveness. What remains is one branch of
criminal science, among many others, of which it is not the most important.

From another standpoint, the new social defense is opposed to positivist
determinism. This opposition covers both the biological and psychological
determinism advocated by the Italian school and certain other Continental
criminologists, and also the sociological determinism upheld by other criminologists which is now supported, more or less firmly, by many American authors.
Social defense retains the fundamental notion of responsibility, but this is no
longer the presumed and abstract responsibility of traditional criminal law, that
is to say, a quality which a reasonable man is deemed to possess, irrespective of
his personal characteristics. Social defense takes into account the deep-seated
feeling of responsibility that exists even in criminal offenders who are held
theoretically irresponsible, because such a feeling exists in every human being.
Every member of society possesses this individual feeling, which is therefore
a psycho-social reality on which a rational system of social reaction against
crime must be based. It is precisely this rational system of reaction against
crime that social defense wishes to develop. At the same time, the new doctrine
of social defense is a reaction against the amoral character of positivism. The
doctrine wants to bring to the struggle against crime the moral values and
ethical considerations which the positivists, for the sake of an immediate result,
were content to brush aside.

In so far as it tries to create a rational system of reaction against crime,
social defense is a link between criminal law and criminology. . . .

Until the end of the nineteenth century, lawyers spoke of psychiatry
and of sociology as auxiliaries of the criminal law. When these sciences expanded
and when at the beginning of the twentieth century criminology established
itself in its own right, there arose in consequence an antagonism between law
and the criminological sciences, and also a more specific hostility between
lawyers and judges on the one hand and medical practitioners on the other.
Social defense claims to put an end to this antagonism, so as to build up modern
criminal policy, that is to say a system which should guide the legislator, judges
concerned with criminal cases, and the administrators of penal institutions, in
a common criminological perspective.

Social defense argues that today neither criminal law nor penal policy
can afford to disregard the unconscious motivations revealed to us by psychoanalysis or depth psychology: the law and its administration must be aware of

what modern criminologists call the "dynamic of crime" and they should be
concerned not with the apparent character of the offender but with his own
personality. This personality makes up a particular human entity that can be
understood only by a scientific study which draws on many different disciplines
and which therefore requires the cooperation of specialists in the different
sciences concerned with the human being. Social defense believes it is essential
that the offender's personality should be known during the proceedings when
sentence is imposed, and afterwards for the application of the court's decision,
which should be the starting point of *a treatment of social readaptation (re-
socialization)*.

In this connection, moreover, social defense observes that great progress
has been made in recent years, especially in the fields of juvenile delinquency,
the treatment of young persons, the detection and care of psychopaths, and
prison administration in general. New ideas have emerged, such as the notion
that the offender should be protected, which was first applied to children and
young offenders; and the idea that a convicted person should be treated with a
view to his readaptation to a free life in society: the problem is to turn the
criminal offender into a law-abiding citizen.

However, social defense believes that this tendency cannot triumph unless
certain conditions are fulfilled. We will merely draw attention to three of the
most important. First, the efforts of scientists and lawyers should be coordinated.
There must be a genuine and sustained medico-legal collaboration which brings
together and draws upon the experience of both sides.

Secondly, these efforts should be pursued on the international level. Social
defense does not, in any way, seek an artificial and impracticable unification
of national laws; it mistrusts the empirical imitation of one legal system by
another, but it believes that scientists and lawyers must join forces to seek valid
answers to the criminal problem envisaged as a social and human question. . . .

Thirdly and finally, social defense believes that in the light of this cooperation, both scientific and international, fundamental reforms of criminal law
and procedure should be undertaken. Such reforms will necessarily be national
in character, but they should be inspired by the spirit of social defense and
rooted in criminological teaching and experience. . . .

As has already been said, the new doctrine of social defense firmly ad-
vocates the maintenance of the rule of law (*regle de la legalite*). It also insists
upon a system of criminal investigation and procedure which guarantees the
rights of the accused and the liberty of the defense. Finally, it wants to make
very wide use of the sense of responsibility which ought logically to be the
creative principle of social readaptation. . . .

What social defense hopes to do, therefore, is to elaborate a system where
criminal justice, inspired by criminology, sets in motion a social reaction which
actively prevents crime, instead of passively waiting to repress the criminal. It
wants to protect both the individual—even the delinquent individual—and

society. The penal philosophy of social defense is centered on the belief that all our efforts ought to be directed, not to the exclusion of the delinquent from the community, but to his reintegration therein, so that after individualized and appropriate treatment which the criminological sciences should enable judges to prescribe and penal officers to apply, the offender can recover his place as a free man in that society of which he will no longer feel himself the enemy. . . .

The aim of this philosophy is to organize the reaction against crime— against the offense and the offender—in such a way as effectively to realize the purposes which such a social reaction sets itself. This approach supposes a funda- mental penal philosophy and such a return to a group of coordinated basic ideas seems essential to modern social defense.

These basic ideas are: individual responsibility having its source in man's subjective sense of responsibility as a being endowed with reason; the search for a general system of safeguards, both individual and social; and a resolute orientation of the penal sanction towards the social rehabilitation of the offender. However, this general scheme is not the abstract construction of legal dogmatism: on the contrary, it is a patient effort based on the scientific study of crime and the criminal. The two fold consequence of this method must be made clear in concluding this paper.

First of all, in the system of social defense, there is no longer any conflict between criminal law and criminology, but, on the contrary, a sustained and necessary cooperation. The result is that criminal law can no longer dwell in the condition of splendid isolation typical of the traditional lawyer. . . .

In the second place, and conversely, criminologists must rid themselves of the sort of superiority complex which they have too often displayed towards lawyers. Criminology can no more ignore the criminal law than the criminal law can ignore criminology. If crime is a human and social phenomenon, it is also, in our system of the rule of law, a legal phenomenon. Therefore, the reaction against crime can be organized only by the law and within a legal framework. . . . Criminologists must not think of themselves as the masters, but as the colleagues of the lawyers. . . .

# Epilogue: The Present and the Future of Criminological Theory

## Richard D. Knudten

As Stephen Schafer made clear in his Introduction, the development of criminological theory has been somewhat sporadic despite the fact that men have always been concerned about deviant behavior and the control of that conduct. Attempts to understand the causes of delinquency and crime have ranged from early supernaturalistic explanations, which assumed that criminal deviance was due to the actions of demons or the devil, to more specific biological, psychological, social psychological, or sociological explanations. Whatever their content, explanations of criminal behavior have rarely been integrated into a consistent theoretical conception.

From primitive times to the Renaissance, attempts to explain crime conceived of the problem in terms of sin, demons, or perverted will. But with the release of a humanistic concern in the Renaissance, a new positivist spirit challenged these conceptions of the problem. The explanation of crime moved to an emphasis on the effect of events and environment upon criminal conduct. As a result, some theorists came to see crime as a product of the general social system and the development of the state. Others located its cause in hereditary forces and the individual's psychological capacities.

## Contemporary Explanations of Criminal Conduct

Although nearly a century has passed since Lombroso challenged Beccaria's theory, the debate as to whether crime is a product of free will (Beccaria) or of environment and heredity (Lombroso) persists. Beccaria's ideas underlie the demand for a return to harsh physical punishment; Lombroso's beliefs support the notion of differential assistance to and humane treatment for the criminal. While both camps have their supporters, a review of theoretical developments since the turn of the century indicates that most contemporary theorizing is closer to the work of Lombroso than to that of Beccaria.

### Physical and Psychological Explanations

Ties to the past are evident in the work of Sheldon and Eleanor Glueck, who utilized William H. Sheldon's method of body-typing, itself influenced by the ideas and work of Cesare Lombroso and of Ernst Kretschmer, in their effort

227

to unravel the causes of juvenile delinquency. The Gluecks find a high correlation between mesomorphy and delinquent conduct. Because the mesomorph
is impulsive, possesses a strong nervous, physical, and emotional structure, and
is a man of action, he is inclined to solve problems within an action context.
Although the ectomorph, a thinker and brooder, and the endomorph, sensitive
and aesthetic, also engage in delinquency to varying degrees, they either fail to
act decisively or are inhibited, tense, or conflict-ridden.

However, the Gluecks concluded as a result of their more recent studies,
delinquency is not merely a product of the individual's physical traits. Hostility,
unconventionality, parental inadequacy, a feeling of not being appreciated,
defensive maternal attitudes, alcoholism, culture conflict, family financial
dependence, a tendency toward fantasy, a lack of family self-respect, and
emotional conflict at home are important factors in the development of delinquency patterns. At some points, cultural factors stimulate antisocial trait
formation. The development of delinquency is related to the differential con-
tamination of a youth rather than to his differential associations, as suggested
by Edwin H. Sutherland. Environmental influences, the Gluecks conclude, even
when excessively criminogenic, propel selectively an adolescent toward maladjustment and delinquency. The speed with which this occurs partially depends
upon the general vulnerability of the youth to such traits.[1]

Fritz Redl and David Wineman focus upon the aggressive child whose ego
is out of touch with the demands of society. Such a child reacts aggressively to
fear, anxiety, or insecurity. Aggression represents, Redl and Wineman contend,
guilt feelings and an individual's inability to fulfill himself through recreation
or other similar activities. While the ego in his case is unable to control the
desire for immediate gratification, it is able to buffer the individual against
extreme forms of impulse gratification. The aggressive child strives to identify
with others possessing similar ego attitudes. Delinquency, therefore, is a product
of the juvenile's inability to achieve self-control.[2]

Freudian psychologists argue even today that behavior is largely a product
of biosocial drives that are unrecognized, unconscious, and generally not understood by the violator. Criminal conduct is frequently an expression of repressed
instincts and faulty socialization. Because criminal behavior is often thus
grounded in the unconscious, the offender can learn to control his activity
only if he gains insight into the nature of his unconscious.[3] The physician-
psychiatrist Walter Bromberg sees crime as an act of self-assertion springing
spontaneously from the violator's impulses and inner needs. The meaning of
criminal behavior is related to the state of "acting." As a result, crime and
punishment must take into consideration the entire personality of the offender,
including his defenses, personality traits, unconscious conflicts, habits, conscious and subliminal motivations, wishes, fantasies, rationalization, displace-
ments, projections, and other related elements. Crime is a form of spontaneous
self-assertion that reveals the inner needs and impulses of the violator. Some

criminals are aggressive and carry out crimes of single or mass murder, assault, and forcible rape; others reveal passive-aggressive tendencies in the form of burglary, larceny, embezzlement, or arson. Those who disclose physiopsychological criminal responses are typically responsible for homosexuality, exhibitionism, pedophilia, public indecency, and prostitution.[4]

Reconceptualizing many of the earlier Freudian assumptions, David Abrahamsen suggests that criminal behavior is related to an interplay of causative factors. Although socioenvironmental factors have an influence on the individual, his psychological and personality characteristics strongly affect how he will react to his environment. Criminal behavior, it is important to recognize at the outset, is a result of many causative factors. A criminal act ($C$) is the sum of a person's criminalistic tendencies ($T$) plus his total situation ($S$) divided by the resistance ($R$) of which he is capable:

$$C = \frac{T + S}{R}$$

The external criminal situation, according to Abrahamsen, is the total environmental situation, including all the stresses and strains that contribute to the mobilization of a person's criminalistic tendencies. The internal criminal situation, on the other hand, is the individual's psychological state. His ability to resist is related to his emotional, intellectual, and social conditioning, which have an impact on his superego, and to the response of his ego to the situation confronting him. The degree to which an individual is able to resist criminogenic factors depends upon the extent of his previous resolution of his unconscious incentuous desires and his degree of emotional maturity.[5]

*Cultural, Social, and Environmental Explanations*

Recent theorizing in the cultural, social, and environmental realm has moved well beyond the assumptions of the psychological-psychiatric-physiological school. The late Donald R. Taft related delinquency and crime to a dynamic, complex, competitive, and materialistic society. A culture tends to reward those who succeed according to the prescribed rules of that culture. Those who are unable or unwilling to compete in the defined manner are likely to be unrewarded. Because schools stress competition rather than socialization, they cause already marginal students to become even more marginal. When the aspirations of large segments of the nonprivileged classes are prohibited by law, delinquency and crime are a probable byproduct of the criminogenic culture.[6]

In his pioneering study of street-corner society, William F. Whyte discovered that crime may be related to a lack of integration of an urban slum into the structure of surrounding society. A potential offender participates in rackets and local politics because they offer him more realistic and meaningful rewards than are provided by the legitimate opportunity structure. Participation in rackets yields prompt recognition even though the participant is only a marginal member of the larger community.[7]

In his differential association and learning theory, Edwin H. Sutherland, as noted earlier in this book, proposes that criminal behavior is learned through an associational relationship with other people. Albert K. Cohen suggests a somewhat broader hypothesis, affirming that delinquency is neither innate nor a self-acquired disposition but is, rather, a form of conduct children learn as they become members of groups that share a delinquent subculture. The delinquent subculture not only is largely nonutilitarian, malicious, and negativistic, but also is based upon norms taken from a larger culture and inverted to delinquent ends.[8] Richard A. Cloward and Lloyd E. Ohlin assert that such subcultures take a criminal, conflict, or retreatist form. Each form is related in some degree to the availability and openness of legitimate opportunity structures, which influence the eventual conduct of nondelinquent and delinquent youth.[9]

Walter B. Miller views delinquency in terms of lower-class culture and delinquent subcultures. The lower-class culture is disproportionately influenced by the focal concerns of trouble, toughness, smartness, excitement, fate, and autonomy. Delinquency among the lower class is a product of an external clash of cultural codes. The lower class emphasizes distinctive values, expressed in many of these focal concerns, which vary markedly from the middle-class values that are the primary supports for the criminal code. Given this context, the mere acting out of lower-class values may automatically encourage violations of criminal law. Because modern education emphasizes the imparting of middle-class values to lower-class youth, much of what is taught by the educational system is held by the lower-class adolescent to be unrealistic and useless in his future life. Consequently, Miller contends, schools should train lower-class youth for a law-abiding lower-class way of life, which may be thoroughly different from middle-class normative life-styles. If the educational system can capitalize upon lower-class focal concerns, values, or preoccupations, much of the youth's interest in deviant conduct can be rechanneled.[10]

Irving Spergel discusses the idea of delinquent subcultures more fully in his examination of "Racketville" (racket subculture), "Slumtown" (conflict subculture), and "Haulburg" (theft subculture). Those youths who attempt to fulfill their aspirations when legitimate opportunities are limited may participate in the racket subculture, engaging in numbers, gambling, or loan-sharking activities. Youths in the conflict subculture of "Slumtown," on the other hand, fulfill their aspirations through gang warfare. Those influenced by the theft subculture of "Haulburg" pursue success goals through acts of burglary, joyriding, car theft, and similar crimes. Although each subculture may have elements of the other two, the primary orientation of each is, according to Spergel, to the racket, conflict, or theft orientation.[11]

Marvin E. Wolfgang and Franco Ferracuti find that some countries or parts of countries have a subculture of violence, composed of a cluster of values related to life-style, socialization processes, and individual interpersonal relationships, all influencing human conduct. Violence is a reflection of basic values which differ from the dominant, central, or parent culture. Expressions of violence, they argue, not only are part of a subcultural system but also reflect the psychological characteristics and traits of the subculture's participants. When violence is made a subcultural norm, the failure to be violent under defined circumstances may result in group ostracism. When violence becomes part of a life-style and a subculture, it becomes normative and an expected behavior response, allowing the violence-prone individual to act out his tendency without feeling guilt.[12]

Arguing in opposition to the gang-subculture hypothesis, Lewis Yablonsky maintains that gangs really represent near-groups. Their conflict-filled activity generates group cohesion and identity. As a near-group, the gang is structurally more than a fleeting mob of individuals and less than a stable organization. Near-group members share diffuse role definitions, limited cohesion, impermanent relationships, minimal normative consensus, shifting membership patterns, disturbed leadership, and a limited definition of membership requirements. In contradistinction to Yablonsky, H.W. Pfautz argues that the violent adolescent gang is not a delinquent subcultural group but is rather a group participating in a social movement.[13]

Terence Morris contends that the delinquent is not always maladjusted and that delinquency is more closely related to the lack of planning or social organization and to the lessened emphasis upon the individual family cultural unit within high delinquency areas. While he questions the validity of the earlier ecological studies of deviance by Shaw and McKay, Morris finds the three highest delinquency rates in Corydon, a county borough near metropolitan London, to be in wards including and surrounding the central business district. The juvenile offender is frequently a member of a family that possesses low social aspirations and lives in close proximity to families of similar type. Morris contends that delinquency is related to membership in the proletarian social class.[14]

But David M. Downes, as a result of a study of two other English communities, disagrees, concluding that crime is related to the physical, economic, and sociocultural characteristics of a high crime area. Adult crimes in the unintegrated slum area of Stepney especially tend to be highly individualistic, unorganized, petty, and poorly rewarded. Delinquency, Downes contends, is related to limited family mobility, family overindulgence, and a desire for immediate gratification. Because socioeconomic conditions determine in part the school and work conditions of the working-class male adolescent, those

finding them unsatisfactory may become generally frustrated or thoroughly
alienated. Not only does the school system irritate and alienate the children of
this group; it also produces many marginal low-skill workers at a time when
demand is decreasing in this manpower category. Delinquency and crime are
therefore related to the facts that many urban slum young males have no
prospect of reaching manhood through work, and they sense that society neither
needs nor wants them. When such youth are forced into a humiliating subordinate role, they may respond with delinquent or criminal acts.[15]

Solomon Kobrin finds that delinquency pockets include both conventional
and criminal conduct norms. In some communities the legitimate norms are
dominant; in others criminal norms have priority. The conventional and criminal
value systems are in constant opposition. Which one dominates depends upon
population, class, ethnic, or racial factors. Because the criminal value system
does not integrate the community even when it is dominant, a criminal violator
is left without the integrating controls of either the criminal group or the
conventional community. The growth of street-corner groups is a natural byproduct of the lower-class juvenile male's attempt to resolve adolescent problems.
Street-corner youth tend to deprecate adult authority and conventional behavior, anticipate physical contact in combat, reject school discipline, take
sexual liberties, and participate willingly in delinquency.[16]

While emphasizing the subcultural transmission of values to lower-class
members, William C. Kvaraceus and Walter S. Miller hold that delinquent
adolescents are essentially normal lower-class youth. Only a small portion of the
delinquent population has some emotional problem; probably an even greater
number of nondelinquents share the same emotional characteristics. Delinquency
is related to the violator's frame of reference, social class, and general aspirations.
Whether he will be nondelinquent depends upon whether his aspirations are
feasible, his personality equal to his aspirational success, and his early family
training directed toward nondelinquent ends.[17]

*Social-Psychological Explanations of Crime*

Theorists of the social-psychological school emphasize the convergence of social
and psychological factors in the formation of criminal and delinquent conduct.
Émile Durkheim pointed out that criminal conduct is a normal function of
societal operations and is merely a differentiation of undesired from desired
behavior. Because the definition of crime by its very nature delimits the range
of actions that a person may legally engage in, the passage of a law may automatically result in the labeling as criminals of people who are doing nothing
more than what they were doing before the law was passed. Although society
may desire to eliminate or at least reduce the volume of criminal conduct, to
do so would cause stagnation within a society since much of what is called
criminal conduct is a forerunner to social change. If conformity is overem-

phasized, it may lessen human creativity. On the other hand, if the social rules do not have authority and a man is unable to fulfill his aspirations, a state of anomie (normlessness, nonbelonging) may prevail. When societies undergo rapid technological change, economic challenges, theological crises, and rapid technological advances, men frustrated in their efforts to reach desired goals may participate in delinquent or criminal acts as an anomic response to the conditions of the moment. The problem of anomie can be overcome, according to Durkheim, only if each citizen is permitted to achieve success goals.[18]

Taking Durkheim's ideas further, Robert K. Merton recognizes a cultural structure consisting of approved norms and goals and a social structure composed of human relationships. The breakdown of the close relationship between desired goals and leigtimate avenues of goal fulfillment underlies the condition of anomie. Aberrant behavior is a reflection of the dissociation between the culturally described aspirations and the socially structured avenues for realizing such aspirations. Criminal conduct is evidence of the disjunction between cultural goals and the prescribed means for achieving such goals. Individuals respond to this disjunction through conformity, innovation, ritualism, retreatism, or rebellion.[19] But Richard A. Cloward and Lloyd E. Ohlin argue that deviant conduct depends upon the nature of the situation and the opportunity of the individual to participate in deviant or criminal acts. Opportunities are not equally available to every person. Lower-class boys do not have access to legitimate means of achieving success values and goals to the same degree as middle and upper-class youth. At the same time, middle and upper-class adolescents do not have to face the strong pressures to participate in deviant conduct which the disjunction between aspirations and means of achieving goals causes. Criminalistic, conformist, and retreatist subcultural responses by youth represent their answers to the apparent opportunity structures available to them.[20]

Alienation may also play a part in the development of delinquent or criminal conduct. According to Frank Tannenbaum, criminals are created through an elaborate process of tagging, defining, identifying, segregating, describing, emphasizing, and stigmatizing youth and adults. Adult disapproval increases the probability of stigmatization and through it alienation. As an offender is separated from others for specialized treatment, his alienation is enhanced. When an isolated child is separated from his more normative counterparts, he becomes dependent upon the security offered by his deviant peer group. However, Karl Marx relates social deviance to the growth of capitalism which, in turn, stimulates an alienated proletariat.[21]

Thorsten Sellin relates criminality to conflicts in conduct norms. The mass character of society exposes each individual to a variety of conduct norms, which are often at odds with each other. Brought about by social change and resultant social disorganization, culture conflict is a representation of a disequilibrium or disintegration of societal integration. Until normative conflict is resolved, forms of criminal deviance are likely to continue.[22]

Walter C. Reckless and Shlomo Shoham explain criminal deviance in terms of a theory of norm containment, which suggests that norms, in the form of laws, duties, moral codes, social principles, or performance standards, can be circumscribed and made ineffective. If norms are not effectively transmitted to each generation and are eroded, deviant conduct may result. Undesirable norms may even eventually replace culturally prescribed norms. Not all human systems or nuclear groups are able to resist deviance or to conform to normative goals to the same degree. Some societal organizations or communities (societal or external containment) are better able to bring about conformity than others. At the same time, individuals vary in their ability to follow expected norms without external constraints (inner containment). When external and/or inner containment is rendered ineffective, potential deviators may be more responsive to the pressures leading toward delinquent or criminal responses.[23] Reckless and Simon Dinitz further contend that delinquency is due in part to a poor self-concept, which, in effect, makes slum youth susceptible to the negative influences of delinquent companions, a delinquent subculture, or deviant acts.[24]

Gresham M. Sykes and David Matza contend that delinquency stems from the youth's neutralization of conventional norms. Youths are more likely to view norms as situational guides than as absolute requirements for conduct. Through a process of neutralization, each is able to repudiate socially accepted rules and rationalize his own delinquency. It is not uncommon for a youth to redefine existing social rules so as to be able to achieve desired goals. In order to overcome the demands of the dominant social order, adolescents may establish a delinquent subculture through which they neutralize the content and purpose of conventional norms and thus become able to engage in deviant acts without feeling psychologically maladjusted. Neutralization occurs either before or during the period of participation in delinquent conduct. It usually involves a denial of responsibility, of injury, or of the victim, condemnation of the condemners, or an appear to a higher loyalty.[25]

David Matza carries the idea of neutralization even further in his notion of "delinquency and drift." Some people, Matza presupposes, exist in drift, a condition midway between freedom and restraint. In such a state, an individual drifts between conventional and criminal action. Most delinquents are merely drifters who share in a subculture of delinquency through which they neutralize many legal prohibitions and minimize the sense of responsibility for their acts. Once the norms have been neutralized, the context in which the youth exerts his will is largely free of social restraints. Once legal constraints are neutralized and the youth has come to the point of drift, he is likely to accept infractions of law as acceptable conduct.[26]

Donald R. Cressey relates certain forms of criminal conduct to rationalization, rather than neutralization, which permits a person to maintain his self-esteem even while violating a position of trust. The individual sees himself as basically honest and rationalizes his illegal conduct. Embezzlers, Cressey finds, usually have a financial problem that cannot be shared, are in a position to resolve their problem secretly through violation of the trust given them, and do not conceive of their actions as those of dishonest men. Edwin M. Lemert finds that check forgers, who face a crisis situation, will turn to forgery as a means of solving their problem. As closure or isolation occurs, the violator acts, probably without any sense of rationalization, to resolve his problem through forgery.[27]

In *Juvenile Delinquency: An Introduction,* Stephen Schafer and Richard D. Knudten suggest that delinquency and crime are a product of the interaction between an individual's socioethical resistance capability (SER) and the pressures to participate in crime (CP), which reveals the degree of the individual's limited socioethical responsibility (LSER). In the form of an equation, the relationship is

$$\frac{SER}{CP} = LSER$$

When socioethical resistance and crime pressures are of equal strength, they may cancel each other out and leave a criminometric average that may be balanced or weighted in favor of one or the other factor. If the criminometric average tends to favor crime pressures, criminal conduct is likely to occur. On the other hand, if it is balanced or is weighted in favor of socioethical resistance, the tendency for crimes to occur is lessened.[28]

John Mays relates crime and delinquency to the personality of the individual and the situation he is part of. Delinquency in large cities, Mays theorizes as a result of his study of Liverpool, is related to the psychological and environmental pressures the individual must respond to. Delinquency and crime are best understood in terms of two equations:

$$Personal + Environmental\ Factors = Crime$$

and

$$Environmental + Personal\ Factors = Delinquency$$

Delinquency, Mays contends, is a form of subculturally prescribed behavior that boys in a community participate in and that ultimately brings them to the attention of the police. The majority of slum youths tend to outgrow their delinquency, but a few do not. Later criminal acts are due primarily to psychological or social adjustment problems that have permanently affected the individual and that he has not outgrown.[29]

Herbert A. Bloch interprets crime as a reflection of the personality structure, itself determined primarily by class, subcultural, or ethnic conditions, which define culturally oriented needs and functions for the individual. Social tropisms represent broad personality structures that determine the individual's movement toward and away from other individuals. They serve as tendencies toward action and are expressed in egoistic, aggressive, withdrawal, or isolation personality states. As such, they are expressions of the individual's self-concept or generic status, which reflects the personality structure and will either be repudiated or enforced by continuing cultural conditions. If an individual is continually exposed to a series of primary relationships oriented to criminal or illegal conduct, or if the individual is placed in situations that fail to reinforce this generic status while creating areas of tension and conflict, criminal conduct is likely to occur. If primary relationships reinforce his generic status, a person may commit criminal acts. On the other hand, if the same primary relationships create tension and conflict for the individual, he may move to resolve the tension between his self-concept and actual social situations by engaging in criminal conduct.[30]

Bloch and Arthur Neiderhoffer suggest that delinquency is due to a major change in status for the adolescent. Deviant conduct is a product of crises that arise during the unsuccessful transition of adolescents to adulthood. While youths are taught to aspire to adult status and privileges, many are placed in positions of marginality, which themselves exert pressures toward deviant acts. Often, youth will commit acts that are common among adults but are held to be deviant when committed by youths.[31]

Lowell J. Carr sees delinquency in terms of shortcomings of personality, environmental pressures against conformity, and the interaction of personality in the environment. If factors encouraging conformity outnumber pressures leading to deviance, a youth is likely to conform to social mores. The reverse, of course, is true if pressures encouraging deviance outnumber pressures supporting conformity. In any case, conforming and deviating factors are products of both the individual and the environment. Carr's deviation-differential hypothesis suggests that the product of the internal and environmental conforming factors minus the product of the internal and environmental deviating factors yields a dominant conforming or deviating differential. The former leads to conforming behavior; a dominant deviating differential leads to delinquent and criminal conduct. In short, delinquency occurs, Carr suggests, when factors supporting deviation exceed those encouraging conforming behavior.[32] Expressed in formular form, Carr's theory reads:

$$\text{CF}(I \times E) - \text{DF}(I \times E) = \begin{Bmatrix} \text{CD} \\ \text{or} \\ \text{DD} \end{Bmatrix} \begin{array}{l} \rightarrow \text{(CB)} \\ \\ \rightarrow \text{(DB)} \end{array}$$

## The Future of Criminological Theorizing

From the foregoing, it should be obvious that current criminological theorizing continues its rich diversity even while it retains its debts to the previous four decades. The fact that Lombroso's work remains highly influential even today in much of Europe and South America and that Sutherland's differential association and learning theory still dominates American theoretical and research efforts testifies to the need to reconceptualize criminological theory. For far too long, criminological theorists have theorized in limited terms that are not applicable to all forms of criminal conduct or even to every culture in which a given violation occurs. The need to define middle-range theories of causation consistent with the known facts about criminal conduct and crime control is urgent.

An example of the future direction for theoretical development is presented by this writer in the "Theory of Relativity" (see page 241). In its revised version, the theory assumes that causation theorizing should not be applicable merely to one crime, one society, or one culture; that there is a need to organize theoretical knowledge; that human communities differ in their conceptualization of crime, the criminal, and the solution to criminal deviance; and that in any criminal event the multiple dimensions of culture, social organization, small groups, and the individual interact in a distinct, relative, and yet holistic manner.

## Notes

1. Sheldon Glueck and Eleanor Glueck, *Unraveling Juvenile Delinquency* (Cambridge, Mass., 1951); Glueck and Glueck, *Physique and Delinquency* (New York: 1956); and Glueck and Glueck, *The Family, Environment and Delinquency* (Boston: 1962).

2. Fritz Redl and David Wineman, *Children Who Hate* (Glencoe, Ill.: 1951), pp. 18-20; and Fritz Redl, *Controls from Within* (Glencoe, Ill.: 1951), pp. 15-19. Menninger and Nayman call this condition "impulse dyscontrol," a state at which the ego is no longer able to contain the surge of emotions underlying the expression of aggression. Karl Menninger and M. Nayman, "Episodic Dyscontrol: A Third Order of Stress Adaptation," *Bulletin of the Menninger Clinic* 20 (July 1956): 153.

3. Richard K. Knudten, *Crime in a Complex Society* (Homewood, Ill.: 1970), pp. 238-240.

4. Walter Bromberg, *Crime and Mind* (New York: 1965), pp. 9-54.

5. David Abrahamsen, *The Psychology of Crime* (New York: 1960), pp. 30-38.

6. Donald Taft and Ralph England, Jr., *Criminology* (New York: 1964), pp. 276-277.

7. William F. Whyte, *Street Corner Society* (Chicago: 1955), pp. 272-275.

8. Edwin H. Sutherland, *Principles of Criminology* (Philadelphia: 1947), pp. 6-7; and Cohen, *Delinquent Boys* (Introduction, n. 27), pp. 11-100.

9. Cloward and Ohlin, *Delinquency and Opportunity* (Introduction, n. 27), pp. 1-150.

10. Walter B. Miller, "Lower Class Culture as a Generating Milieu of Gang Delinquency," *Journal of Social Issues* 14, no. 3 (1958): 8–13.

11. Irving Spergel, *Racketville, Slumtown, Haulburg* (Chicago: 1964), pp. ix–xviii; and Spergel, "An Exploratory Research in Delinquent Subculture," *Social Services Review* 35 (March 1961); 33–47.

12. Marvin E. Wolfgang and Franco Ferracuti, *The Subculture of Violence* (New York: Tavistock Publications, 1967), pp. 156–159.

13. David M. Downes, *The Delinquent Solution* (Glencoe, Ill.: Free Press, 1966), pp. 16–17.

14. Terence Morris, *The Criminal Area* (New York: The Humanities Press, 1958), pp. 29–30.

15. Downes, *The Delinquent Solution,* pp. 141–260.

16. Solomon Kobrin, "Conflict of Values in Delinquency Areas," *American Sociological Review* 16 (October 1951): 657–659; and "The Impact of Cultural Factors on Selected Problems of Adolescent Development in the Middle and Lower Class," *American Journal of Orthopsychiatry* 32 (April 1962): 387–389.

17. William C. Kvaraceus, Walter S. Miller, et al., *Delinquent Behavior: Culture and the Individual* (Washington, D.C.: National Education Association, 1959), pp. 55–56.

18. Émile Durkheim, *Suicide: A Study in Sociology,* trans. by J.A. Spaulding and George Simpson (Glencoe, Ill.: Free Press, 1951), pp. 247–257.

19. Robert K. Merton, *Social Theory and Social Structure* (New York: Free Press, 1957), pp. 131–136; and "The Socio-Cultural Environment and Anomie," *New Perspectives for Research on Juvenile Delinquency,* edit. by Helen H. Witmer and Ruth Kopinski (Washington, D.C.: U.S. Department of Health, Education, and Welfare, 1955), pp. 24–50.

20. Richard A. Cloward and Lloyd E. Ohlin, *Delinquency and Opportunity: A Theory of Delinquent Gangs* (New York: Free Press, 1960), pp. 1–150.

21. Karl Marx and Friedrich Engels, *Capital* (New York: Random House, 1906).

22. Thorsten Sellin, *Culture Conflict and Crime* (New York: Social Science Research Council, 1938), pp. 13–131.

23. Walter C. Reckless and Shlomo Shoham, "Norm Containment Theory As Applied to Delinquency and Crime," *Excerpta Criminologica* 3 (November-December 1963): 637–643.

24. Simon Dinitz, Frank Scarpitti, and Walter C. Reckless, "Delinquency and Vulnerability: A Cross-Group and Longitudinal Analysis," *American Sociological Review* 27 (August 1962): 517.

25. Gresham M. Sykes and David Matza, "Techniques of Neutralization: A Theory of Delinquency," *American Sociological Review* 22 (December 1957): 712–719; and "Delinquency and Subterranean Values," *American Sociological Review* 26 (October 1961): 712–719.

26. David Matza, *Delinquency and Drift* (New York: John Wiley & Sons, 1964), pp. 27–183.

27. Edwin M. Lemert, "An Isolation Enclosing Theory of Naive Check Forgery," *Journal of Criminal Law* 44 (September-October) 1953): 29–307.

28. Stephen Schafer and Richard D. Knudten, *Juvenile Delinquency: An Introduction* (New York: Random House, 1970).

29. Morris, *The Criminal Area.*, pp. 78–104.

30. Herbert A. Bloch and Gilbert Geis, *Man, Crime and Society* (New York: Random House, 1962), pp. 125–128.

31. Herbert A. Bloch and Arthur Neiderhoffer, *The Gang: A Study of Adolescent Behavior* (New York: Philosophical Library, 1958), pp. 15-19.

32. Lowell J. Carr, *Delinquency Control* (New York: Harper and Brothers, 1950).

# A Theory of Relativity: An Integrated Middle-Range Conception of Delinquents and Criminal Behavior

*Richard D. Knudten*

## Introduction

*The definition, character, and incidence of delinquency and crime are relative to the cultural, social, organizational, small-group and personality factors and forces which produce and shape them.*

## Relativity and Culture

The definition, character, and incidence of delinquency and crime, while often similar in a number of other cultures, are relative. They are interactional products of environmental, cultural, societal, associational, small-group, and personality factors. Societal reaction to delinquent or criminal behavior depends upon the definition of criminal deviance; the time, place, and situation of its occurrence; and the person(s) involved. Although norms are delimited by culture, different segments of society will modify many norms to make them more relevant and realistic for their members.

Because delinquency and crime, whether serious or less serious, are by definition violations of some normative legal code, they are relative to normative social definitions. Normative content, however, varies in relationship to such factors as social class; subcultural, occupational, and religious community; political preferences; familial characteristics; economic capabilities; ethnic and racial membership; geographic region; community characteristics; and educational achievements. How they will be processed will depend upon the victim–offender relationship, the degree of seriousness attached to the act, the value of the target imagined and evaluated by legislators, the philosophy of law enforcement in the area, and the like.

Although crimes of young adults are specific violations of the criminal code, delinquent offenses, while also specified in law, are generally more exten-

This is the second version of the theory first published by the author in 1970. He acknowledges the contributions of Vernon Fox of Florida State University, Daniel Glaser of the University of Southern California, George Homans of Harvard, and Stephen Schafer of Northeastern University; of his former Valparaiso colleagues William Cross, LeRoy Martinson, and Nancy Sederberg; and his undergraduate and graduate students and colleagues in the field generally in the formulation and reformulation of this theory. Critical assistance has been provided by Mary S. Knudten.

241

sive and cover behavior often permitted adults. However, the number of delinquent and criminal offenses known to the police are only a fraction of the total volume of such violations in both delinquency and crime categories. Those apprehended, judged, and sentenced represent only a sample of the total volume of continuing offenders.

Because every cultural system is composed of multiple normative and deviant subsystems, crime for some persons within a social or cultural system is a functional act for attaining major social and cultural goals. However, what is functional to one person or group is often dysfunctional to another. What system(s) the individual participates in will be determined in large degree by opportunity and status factors over which the youth has little control during his/her childhood. While his/her delinquency is closely related to a lack of social planning and system integration and a lessened emphasis upon the family sociocultural unit, the family in some instances may be supportive of delinquency and crime.

Delinquency is often a product of social roles provided and supported within a subculture of delinquency, which may be of different types. Subcultures of delinquency (sometimes called contracultures) may be partially described in terms of the following ideal types which are defined in relationship to existing opportunity structures:

1.  Criminal subcultures (that is, gangs oriented to theft, extortion)
2.  Retreatist subcultures (that is, drug)
3.  Conflict subcultures (that is, manipulative violence)

Among the clearly adult subcultures of criminality are the (a) confederational or organized and (b) professional, in addition to the adult variations of the three juvenile subcultures mentioned here.

On another level, a subculture of violence, composed of a cluster of values related to life-styles, to the socialization process, and to interpersonal relations, also exists in some regions or among some group(s).

Where delinquent and criminal conduct are more a product of cultural rather than personality factors, decreased functioning of normative social controls, increased value conflicts, and greater social disorganization are likely to exist. Some slum dwellers rationalize their situation in a form of "inverted snobbery" and express a preference for slum living despite existing deficiencies in social control, value conflicts, and social disorganization. However, delinquency and crime may also exist and grow in areas where these problems do not exist in the same degree. The lower volume of reported suburban delinquency is most likely due to lessened reporting of deviance in such areas as compared with those of high social disorganization or blight.

Some delinquent behavior is an anticipated outcome of "normal" adolescent socialization because the totality of culture is always greater than the individual or group's ability to comprehend and command that culture. Delinquent and criminal groups will reveal distinct patterns which are not found to the same degree among more norm-maintaining elements of society. Inasmuch as the process of socialization includes cognition and the application of skills as well as learning through trial and error, delinquent conduct, especially among males, may be expected as juveniles mature. However, because much of the actual delinquency that occurs goes undetected and unreported, questions arise as to: By what process do delinquents overcome their deviance and assume normative patterns? Are current procedures for identifying, processing, and treating juveniles obstacles to the overcoming of delinquency?

Social factors act selectively upon delinquents who possess or are excessively exposed to certain personal traits and/or who belong to certain stigmatized ascriptive (born-into) categories. These include the traits and categories of hostility, unconventionality, feeling of being unappreciated, sense of parental inadequacy, defensive maternal attitudes, family financial dependence, unstable home life, lack of familial and personal self-respect, and physical impairment. Delinquent conduct is related to differential exposure to ascribed environmental factors, as well as to the differential association of youth with delinquency-prone groups.

Male juveniles often engage in "conspicuous masculinity," proving their manhood by malicious and destructive acts. Female juveniles are more apt to express their "conspicuous femininity" through obvious sexual or runaway activity. Lower class male juveniles' focal concern for trouble, toughness, smartness, excitement, autonomy, and fate underlies a disproportionate part of its deviant conduct. These focal concerns, however, may or may not encourage deviant conduct. If such concerns (or values) are channeled effectively into normative ends, normative conduct may be expected. In addition, the same focal concerns may be expressed in many different ways by members of the various social classes.

As the distance between social classes has narrowed, forms of class delinquency and crime will become less well defined. As lower-class juveniles, for example, transmit their concerns to middle-class youth, norm-violating behavior in a form common to lower-class youth may become more prevalent among these youths and vice versa. Lower-class mobility has created status inconsistency and blurred the boundaries of class delinquency. The volume of delinquency and crime, therefore, tend to increase in direct relationship to a variety of crime-encouraging factors present in a culture, society, or subculture. These factors may include the number of adolescents and young adults in the population, the volume of new legislation relating to delinquency and crime, the ease with which such deviance may be committed, the supply of produced consumer goods, the number and efficiency of law enforcement personnel and the philosophy of enforcement, the character and efficiency of justice in the

courts, the public's concern for delinquency and crime, the structured strain
between ideals and institutional means for reaching these goals, the methods
used to record these offenses, pressures in favor of deviance within one's peer
groups, and the nature of parent-child relationships. Each of these factors is
relative to a particular cultural system.


### Relativity and Social Organization

Delinquent or criminal conduct influences the social organizational form such
conduct takes; the organizational structure in turn helps to determine the
eventual success of the delinquent or criminal group as it acts deviantly. Each
function and organization is influenced or shaped in relation to the other and
is, in effect, a product of interaction. Some delinquency and crime functions
are manifest (intended) and others are latent (unintended) consequences of a
completed action. Each planned action may possess both expected and unexpected consequences. Inasmuch as all functions are performed in a social
equilibrium at the time of enactment, a change in one element of a functioning
normative or deviant system will result in the modification of other facets of the
same system. Similar changes will also occur if the existing social equilibrium
is composed of a dysfunctioning or deviant system.

Social structures frequently exert pressures upon some persons, especially
the poorly socialized, to participate in nonconforming rather than conforming
actions. Because delinquent or criminal social groups are fundamentally systems
of interaction, the relationship between the deviant actors within that group
represent the structure of the social system. Deviant and normative social structures and systems are composed of role relationships which include role trans-
actions and role bargaining. Because the individual's total role obligations are
highly idealized and overdemanding, they are frequently contradictory, inconsistent, or conflicting. Nevertheless, each deviant actor is located within the
delinquent-criminal group in terms of status roles. While status locates the
individual in the group or in a society in relation to other participant actors,
roles define the various tasks he is to perform. If the delinquent or criminal
offender's status is low, he may complete legal or illegal acts to achieve status
goals. If his status is high, he may respond to peer pressures or other forces.
The greater the lower-class domination of the community, the greater the
chances of a delinquent life for boys of any social status. Delinquency and
crime, however, cannot be correlated with a condition of poverty.

The stability and the orderly development of the delinquent-criminal social
system depend upon the meeting of a minimum number of needs for a majority
of criminal or delinquent actors, the maintenance of a minimum of control over
potentially disruptive behavior, and the continued internalization of a personality level adequate for one's participation within that system. The amount of

functional or actual crime will tend to vary according to the total number of opportunities available for normative or delinquent-criminal conduct and the tendency of a social system to support such conduct.

Delinquency and crime are potential status equalizers in a competitive society. In the United States, both delinquency and crime tend to be consistent with a cultural emphasis upon competition and achievement. As individuals, delinquents and criminals reveal a tendency to seek immediate gratification and an inability or unwillingness to defer their desires for fulfillment. The basic delinquent-criminal interests of the juvenile or adult offender are determined in large degree by whether he/she is pursuing his/her own private interest or one which he/she shares with others. Only gangs, organized crime or other con-federational groups, and professional offenders units appear to be successful in motivating their members to defer their desires for immediate gratification in order to achieve larger group goals.

## Relativity and the Small Group

Socialization to delinquency and crime generally occurs in small groups which share a dynamic social equilibrium and possess true uniformities in *activity* (what group members do), *interaction* (relation of one member to another), and *sentiment* (sum of interior feelings or codes of behavior which groups adopt). Each delinquent or criminal group participates within an external system (relationship between group and environment) and an internal system (group sentiments to another which have implications for behavior). Each system, external or internal, consists of activity, interaction, and sentiment. While the environment affecting the deviating group's external system may be primarily physical, technical, social, or a combination thereof, the internal system of the deviating group emerges from within the external system and reacts upon it. What acts and reacts is not a single part or function or a combination of parts or functions but the mutually interdependent system as a whole.

When individuals interact within a delinquent or criminal group or system, they are more likely to hold similar norms, believe themselves to be distinct from other persons or subgroups, and participate in similar activities. Peer discipline serves to establish order in disorder, although the new order may be radically opposed to legal codes and middle-class values. While the degree of individual participation within such a group or system varies in intensity, priority, duration, and frequency, individual actions will be frequently influenced by feelings within the group which have no direct bearing on the group's relation to its environment. The number of persons in the delinquent or criminal group and the nature of the group itself are variable and relative. The possibility that a few youth will complete a delinquent act depends upon the characteristics of the other members of the friendship dyad or triad. In other instances, the scope of delinquency will depend upon the character of the larger social unit. Although many play groups or gangs do not participate in delinquency, others encourage its development through undifferentiated play life. Gangs of older youth (also known as "near-groups") that engage in conflict do so in order to demonstrate manhood and generate cohesion and personal and group identity. And yet, they are generally characterized by diffuse role definitions, limited cohesion, impermanence, minimal consensus of norms, shifting membership, disturbed leadership, and limited membership expectation. All gangs are a social device which allows youth to find the power necessary for manhood through interaction with peers. Street-corner groups tend to deprecate adult authority and conventional conduct, emphasize readiness for physical combat, reject school discipline, accept sexual aggression, and participate willingly in delinquency.

Although inherited physical characteristics provide the raw material from which personality is formed through a process of socialization in multiple social groups, most crimes are products of all the processes involved in learning. Deviant actions are partially a product of personal attitudes, imitation processes, reference group commitments and associational relationships. New attitudes, motives, drives, and rationalizations are created through learning, usually in relationship to definitions of legitimate and illegitimate conduct. On the other hand, some delinquency and crime, as in the case of the mental defective or senile adult, are a consequence of incomplete or inadequate socialization; and still others a result of passion and emotion which lessens rational-normative personality controls.

## Relativity and the Individual

While some delinquency or crime may be conceived as a substitute or symbolic expression of a repressed personality structure and may be viewed as a product of guilt or anxiety resulting from a conflict in the unconscious mind, other explanations hold greater meaning. Faulty socialization or the failure to develop a meaningful sense of socioethical responsibility may offer a better explanation of criminal deviance. Consequently, delinquency and crime causes are relative in relation to physical, psychological, social psychological, and sociological factors.

The processes of stigmatization and alienation play an important part in the development of delinquent or criminal personalities. Once stigmatization of a youth as "bad" or an adult as "criminal" occurs, the person may become fully alienated and increasingly isolated, and may become dependent upon the security offered by persons with similar problems and interests. To overcome the alienation components of powerlessness, meaninglessness (confusion), normlessness (inadequacy of approved norms), isolation (feeling separation from society), and self-estrangement (inadequate rewarding activities for the integration of life), the violator may seek a new normative security with deviant persons or deviant groups.

Deviating behavior in the form of delinquency and crime may also represent a product of dissociation between culturally prescribed aspirations, and socially structured avenues for realizing these aspirations. When cultural constraints produce satisfactions for the individual, they will tend to be upheld. On the other hand, when achievement goals and the institutionalized means by which to reach them no longer coincide, new rules may be devised by persons or groups for attaining these ends. In such instances youths and adults will seek out both illegitimate and legitimate means to reach such goals.

Because delinquents and criminals are unable to accept continued tension and/or conflict throughout their lives, they will make every effort to reduce inconsistency (dissonance). This may be done throug the neutralization of conventional norms or through the development of new deviant commitments which are reinforced by new norms. If neutralization occurs, it may take the form of offender denial of responsibility, denial of injury, denial of the victim, condemning of the condemnors, or an appeal to higher loyalties.

The move to lessen inconsistency (dissonance) and achieve consistency (consonance) will include attempts to avoid situations or information which produce or increase dissonance and to unify one's cognition about one's self, one's behavior, and one's environment. However, the desire to reduce dissonance will often produce attitudes and actions which are frequently irrational and inconsistent with the person's previous behavior patterns. Adolescents and adults may specifically associate with gangs and groups of criminals in order to reduce dissonance and to reinforce consonance. However, many will merely drift in commitments, making the condition of drift a commitment in itself. Drift also makes infractions possible by removing restraints and permitting a minimum feeling of guilt. Norms may similarly be contained and rendered ineffective.

Because the delinquent or criminal's sense of reality will bring pressures to bear upon his person to bring appropriate cognitive elements into line, the situations which are real in their consequences will be those which persons define as real. Following a decision favorable to committing an offense, the decisionmaker actively seeks out information which produces a consistent (consonant) cognition with the action decided upon. As a result, the questioning of the original decision to violate tends to decrease, making it more difficult to reverse the decision once it has been made. Dissonance-reducing cognition is sought while dissonance-increasing cognition is avoided.

Delinquents or criminals who become personally demoralized or socially deinstitutionalized may adapt to their social context through innovation; ritualism, often called overconformity; retreatism or withdrawal; isolation, and rebellion or aggression. Whatever the response, it is influential in relieving a condition of anomie (nonbelonging, rootlessness, normlessness).

Although the greater number of juveniles overcome delinquent tendencies, many continue into adult crime. Once entrance is made into a system of juvenile or later adult justice, the institutional system tends to retain many offenders within its limits through the ensuing stigmatization of the offender and institutional maintenance processes. However, those officially coming to the attention of, and remaining within, the system of justice represent only a sample of the total volume of delinquent and criminal deviance.

The violator's success or failure in overcoming delinquency and crime depends in large degree upon his/her ability to bargain and upon the assets he/she has to bargain with when he/she comes into contact with the police, the courts, or the systems of correctional intervention. All persons do not share equal skills, status, and prestige and are, therefore, not subject to the processes of justice to the same degree. As a result, those most likely to continue in criminal conduct are those individuals who fail to follow the norms prescribed in criminal law and who have only limited resources with which to negotiate their future with the criminal justice system or its agents.

## Conclusion

*Delinquency and crime are relative and depend upon the situation in which criminal norms and action are located; the individuals' tendency to ignore or to neutralize limits placed upon their actions by the culture, society or subculture; their social class or social status; their ability to resist pressures which call for violation placed upon them by their group roles; and their individual personality characteristics which largely determine their tendencies toward deviant or criminal action. Delinquency and crime are relative products of cultural, social organizational, small-group, and individual characteristics.*

# Postscript

Criminological theory, while dependent upon the past, has now to free itself
to develop new postulates for the future. No longer is it enough to describe
the causes of crime in terms of "born criminals," mental deficiencies, faulty
socialization, poverty, powerless, economic servitude, generic status, pressing
events, or value neutralization and drift. Much more is involved. No crime takes
place within a social vacuum; rather, crime is a product of all elements involved
in human association, growth, and interaction. Future criminological theorizing
should speak to these complex issues and not merely add more fragments to
an already fragmented field of theory. What is needed now are theories that
bring order out of diversity and multiplicity.

## About the Editors

**Stephen Schafer** was professor of criminal justice at Northeastern University (Boston). A native of Hungary, Schafer was on the faculties of Ohio University (Athens) and Florida State University before joining the sociology and later criminal justice faculty at Northeastern. He was widely known for his work in victimization and victimology, and political crime. Among his many works are *The Victim and His Criminal; An Introduction to Criminology; Theories of Criminology; Juvenile Delinquency: An Introduction; Juvenile Delinquency: A Reader; Social Problems in a Changing Society;* and *The Political Criminal.* Dr. Schafer died on July 29, 1976.

**Richard D. Knudten** is professor of sociology and director of the Center for Criminal Justice and Social Policy at Marquette University (Milwaukee). He has conducted extensive research in the area of victim and witness attitudes, beliefs, problems and needs, is an associate editor of *Victimology: An International Journal,* and is the retiring editor of the *Review of Religious Research.* Knudten has authored *Crime in a Complex Society; Crime, Criminology and Contemporary Society; Juvenile Delinquency: An Introduction* and *Juvenile Delinquency: A Reader* (with Schafer); *Social Problems in a Changing Society* (with Mary S. Knudten and Schafer); *Criminological Controversies,* and a wide range of other works. He also serves as president of Evaluation/Policy Research Associates, Ltd. of Milwaukee, Wisconsin.

## DATE DUE

| DATE DUE | | | |
|---|---|---|---|
| NOV 30 '84 | | | |
| DE 15 '90 | | | |
| | | | |
| | | | |
| | | | |
| | | | |
| | | | |
| | | | |
| | | | |
| | | | |
| | | | |
| | | | |
| | | | |
| | | | |
| | | | |
| | | | |
| | | | |
| | | | |
| | | | |
| GAYLORD | | | PRINTED IN U.S.A. |